Deep Learning

Deep Learning

A Comprehensive Guide

Shriram K. Vasudevan

Sini Raj Pulari

Subashri Vasudevan

CRC Press
Taylor & Francis Group

A CHAPMAN & HALL BOOK

First edition published 2022
by CRC Press
6000 Broken Sound Parkway NW, Suite 300, Boca Raton, FL 33487-2742

and by CRC Press
2 Park Square, Milton Park, Abingdon, Oxon, OX14 4RN

Library of Congress Cataloging-in-Publication Data
Names: Vasudevan, Shriram K., author. | Pulari, Sini Raj, author. | Vasudevan, Subashri, author.
Title: Deep learning: a comprehensive guide / Shriram K. Vasudevan,
Sini Raj Pulari, Subashri Vasudevan.
Description: First edition. | Boca Raton: Chapman & Hall/CRC Press, 2022. | Includes index. |
Summary: "Deep Learning: A Comprehensive Guide focuses on all the relevant topics in the
field of Deep Learning. Covers the conceptual, mathematical and practical aspects of all
relevant topics in deep learning Offers real time practical examples Provides case studies.
This book is aimed primarily at graduates, researchers and professional working in
Deep Learning and AI concepts – Provided by publisher.
Identifiers: LCCN 2021031713 (print) | LCCN 2021031714 (ebook) |
ISBN 9781032028828 (hardback) | ISBN 9781032028859 (paperback) |
ISBN 9781003185635 (ebook)
Subjects: LCSH: Deep learning (Machine learning)
Classification: LCC Q325.73 .V37 2022 (print) |
LCC Q325.73 (ebook) | DDC 006.3/1–dc23
LC record available at https://lccn.loc.gov/2021031713
LC ebook record available at https://lccn.loc.gov/2021031714

ISBN: 978-1-032-02882-8 (hbk)
ISBN: 978-1-032-02885-9 (pbk)
ISBN: 978-1-003-18563-5 (ebk)

DOI: 10.1201/9781003185635

Typeset in Minion Pro
by Newgen Publishing UK

Access the companion website: www.routledge.com/9781032028828

Contents

Preface

EVER SINCE ARTIFICIAL INTELLIGENCE (AI) became popular, there has been a surge in worldwide automation. Be it in the automobile industry, finance or farming, automation finds its place everywhere. The more the applicability, the higher will be the demand. Machine Learning (ML) and Deep Learning (DL) being subsets of AI, most reputed universities began offering courses on them. With a little exposure to programming and analytics, one can deep dive into these subjects and become an expert in no time.

This book aims to make the readers proficient in the DL concepts/ mechanisms and also enables them to build products right away. The book provides lots of real-world examples and explains the steps to build applications from scratch. The tools required, application setup needed, input data, expected output – everything is provided in a simple manner. We are sure this book is going to be a one-stop solution for every aspiring DL enthusiast.

The book is arranged in the following manner. Chapter 1 covers the introduction to DL. It has all the basics explained in a down-to-earth way and prepares the readers for a smooth DL journey. Chapter 2 comes with the details of tools required for building products and a step-by-step installation guide. Chapter 3 deals with the ML fundamentals that go hand in hand with DL. Chapter 4 covers the DL framework, while Chapter 5 touches upon the ins and outs of Convolution Neural Networks (CNN). Chapter 6 explains the CNN architectures that lay the foundation for DL, followed by Recurrent Neural Networks (RNN) in Chapter 7. Autoencoders are discussed in Chapter 8. Chapter 9 touches upon Generative Adversarial Networks. Chapter 10 comes with a beautiful concept called "Transfer Learning" which has been gaining popularity over the years. OpenVino is an Intel product that comes with a lot of useful features for building various DL products, and the same is discussed in Chapter 11. And at last, Chapter 12 comes with a handy reference to the interview questions for aspiring DL candidates.

We would like to thank Sunandhini Muralidharan and Nitin Dantu for their efforts throughout in shaping this book.

The Authors

Shriram K. Vasudevan
An academician with a blend of industrial and teaching experience for 15 years. Authored/co-authored 42 books for publishers around the world. Authored more than 120 research papers in international journals and 30 papers for international/national conferences. He is an IETE Fellow, ACM Distinguished Speaker, CSI Distinguished Speaker, and Intel Software Innovator. He has a YouTube channel – Shriram Vasudevan – through which he teaches thousands of people all around the world.

Recognized/awarded for his technical expertise by Datastax, ACM, IETE, Proctor and Gamble Innovation Centre (India), Dinamalar, AWS (Amazon Web Services), Sabre Technologies, IEEE Compute, Syndicate Bank, MHRD, Elsevier, Bounce, IncubateIND, Smart India Hackathon, Stop the Bleed, "Hack Harvard" (Harvard University), Accenture Digital (India), Nippon Electric Company (NEC, Japan), Thought Factory (Axis Bank Innovation Lab), Rakuten (Japan), Titan, Future Group, Institution of Engineers of India (IEI), Ministry of Food Processing Industries (MoFPI – Government of India), Intel, Microsoft, Wipro, Infosys, IBM India, SoS Ventures (USA), VIT University, Amrita University, Computer Society of India, TBI – TIDE, ICTACT, *Times of India*, the Nehru Group of institutions, Texas Instruments, IBC Cambridge, Cisco, CII (Confederation of Indian Industries), Indian Air Force, DPSRU Innovation & Incubation Foundation, ELGi Equipments (Coimbatore), and so forth. Listed in many leading biographical databases.

Notable honors:

- First Indian to be selected as HDE (Huawei Developer Expert).
- NVIDIA Certified Deep Learning Instructor.
- Winner of the Harvard University "Hack Harvard" Global, 2019 and World Hack, 2019. Winner of 50-plus hackathons.
- Selected as "Intel IoT Innovator" and inducted into the "Intel Software Innovator" group. Awarded "Top Innovator" award – 2018, "Top Innovator – Innovator Summit 2019".
- World Record Holder – With his sister, Subashri Vasudevan (Only siblings on the globe to have authored nine books together: *Unique World Record Books*).
- Entry in Limca Book of Records for National Record – 2015.
- Entry in India Book of Records – National Record and Appreciation – 2017.

Sini Raj Pulari
Professor in a government university in Bahrain, with 14 years of experience in various Indian universities and industry, with contributions to the teaching field and carrying out activities to maintain and develop research and professional activities relevant to Computer Science Engineering. Research interests include areas of Natural Language Processing, recommender systems, Information Retrieval, Deep Learning, and Machine Learning.

She has authored 17-plus Scopus Indexed publications; guided over 30 UG and PG students for various innovative product-based and algorithmic ideas; and was an active member of the Funded Project – Early Warning and Monitoring System of Elephants – Amrita University. Member of the International Association of Engineers (IAENG) and the Computer Society of India (CSI). Delivered various lectures on the emerging technological topics. Actively participated in the board of studies. Organized, presented, and participated in various national and international technical events, conferences, workshops, and hackathons and has been on the international advisory committees of various international conferences.

Subashri Vasudevan

Subashri holds an M.Tech in CSE and was associated with Cognizant Technology Solutions for more than eight years. She was a senior developer and has exposure to various DOTNET technologies and reporting tools. She has coauthored more than twenty-five technical books for publishers around the world, including titles on software engineering, C# programming, C++ programming, and so forth. Her name is featured in the Limca Book of Records for the number of books authored by siblings. She has recently developed an interest in the IoT and ML areas and began contributing to projects involving these technologies. Teaching is her passion, and she wants to make technology simpler for the students. She also manages a technical YouTube channel ("All about BI") for Azure-related concepts and has delivered dozens of lectures in various educational institutions.

## CHAPTER 1

Introduction to Deep Learning

LEARNING OBJECTIVES

After reading through this chapter, the reader will understand the following:

- The need for Deep Learning
- What is the need of transition from Machine Learning to Deep Learning?
- The tools and languages available for Deep Learning
- Further reading

1.1 INTRODUCTION

Artificial Intelligence and Machine Learning have been buzz words for more than a decade now, which makes the machine an artificially intelligent one. The computational speed and enormous amounts of data have stimulated academics to deep dive and unleash the tremendous research potential that lies within. Even though Machine Learning helped us start learning intricate and robust systems, Deep Learning has curiously entered as a subset for AI, producing incredible results and outputs in the field.

Deep Learning architecture is built very similar to the working of a human brain, whereby scientists teach the machine to learn in a way that humans learn. This definitely is a tedious and challenging task, as the

DOI: 10.1201/9781003185635-1

working of the human brain itself is a complex phenomenon. Our research in the field has resulted in valuable outcomes to makes things easily understandable for scholars and scientists to build worthy applications for the welfare of society. They have made the various layers in neural nets in Deep Learning auto-adapt and learn according to the volume of datasets and complexity of algorithms.

The efficacy of Deep Learning algorithms is in no way comparable to traditional Machine Learning algorithms. Deep Learning algorithms may be bit time consuming in training of data, but still it executes faster on a new set of data. Deep Learning helped industrialists to deal with unsolved problems in a convincing way, opening a wide horizon with ample opportunity. Natural language processing, speech and image recognition, the entertainment sector, online retailing sectors, banking and finance sectors, the automotive industry, chat bots, recommender systems, and voice assistants to self-driving cars are some of the major advancements in the field of Deep Learning.

1.2 THE NEED: WHY DEEP LEARNING?

Deep Learning applications have become an indispensable part of contemporary life. Whether we acknowledge it or not, there is no single day in which we do not use our virtual assistants like Google Home, Alexa, Siri and Cortana at home. We could commonly see our parents use Google Voice Search for getting the search results easily without requiring the effort of typing. Shopaholics cannot imagine shopping online without the appropriate recommendations scrolling in. We never perceive how intensely Deep Learning has invaded our normal lifestyles. We have automatic cars in the market already, like MG Hector, which can perform according to our communication. We already have the luxury of smart phones, smart homes, smart electrical appliances and so forth. We invariably are taken to a new status of lifestyle and comfort with the technological advancements that happen in the field of Deep Learning.

1.3 WHAT IS THE NEED OF A TRANSITION FROM MACHINE LEARNING TO DEEP LEARNING?

Machine Learning has been around for a very long time. Machine Learning helped and motivated scientists and researchers to come up with newer algorithms to meet the expectations of technology enthusiasts. The major limitation of Machine Learning lies in the explicit human intervention for the extraction of features in the data that we work (Figure 1.1). Deep Learning allows for automated feature extraction and learning of the model adapting all by itself to the dynamism of data (Figure 1.2).

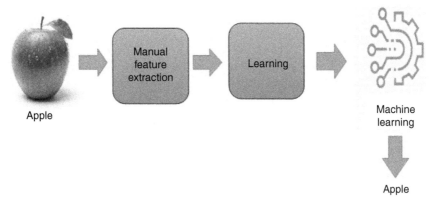

FIGURE 1.1   Limitation of Machine Learning.

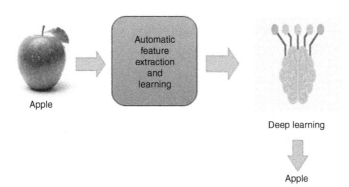

FIGURE 1.2   Advantages of Deep Learning.

Deep Learning very closely tries to imitate the structure and pattern of biological neurons. This single concept, which makes it more complex, still helps to come out with effective predictions. Human intelligence is supposed to be the best of all types of intelligence in the universe. Researchers are still striving to understand the complexity of how the human brain works. The Deep Learning module acts like a black box, which takes inputs, does the processing in the black box, and gives the desired output. It helps us, with the help of GPUs and TPUs, to work with complex algorithms at a faster pace. The models developed could be reused for similar futuristic applications.

1.4 DEEP LEARNING APPLICATIONS

As introduced earlier, there is an excess of scenarios and applications where Deep Learning is being used. Let us look at few applications in Deep Learning for a more profound understanding of where exactly DL is applied.

1.4.1 Self-Driving Cars

The advent of autonomous cars has had a great impact in the field of Deep Learning. Major companies like Uber and Google have been researching and developing autonomous cars for more than 22 years. MG Hector and MG Gloster are already in market with an advanced driver assistance system (ADAS). ADAS provides greater assistance to drivers by reducing the chance of accidents on the road. Hands-free automatic parking, automatic emergency braking and adaptive cruise control are something that we can see in latest cars out in the market. The data gathered through various sensors, like radar and cameras, to identify the front and back distances between other vehicles adjacent (Figure 1.3). Radar-based features in automatic emergency braking systems constantly monitor the possibility of a head-on crash.

FIGURE 1.3 Autonomous cars with various sensors.

Self-driving cars guarantee a greater reduction of pollution, helping to maintain a balanced ecosystem. This also demands a raise in the need for knowledgeable persons in the automobile industry. Automatic parking of cars will become a great feature. Uber has come out with the newest strategy of utilizing self-driving cars for food delivery.

1.4.2 Emotion Detection

Feelings are an integral part of human communications, which contributes to understanding. Facial expressions normally show whether a person is angry, surprised, depressed, sad, joyful and so forth. Sarcasm is one of the toughest emotions to be identified by AI. Lots of applications have used photos and videos for the detection of the emotions of humans. In the 1970s Loufrani came out with the first smiley design. Later, he started the company, named Smiley, which is still in market, always with a roaring success with the newest pack of emoticons. There were lot of projects using emotion detection, from capturing the emotions of a student in a class to capturing the emotions of a customer while crossing the traffic lane. There are numerous applications using both photo captures and videos. If the videos are captured, then it needs to be converted to frames for further pre-processing. The frames are classified by applying various Deep Learning algorithms for emotion detection. The emotions are identified and displayed according to the images. A simple diagram for emotion detection is shown below (Figure 1.4). Convolution Neural networks are commonly used for emotion detection applications in Deep Learning.

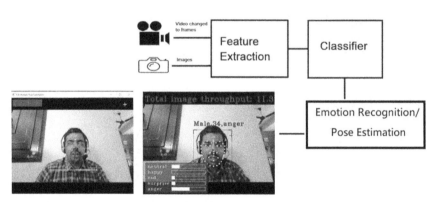

FIGURE 1.4   How emotions are identified.

1.4.3 Natural Language Processing

Natural language processing (NLP) has become one of the greatest areas of research in the field of artificial intelligence. Even if we are new to a completely new place on earth, we don't need to worry about it because of the greatest NLP application by Google, Google Translate. It is a multilingual application where texts or speech in any language can be converted to any other language (Figure 1.5).

FIGURE 1.5   Google Translate an example.

Google gives lot of recommendations while doing a search in the Google search engine. You would have experienced this while searching for needed data from a Google server something like this shown below (Figure 1.6):

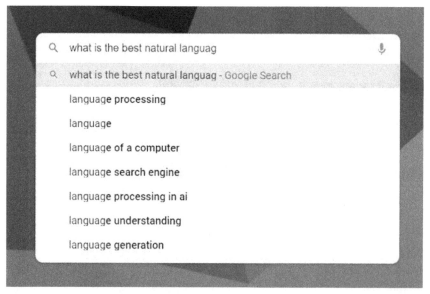

FIGURE 1.6   Google helping us by giving recommendations for the search text.

The indispensable feature, "Voice Search," purely comes under natural language speech processing (Figure 1.7). Whatever people say would be converted as voice signals from which the algorithms encode and decode what exactly a person has asked for. Viterbi algorithms are commonly used here. This feature is mainly used for Google Search to retrieve the data needed from a server by giving simple voice input. This feature is very commonly seen as subtitles for YouTube videos and multilingual cinemas, too.

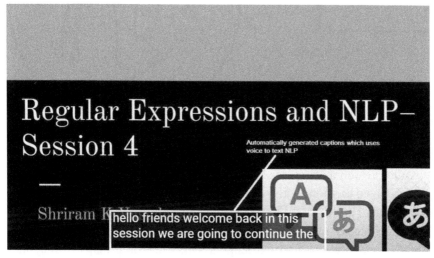

FIGURE 1.7   Automatic captions generated for our YouTube channel.

Even the young people in this era are accustomed to Alexa, Hello Google, Cortana, Siri and so forth This comes under the wide window of natural speech processing.

1.4.4   Entertainment

Deep Learning is extensively used for abstraction of videos, cinema, and Web series. This technique is widely used for the analysis of video footage in sports and to generate highlights of games (Figure 1.8). Research is going on to produce the best highlights, applying various algorithms. This is also used for the analysis of major points for crime analysis in real situations. Sometimes humans may miss the hours and hours of inactive video footage with a relevant information. However, even minor changes could be captured by deep video analysis. This helps people by saving time, energy and effort, still helping in gathering the required information without missing it. Deep Learning paves the way for editing the content in an effective way, generating content automatically and even virtual characters in the process of animated films.

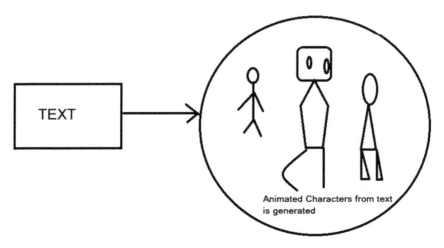

FIGURE 1.8 Characters generated from text.

Auto cartoon makers are on the rise, and we have seen researchers superimposing old cartoons with variety of new sounds to make it more comical. All these are done using Deep Learning algorithms. These algorithms will become effective on multiple training data sets, which consist of a wide range of video clips of varied lengths. Deep Learning helps in mapping videos to corresponding words. The algorithms are also responsible for identifying the best parameters in the video. There are also algorithms that convert text into video or animated clips.

1.4.5 Healthcare

Healthcare is an area where Deep Learning is used for extremely arduous tasks. Even during the 2020's pandemics, artificial intelligence has played a significant role in the testing for novel corona virus (Figure 1.9). Thus, Deep Learning proved its presence in finding cures for untreatable diseases. Apart from drug discovery, Deep Learning is often used in developing assistance for children with speech disorders, developmental disorders and autism. Deep Learning helps to analyze data and bring early detection of these disorders. This helps victims in many ways to perform an early course correction. This helps them to tackle situations ahead in a much better way. Course correction may contribute to the physical, emotional and mental well-being of the children. There are various research labs that specifically work under this category.

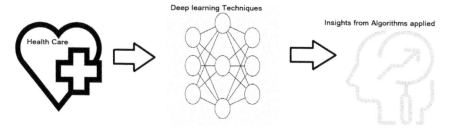

FIGURE 1.9 Medical insights generated through Deep Learning techniques.

The only caveat still considered a major challenge by physicians is that they remain skeptical about the accuracy of the techniques used, as they lack a large amount of data to work on. Major data training brings huge precision to the table. Moreover, Deep Learning is widely used for the analysis of the treatments already done on patients. Most of the patients with Alzheimer's Disease use lot of AI powered instruments, which help to ease the challenges they face.

There are various other applications, like image reconstruction, which could be done by using Convolutional Neural Networks, automatic text generation and summarization where Recurrent Neural Networks could be used, algorithms which uses Generative Adversarial networks (GAN) help in applications like auto aging, fake or real image detection and so forth. There are also lot of studies that use VGG Face for emotion detection and other similar applications – thanks to pre-trained models in Keras, which helps developers work on various applications without coding from scratch.

YOUTUBE SESSION ON DEEP LEARNING APPLICATIONS

https://youtu.be/h4Vvuc2mXKc

KEY POINTS TO REMEMBER

- Deep Learning can work on complex datasets and can use complex processes to get the most desired output.
- The need of Deep Learning is on the rise as time passes. Machine algorithms help in classification-based problems.
- Deep Learning techniques help to do automatic feature extraction and adaptive learning, which clearly define the need for a transition from ML to DL.

- Various Deep Learning applications include autonomous cars, emotion detection, natural language processing, and entertainment and healthcare applications.

QUIZ

1. Define Deep Learning.

2. Explain how Deep Learning is different from machine Learning.

3. State a few reasons why Deep Learning is significant.

4. List a few real-time applications of Deep Learning that you use on a daily basis.

5. Can you think of some healthcare applications where Deep Learning could be useful?

6. If you are asked to help the professor in getting feedback for his class, how will you engage Deep Learning techniques to get it done automatically? You may use any gadgets you want. Widen your imagination and come out with the best solution for the professor.

FURTHER READING

✓ Grigorescu, Sorin, et al. "A survey of deep learning techniques for autonomous driving." *Journal of Field Robotics* 37.3 (2020): 362–386.

✓ Lateef, Fahad, and Yassine Ruichek. "Survey on semantic segmentation using deep learning techniques." *Neurocomputing* 338 (2019): 321–348.

✓ Kanjo, Eiman, Eman M.G. Younis, and Chee Siang Ang. "Deep learning analysis of mobile physiological, environmental and location sensor data for emotion detection." *Information Fusion* 49 (2019): 46–56.

✓ Garcia-Garcia, Alberto, et al. "A survey on deep learning techniques for image and video semantic segmentation." *Applied Soft Computing* 70 (2018): 41–65.

✓ Bertero, Dario, and Pascale Fung. "A first look into a convolutional neural network for speech emotion detection." 2017 IEEE International Conference on Acoustics, Speech and Signal Processing (ICASSP). IEEE, 2017.

✓ Liu, Yifan, et al. "Auto-painter: Cartoon image generation from sketch by using conditional Wasserstein generative adversarial networks." *Neurocomputing* 311 (2018): 78–87.

✓ Esteva, Andre, et al. "A guide to deep learning in healthcare." *Nature Medicine* 25.1 (2019): 24–29.

## CHAPTER 2

The Tools and the Prerequisites

LEARNING OBJECTIVES:

After this chapter, the reader will be able to understand the following:

- The tools required to be installed.
- Installing and testing Anaconda.
- Running the first code with Jupyter platform.
- Installing Keras.
- The most frequently used datasets and sources for the same.

2.1 INTRODUCTION

It is always viewed this way. Installation of the tools and prerequisites to learn Machine Learning or Deep Learning is very difficult and is a daunting task. This view is a myth and is to be challenged. The installation process is simple and straightforward. This chapter provides the complete information on the installation process with step-by-step inputs. The next major challenge faced by all Deep Learning/Machine Learning aspirants is "Datasets." Which dataset to use is a question that is frequently asked. This chapter provides the details of the most commonly used datasets with the links for download. Overall, this chapter serves as a foundation for the complete learning provided to the reader.

DOI: 10.1201/9781003185635-2

2.2 THE TOOLS

Deep learning is all about tools. It is all practical. So, this chapter discusses the tools and the prerequisites to be installed in your PC to practice the algorithms and implementations. Let us get our hands on!

2.2.1 Python Libraries – Must Know

The book is full of Python codes. This is a true statement, and we are living in the era of Python. We are going to use Python and the libraries completely. Python has gained popularity as it has very rich library support and community hand holding. The following Python libraries are the frequently used ones, and a brief note on all of them is presented. Wherever the libraries are invoked, explanation is presented there as well. First, let us understand the details of the libraries/packages that will be used throughout the book.

FIGURE 2.1   NumPy.

NumPy is simply powerful, flexible, performance-oriented, easy to use and open-source package for Python (Figure 2.1). It offers very comprehensive math functions, random number generators, support for linear algebra and Fourier Transforms. Thus, it is very powerful and complete by itself. NumPy is very flexible. It can fit well with a variety and wide range of hardware and computing platforms. It can work fine with Central Processing Unit and Graphics Processing Unit (CPUs and GPUs), thus proving handy and versatile. Being powerful and flexible alone is not sufficient. It has to be performance-oriented, and NumPy also stands tall in terms of performance. The core of NumPy is C Code. The speed of C with the flexibility of Python makes it superior.

Any tool or invention, if not easy to use, can get lost in the market. NumPy is very easy to use, and it has very simple and easily remembered syntaxes, thus making it favorite for all the users. Moreover, the most appreciable point is that NumPy is open-source. One can learn more about NumPy from the official website: https://numpy.org/.

FIGURE 2.2   Matplotlib.

Whenever the results are presented or something is analyzed, it is important to have appealing visuals, which makes the interpretations easier and more meaningful. Else, the numbers will remain strange data. Matplotlib is a comprehensive library for creating static, animated, and interactive visualizations in Python (Figure 2.2). The tagline one can read in the Matplotlib official website is interesting: "Matplotlib makes easy things easy and hard things possible." Readers can learn more about this from the website: https://matplotlib.org/

FIGURE 2.3   SciPy.

Scipy is used for the statistical operations and is one of the most preferred (Figure 2.3). Scipy has the fundamental library for the scientific computing. Support for numerical integration, interpolation, optimization, linear algebra, and statistics makes Scipy the preferred option. Again, this is open-source and one can read more about Scipy here: www.scipy.org/. One interesting thing to note is that SciPy uses NumPy internally.

FIGURE 2.4   Pandas.

Pandas is a very powerful, flexible, and easy to use open-source data analysis and manipulation tool, built on top of the Python programming language (Figure 2.4). It handles different formats of the file, such as CSV,

JSON or even SQL. It also helps with providing support for the data manipulation through merging, selecting, and reshaping. It also has a role in data cleaning. One can learn more about Pandas by visiting https://pandas.pydata.org/

FIGURE 2.5   IPython.

IPython is a web-based interactive development environment for the Jupyter Notebook code, and data (Figure 2.5). It is rich and powerful, with interactive visualization options. It is also easy to use. The complete installation procedure is presented in the chapter for the reader to try the same in their respective computers.

2.2.2   The Installation Phase

A.   Anaconda Installation

We need to install Anaconda Distribution first. It is the most preferred and most sophisticated platform with support for everything we need. Beginners will be in the land of comfort installing and using this tool. This is the most suitable tool for all sorts of data-science applications. All the tools and packages discussed in the previous section are all available, inbuilt with Anaconda itself. The reader is presented with step-by-step installation guidelines. The Anaconda has the following, as shown in Figure 2.6, which makes Anaconda special.

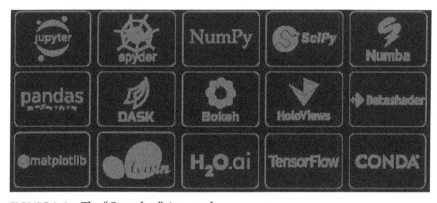

FIGURE 2.6   The "Complete" Anaconda.

1. Visit Anaconda site – www.anaconda.com/distribution/
2. The reader will land on the below page (Figure 2.7):

FIGURE 2.7   The landing page.

3. On clicking the download button, the following screen appears (Figure 2.8).

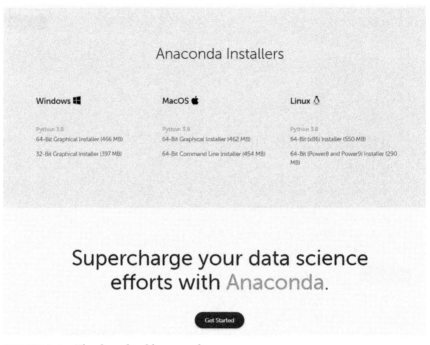

Anaconda Installers

Windows ⊞	MacOS	Linux △
Python 3.8	Python 3.8	Python 3.8
64-Bit Graphical Installer (466 MB)	64-Bit Graphical Installer (462 MB)	64-Bit (x86) Installer (550 MB)
32-Bit Graphical Installer (397 MB)	64-Bit Command Line Installer (454 MB)	64-Bit (Power8 and Power9) Installer (290 MB)

Supercharge your data science efforts with Anaconda.

Get Started

FIGURE 2.8   The download happens here.

4. Select the appropriate version for the download and, on clicking, the download will begin with the screen below appearing in front (Figure 2.9).

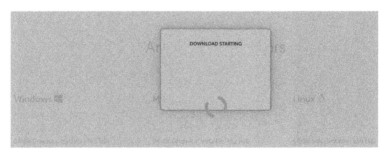

DOWNLOAD STARTING

FIGURE 2.9   The download Progress.

5. One should start the installation by double clicking the installation file. The process is easy to follow and will be simple to complete. The

only point to be remembered is, "The name of the destination folder should not have any space between." **New Folder** cannot be the name, but **New_Folder** is fine to proceed with. One can understand the complete installation procedure by following the guidelines provided in the video lecture created by authors presented in: https://youtu.be/bzaO9SFHJSA

B. Jupyter Installation

1. For the installation of the Jupyter, one should open the Anaconda Prompt. Many beginners will make a minor mistake here. Beginners tend to issue the command in the normal command prompt instead of the Anaconda Prompt. Then the installation will not work, as it is the destined method to be followed. The screenshot below presents the error message one would get if the command is issued in normal command prompt, which should be avoided. Figure 2.10 presents the command prompt followed by the error message being presented as Figure 2.11 when the command for Jupyter installation is issued.

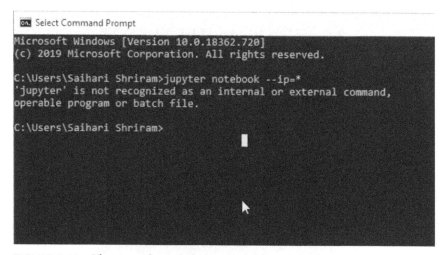

FIGURE 2.10   The normal command prompt.

Command Prompt

```
Microsoft Windows [Version 10.0.18362.720]
(c) 2019 Microsoft Corporation. All rights reserved.

C:\Users\Saihari Shriram>jupyter notebook --ip=*
'jupyter' is not recognized as an internal or external command,
operable program or batch file.

C:\Users\Saihari Shriram>jupyter notebook --ip=*
'jupyter' is not recognized as an internal or external command,
operable program or batch file.

C:\Users\Saihari Shriram>_
```

FIGURE 2.11   The error.

The command to be issued is "**jupyter notebook –ip=***".

2. One should open the Anaconda prompt now and issue the above command. The following screenshots, Figure 2.12, reveal the presence of the Anaconda prompt in the system. Figure 2.13 presents the successful installation note.

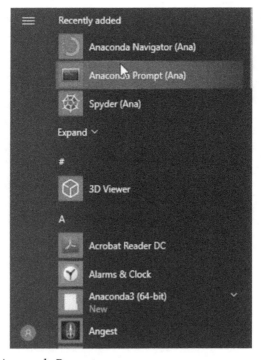

FIGURE 2.12   Anaconda Prompt.

FIGURE 2.13   Anaconda Prompt installation complete.

3. After the installation is complete, one can with ease open and access the notebook with the link obtained. Copying and pasting the link in any of your favorite browsers gets the Jupyter Notebook open (See Figure 2.14).

FIGURE 2.14   How to open the Jupyter?

Or, there is another, easier way, to open and access the Jupyter Notebook. Just type "Jupyter" in the search box. It will display the Jupyter Notebook launcher option as presented below in Figure 2.15. On clicking, the notebook is launched.

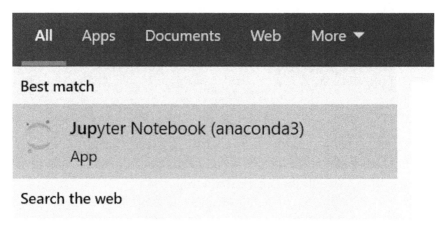

All   Apps   Documents   Web   More ▼

Best match

Jupyter Notebook (anaconda3)
App

Search the web

FIGURE 2.15   Launching Jupyter.

The reader will have the Jupyter launched in a Web browser as presented below in Figure 2.16.

FIGURE 2.16   Jupyter – the first launch.

Now, the installation is complete. It is time to try out the first program.

C. *The First Program with the Jupyter*
  1. After launching the Jupyter Notebook successfully, the user is presented with the below screen. There, one can spot the button "New" as highlighted (Figure 2.17).

FIGURE 2.17   Jupyter – the first program.

2. Once "New" is clicked, the below screen (Figure 2.18) appears, presenting the options. Click Python 3. Then it is good practice to issue a name for the Python Notebook you want to create and run. The same is presented in Figure 2.19.

FIGURE 2.18   The New Python Notebook.

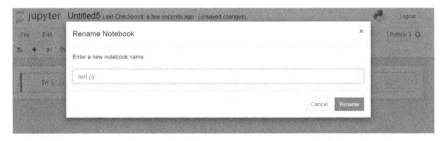

FIGURE 2.19   Name the Notebook.

3. Then, the user is free to type any Python code as required. The option for running (executing) the typed code is also available, and RUN has to be clicked as presented below in Figure 2.20. The output for the first code has come.

FIGURE 2.20   The first code execution.

Once the test is completed, it is always important to logout. The logout option is also highlighted, and the user can click it to sign off. The complete procedure is presented as Demo video @ https://youtu.be/bzaO9SFH JSA. Next in the list is the installation of Keras. It is frequently used in the book, and readers are requested to pay complete attention to the process of installation.

D. Keras Installation

One has to follow the sequence and steps. The first step is presented as a screenshot, as shown in Figure 2.21. From the Windows "Start" button, Click on search "Anaconda Prompt."

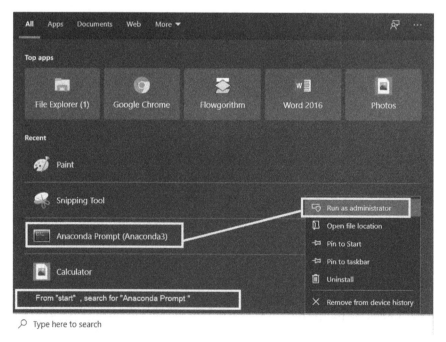

FIGURE 2.21   The Anaconda Prompt.

Next, to install Keras, one has to issue the below command in the command prompt. Once successfully installed, the message "Successfully installed Keras" will appear on screen confirming the completeness of the installation, as shown in Figure 2.22.

> *pip install keras*

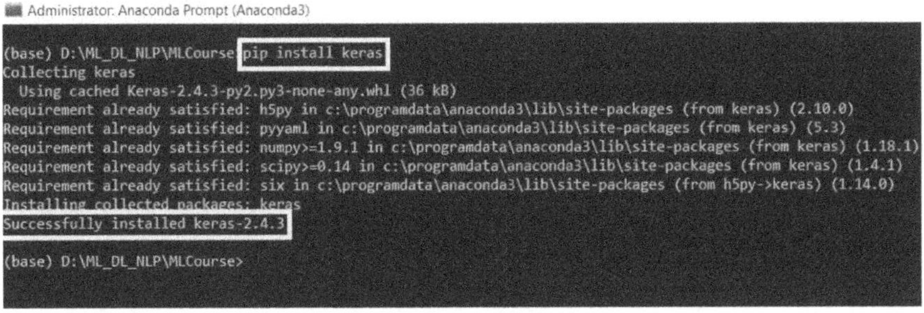

FIGURE 2.22   The Keras installation completion.

If someone has installed Keras already and wants an upgrade, it can be done with the command presented below as Figure 2.23.

>*pip install – upgrade keras*

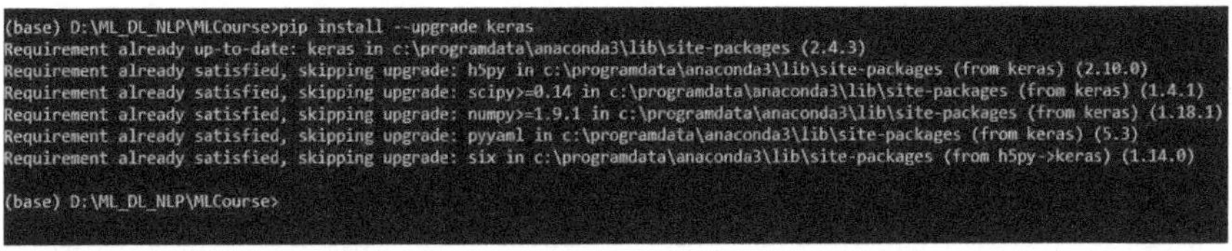

FIGURE 2.23   Keras upgrade.

To validate whether the installation has been done properly, there are some sequences to be followed. Open the Jupyter Notebook with the steps taught earlier in the section through command prompt or through the search-and-find option. Let us try whether Keras works properly in the Jupyter Notebook by running a simple program using Keras.

So, the first step in the flow is to import the Keras. Readers should also understand that the inbuilt datasets from Keras can also be used. Here, in the below code snipped, we have imported the MNIST data set from Keras.

```
In [1]:  ▶  #Simple Example to check whether Keras is Properly Installed
```

```
In [2]:  ▶  import numpy as np                        Importing the Keras Library which is built
            from tensorflow import keras              upon Tensorflow framework
            from tensorflow.keras import layers       Imports the methods to get model
                                                      information like layers
```

```
In [3]:  ▶  # Model / data parameters
            num_classes = 10
            input_shape = (28, 28, 1)
                                                      Load the dataset from keras
            # the data, split between train and test sets
            (x_train, y_train), (x_test, y_test) = keras.datasets.mnist.load_data()

            # Scale images to the [0, 1] range
            x_train = x_train.astype("float32") / 255
            x_test = x_test.astype("float32") / 255
            # Make sure images have shape (28, 28, 1)
            x_train = np.expand_dims(x_train, -1)
            x_test = np.expand_dims(x_test, -1)
            print("x_train shape:", x_train.shape)
            print(x_train.shape[0], "train samples")
            print(x_test.shape[0], "test samples")


            # convert class vectors to binary class matrices
            y_train = keras.utils.to_categorical(y_train, num_classes)
            y_test = keras.utils.to_categorical(y_test, num_classes)

            x_train shape: (60000, 28, 28, 1)
            60000 train samples
            10000 test samples
```

CODE 2.1 Keras import action.

Keras includes various inbuilt models. Data structures in Keras help in organizing the layers. The major ones are sequential and Function API. Most Deep Learning models used in this book are sequential. A sequential model is the simplest model, which helps to stack one layer over another in a simple sequence. This model is not suitable when layers have multiple inputs or outputs. Functional API is used when layers have multiple inputs or outputs.

```
▶  model = keras.Sequential(          Keras provides various model where here
        [                             uses a sequential model
            keras.Input(shape=input_shape),
            layers.Conv2D(32, kernel_size=(3, 3), activation="relu"),
            layers.MaxPooling2D(pool_size=(2, 2)),
            layers.Conv2D(64, kernel_size=(3, 3), activation="relu"),
            layers.MaxPooling2D(pool_size=(2, 2)),
            layers.Flatten(),
            layers.Dropout(0.5),
            layers.Dense(num_classes, activation="softmax"),
        ]
    )                                 Includes input and various layers in a sequence
```

CODE 2.2 Sequential model in Keras.

One can uninstall Keras by referring to the screenshot for easier reference to the following command (Figure 2.24).

>*pip uninstall keras*

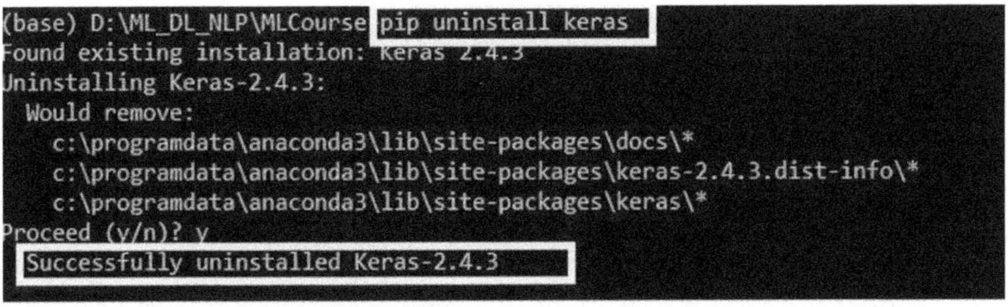

```
(base) D:\ML_DL_NLP\MLCourse pip uninstall keras
Found existing installation: Keras 2.4.3
Uninstalling Keras-2.4.3:
  Would remove:
    c:\programdata\anaconda3\lib\site-packages\docs\*
    c:\programdata\anaconda3\lib\site-packages\keras-2.4.3.dist-info\*
    c:\programdata\anaconda3\lib\site-packages\keras\*
Proceed (y/n)? y
Successfully uninstalled Keras-2.4.3
```

FIGURE 2.24   Keras uninstallation.

The installation procedure is presented as a video in the link: https://youtu.be/7YhBIzXLfKM

2.3   DATASETS – A QUICK GLANCE

Many data sets sources are available. A few are listed below with the corresponding links in Table 2.1.

TABLE 2.1   Datasets and the Sources

S.NO	Name of the dataset	Link for download
1	Kaggle Datasets	www.kaggle.com/datasets
2	Kdd Nuggets	www.kdnuggets.com/datasets/index.html
3	UCI Datasets	https://archive.ics.uci.edu/ml/datasets.php
4	deeplearning.net	http://deeplearning.net/datasets/
5	Visual Data	www.visualdata.io/discovery
6	Carnegie Mellon University Libraries	www.library.cmu.edu/
7	Google Cloud Public Datasets, Google	https://cloud.google.com/public-datasets/
8	Git Hub	https://github.com/awesomedata/ awesome-public-datasets#machinelearning
9	Stanford Common Dataset, Stanford University	https://snap.stanford.edu/data/
10	Datalab	UC Berkeley	www.lib.berkeley.edu/libraries/data-lab
11	Keras.io	https://keras.io/examples/

KEY POINTS TO REMEMBER

- Deep Learning is all about tools. Many tools and libraries are available, and it is essential to know them all.
- NumPy is simply a powerful, flexible, performance-oriented, easy to use, and open-source package for Python.
- Matplotlib is a comprehensive library for creating static, animated, and interactive visualizations in Python.
- Scipy is used for the statistical operations and is one of the most preferred. Scipy has the fundamental library for scientific computing. Pandas is a very powerful, flexible, and easy to use open source data analysis and manipulation tool, built on top of the Python programming language.
- IPython is a web-based interactive development environment for Jupyter Notebook code, and data.
- One can install Anaconda by visiting www.anaconda.com/distribution/
- The command to be issued is "jupyter notebook –ip=*" for the installation of Jupyter from the Anaconda prompt.
- The command "pip install keras" is used for the installation of Keras.

QUIZ

1. Describe clearly the procedure for installation of Anaconda.
2. How can someone install Jupyter over Anaconda?
3. How do we create a notebook in Jupyter and how can the same be run?
4. What is NumPy all about and how is it useful?
5. Why is Pandas so famous and how is it special?
6. How is SciPy handy? List your views.
7. What is the command for the installation of Keras?
8. How is Keras uninstalled?

## CHAPTER 3

Machine Learning: The Fundamentals

LEARNING OBJECTIVES

After reading through this chapter, reader will be able to understand the following:

- What is machine learning?
- Importance of machine learning.
- Types of learning algorithms.
- Machine learning framework.
- Regression.
- Difference between Logistic and Linear Regression.
- Classification techniques.
- Clustering techniques.

3.1 INTRODUCTION

The book is aimed at Deep Learning, and this chapter is about Machine Learning. Why is this needed is the first question a reader would have in mind. The first chapter introduced the reader to the need for Deep Learning and the discussions revolved around it. The present chapter provides the reader with information on Machine Learning concepts and fundamentals

DOI: 10.1201/9781003185635-3

that are essential for any AI aspirant to know. Also, a Deep Learning expert cannot avoid the concepts of Regression or Classification or Clustering. All these are discussed in this chapter, which certainly is an important one. There are cases where one could use the ML concepts in the Deep Learning based systems. There is a lot of interoperability between ML and DL and, hence, the authors have drafted this chapter by embedding much important information.

3.2 THE DEFINITIONS – YET ANOTHER TIME

It is good to recollect the definitions once again, here. Let us define what Artificial Intelligence, Machine Learning, and Deep Learning are about.

- *Artificial Intelligence* –We humans and animals have natural intelligence. Yes, we can think and act. Machines cannot. "If machines can exhibit intelligence and act the way we do, it is called Artificial Intelligence." This is achieved through algorithms and complex math. Deep Learning, Machine Learning, and Natural Language Processing (NLP) have made this possible. (Natural Language Processing is beyond the scope of this book, hence, we do not focus on it.)
- *Machine Learning* – This is a subset of the broad AI umbrella. ML will enable the systems to perform a specific task without explicit interventions or inputs. Decisions will be based on the examples we provided in the past. Based on the patterns in the received data, inferences can be drawn and decisions can be taken. The main aim is to have NO human intervention at all. Let the computer learn automatically and perform.
- *Deep Learning* – Here comes the growth. In Deep Learning the human brain is imitated in processing data and understanding the same. Solutions also are to be in a way similar to how the brain thinks. This is fully based on neural networks (The brain is full of neurons!). People also call this Deep Neural Learning or Deep Neural Networks. This book is completely focused on Deep Learning with Machine Learning fundamentals covered.

To understand the connection between the aforesaid three, a diagrammatic representation is presented below as Figure 3.1.

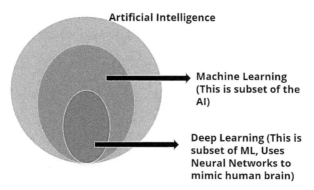

FIGURE 3.1   The AI, ML and DL Connect.

The next immediate topic for the discussion is "Machine Learning Algorithms." There are four categories of ML algorithms (Some say three, but we make it four for enhanced understanding and clarity).

- Supervised Learning
- Unsupervised Learning
- Reinforced Learning
- Evolutionary Learning

We shall learn these in succession, with examples!

3.3   MACHINE LEARNING ALGORITHMS

3.3.1   Supervised Learning Algorithms

This is to be explained with a clear example. Let us, as an instance, take a baby, that is, an infant who is growing. Mother teaches infant everything and infant learns it all. Mother teaches the fruits now. Mom shows apple and teaches child, showing apple as "Apple"; the child remembers the color and the label "Apple." Next, mom shows banana, tells, this is banana. Child will remember the shape, color and name it with the label "banana" in his/her mind. Next time, when an apple is shown, Child will jump and say "apppllleeeee." Similarly, when the banana is shown, Child will shout, "Banana!" Child learns to identify these fruits as he or she is trained to do! Child Learning = Machine Learning. This approach is labelled! The baby knows the Apple and Banana and will identify the labels correctly anytime when coming across the same. This is called Supervised Learning! Figure 3.2 shows exactly how Supervised Learning works.

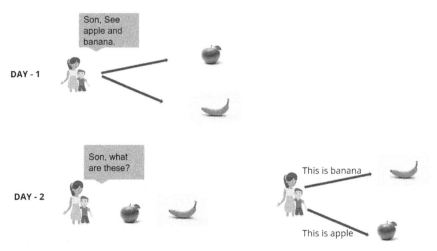

FIGURE 3.2   Supervised Learning with Apple and Banana.

Your data will enable examples for each situation. The data will also specify the outcome for these situations. Training data is used to build the model, and the model will predict the outcome for the new data! (This is done with previous knowledge). If not trained, the results will not be as expected (Figure 3.3).

If not trained, results won't be as expected.

FIGURE 3.3   Supervised Learning: training is everything.

Wrong training leads to wrong results in Machine Learning – it is karma.

If you train wrongly, the system will provide only wrong results. It is like karma and is very powerful. One can refer to Figure 3.4 for a quicker understanding of how important is the proper training. Based on the training, the results come, and that is Supervised Learning.

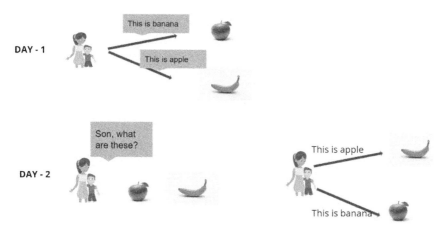

FIGURE 3.4   Supervised Learning: wrong training leads to wrong results.

3.3.2   The Unsupervised Learning Algorithms

It is time to learn the next approach. This approach will not have the knowledge of the outcome variable in the data set. Confusing right, the baby comes to the rescue with the right example – let us see that.

A baby is again taken for reference in Figure 3.5. He is shown a picture with dogs and cats. Baby has not been introduced to dogs or cats before (unsupervised). Baby in no way knows the features of dog or cat. So, no supervisory approach will work here. The baby has no labels for the items before him.

Now, the human approach is to think smart! Baby will somehow look into the similarities of the cats and dogs and will say 1, 2, 4 are dogs and 3, 5, 6, 7 are cats. Baby may not know why and what. But there is a pattern, and it can be grouped. This is called Unsupervised Learning.

FIGURE 3.5 Unsupervised Learning process.

Given a set of data, it will categorize them and give an output. Each category is referred to as a cluster. The labels for the clusters are to be manually tagged later. The categorization is based on features in the data points. The unsupervised learning algorithms are also referred to as clustering algorithms. Consider the same use case discussed for supervised learning. Here the model takes in all images and gives out two clusters. One cluster will be "cat," whereas another cluster will have all the images of "dog." When a new image is given to the model, it will be placed in one of the two clusters based on its features.

3.3.3   Reinforcement Learning

This is a feedback-based learning process. This method of learning is used in most robots and computer-based games. Here the input need not have labelled data. Instead, the model learns by interacting with the environment and getting feedback from it. The first time the model makes a decision based on the feedback, the model learns if its decision was right or wrong. So, this supervised learning eases the task of giving completely labelled data for training. A very common example is a computer chess game: If the computer loses while playing with you, then the program will remember all the steps that the player made, and the system made. Next time, if you use the same strategy it will not work in the system and, eventually, the player will lose to the program.

The baby comes to the rescue again. One can refer to Figure 3.6.

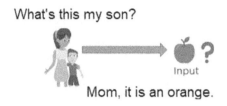

What's this my son?

Input

Mom, it is an orange.

No, My boy, it is Apple.   This is the feedback!

Input

Oh, Apologies mom, I shall correct

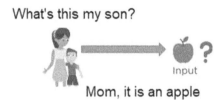

What's this my son?

Input

Mom, it is an apple

FIGURE 3.6   Reinforcement Learning.

3.3.4 Evolutionary Approach

This approach is still evolving and is not an easy one. These types of algorithms imitate natural evolution to solve a particular problem. For an instance, Genetic algorithms can be used to solve a problem. This is beyond scope of this book and, hence, is ignored for now.

3.4 HOW/WHY DO WE NEED ML?

Well, how do we learn? The following example is handy. When we see dark clouds in the sky, we predict it is going to rain. Simple; this is prediction through the training we received from childhood. This is the same concept we use with ML. We train, we get the machine working, repeatedly working, with no human intervention.

So, why do we need ML?

We need ML because we cannot do all the things needed. Nor can we do everything accurately. But machines cannot deny the order you gave. So, make the machines work, but with the intelligence you ask for.

Machines with ML algorithms can also work without intervention. These machines adapt to environments, learn from mistakes, and no such errors will be repeated in the future. In short, the process shall be faster, smoother, and error free. Also, repeated tasks can be done even better with ML in place. Some of the known ML applications the reader has already seen:

- FB recommending you friends.
- Amazon recommending you products.
- Flipkart recommending you products.
- Netflix recommendations.

Netflix makes recommendations with the best series based on your taste, but with ML behind. So, the point is simple. With ML in the picture, a company can identify more opportunities for making good profits.

A Scenario – You are browsing about Thailand Holidays. You did not book any tickets or even confirm the trip. You login to Facebook and get the Thailand holidays related posts. This is ML for you!

It helps in finding new business, enhancing profit and avoiding errors or human intervention. No operator is there to link that Thai AD to a Facebook page yet, so you got it. One can refer to the YouTube lecture by authors on all the above discussed topics @ *https://youtu.be/sQH_jyEkP-8.*

3.5   THE ML FRAMEWORK

Figure 3.7 below is sufficient to understand the flow. Each step needs math, tools, and techniques which we shall be learning here.

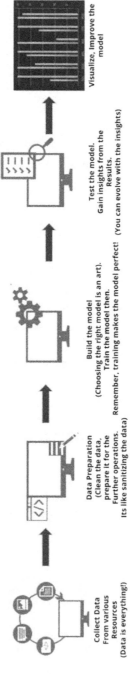

FIGURE 3.7 The ML Framework.

The first step is about collection of the data from all the relevant resources. The data is new fuel. In fact, the data is everything. The better the collected data, the better the model developed will be. The second step is about cleansing the data. It is like sanitizing the data and making it usable. The outliers should be removed, and data should be consistent. Next, model building is the step to be done. Training the model is important and the better the training, the better the results. Just training is not sufficient, so, the next phase is about testing. One can gain insights from the testing results. One can deploy the model and visualize, improving the model as well. This is the flow. One can listen to the video lecture on the ML Framework from the link: *https://youtu.be/3QwkFzofzbI*

3.6 LINEAR REGRESSION – A COMPLETE UNDERSTANDING

We need to learn some math (it cannot be avoided any further). Simple Linear Regression is very useful and most commonly used algorithms in the predictive analytics and Machine Learning. We shall understand what Linear Regression is, how to build a model, and so forth. It is a simple technique used to find the relationship between a dependent variable and an independent variable. That is, simply saying, regression tries to establish a clear relationship between input and output.

- The dependent variable = Output.
- The independent variable = Input.

We can take an example: X Axis with Input, independent variables; Y with Output, Dependent variables. Some simple examples are presented below.

- Mapping/drawing relationship between number of hours worked and salary drawn.
- Number of hours prepared and marks scored.

We now try to draw the relationship between the input and output, that is, the Independent variable and Dependent variable (Figure 3.8).

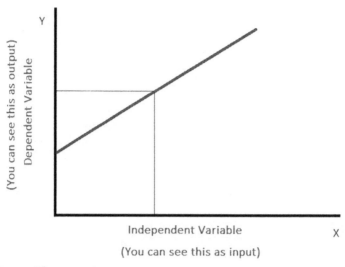

FIGURE 3.8   The regression.

This is the purpose and what Linear Regression does. It derives a relationship between the Independent and Dependent variables. Now, let us understand the possible cases.

Case 1 – Positive Relationship:
What will be the status when the Independent variable changes? When the Independent variable increases and if the Dependent variable increases, we call it positive. See picture below:

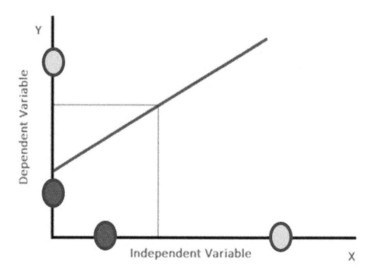

FIGURE 3.9   The Positive relationship.

Here, there is a Positive relationship.

- X – Number of hours worked.
- Y – Wage increase.

If Y increases positively as X increases, it is called a Positive relationship. In this case, the salary increases as the number of hours increase.

Next to learn about is the Negative relationship. One can look at Figure 3.9 to understand what the Negative relationship is about.

Case 2 – Negative Relationship:
When the Independent variable increases and the Dependent variable decreases we call it Negative relationship.

X – Number of hours spent on TV.
Y – CGPA drop.

If Y decreases as X increases, it is called a Negative relationship. In this case, the CGPA decreases as the number of TV hours increase. One can quickly have a look at Figure 3.10.

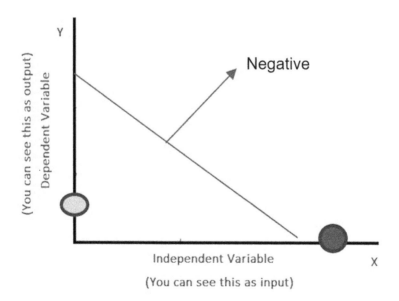

FIGURE 3.10   The Negative relationship.

With the regression, one would aim at drawing a straight line (Need not be straight always). We plot all the observations with dots. Then a line has to be drawn that fits all the different points, and it is called a Regression line. This is drawn through **Least Squares Methods.** The core aim is to minimize error through drawing the Regression line. The Regression line is presented with Figure 3.11, and now one can clearly understand the purpose of this line. One can also walk through the video lecture presented at the YouTube Link, which clearly talks about Linear Regression: *https:// youtu.be/MdHe7Sn6Qt4*

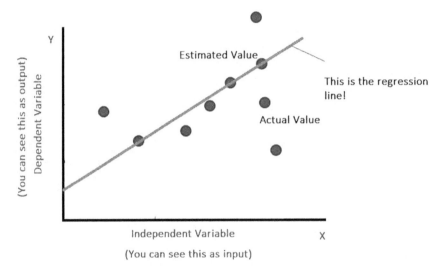

FIGURE 3.11   Regression line.

To understand what errors are about, one can have a look at Figure 3.12, below.

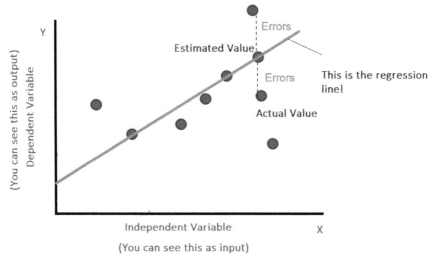

FIGURE 3.12   The error.

The overall aim is to reduce error and keep it to a minimum. It is time to go with a little mathematics. Readers already must be familiar with these fundamental mathematical terminologies and, in that case, it is a recap for the readers. Otherwise, it is important to pay attention to the next couple of sections, where it is all fundamental mathematics. One should refer to Figure 3.13 before getting into the expressions presented below:

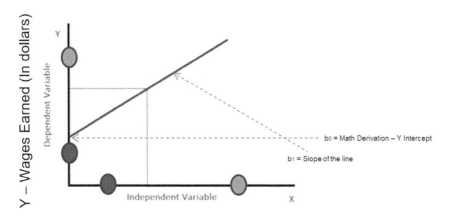

X – Amount of hours worked

FIGURE 3.13   The mathematical connect: positive impact.

One could recollect the Y = MX + C expression, which was learned during school days. The same come handy here.

$$Y = b0 + b1 * x$$

- Y = Estimated Pay
- X = Number of hours worked
- b0 = Y Intercept
- b1 = Slope of the line –
  - Here is positive impact and, hence, is + b1

As the number of hours increase, the pay should increase. Hence, there is a Positive relationship.

- X is an Independent variable. One can only control this.
- Y is the Dependent variable and is the outcome. The salary is dependent on the number of hours worked (This is fully dependent).

$$Y = b0 - b1 * x$$

- Y = Estimated pay
- X = Number of hours worked
- b0 = Y Intercept
- b1 = Slope of the line
  - Here is Negative impact and hence is – b1.

As the number of hours of watching TV increases, the score naturally will come down. Hence, there is a Negative relationship.

- X is the Independent variable. Y is the Dependent variable and is the outcome.

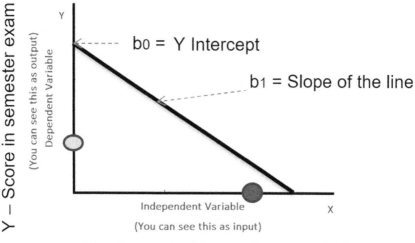

X – Amount of hours Spent on TV

FIGURE 3.14   The mathematical connect: negative impact.

The next step is to understand how to derive Linear Regression with the Least Square Method. This is one of the most commonly followed approaches for Linear Regression calculation/plotting. The first step is to create a simple data set. The process is presented step by step:

Step 1: Get the X and Y. Mark the plot. X is the input and Y is the output. X can be termed as Independent Variable and Y can be termed as Dependent Variable (Table 3.1).

TABLE 3.1   The Data Points

X	Y
1	2
2	4
3	6
4	3
5	5

The immediate next step is to calculate Mean X and Mean Y. Mean X = (1 + 2 + 3 + 4 + 5) / 5 = 3. We also need to calculate Mean Y = (2 + 4 + 6 + 3 + 5)/ 5 = 4.

So, we have arrived at Mean X and Mean Y. It is time for readers to go to the next step in the sequence. Can we make a plot? Yes, the next step is to go for the plotting of the Independent variable versus the Dependent variable. (Figure 3.15)

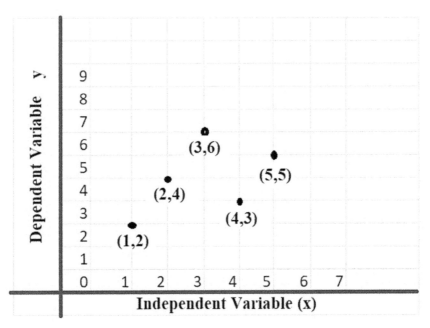

FIGURE 3.15   The x vs. y.

The next step is to plot the mean in the graph presented above in Figure 3.15. One can have a look at Figure 3.16 to understand how the plotting has happened.

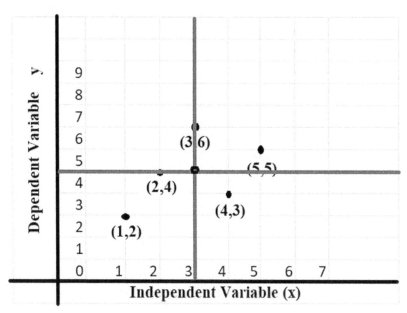

FIGURE 3.16   Mean x and Mean y plot.

The next step in flow is to get the slope and the Y intercept plotted. These are to be taken forward from the previously presented graph shown in Figure 3.17.

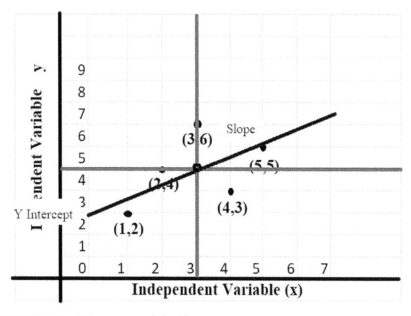

FIGURE 3.17   Y Intercept and the Slope.

The above plots have given the visualization of the data in form of the graph, and it is mandatory to visualize data points in an understandable manner. Now, we need to call for the distance. The distance from x value to X mean and the y value to Y mean is to be calculated. Table 3.2 presented below keep growing step by step and are easier to understand.

TABLE 3.2   Calculation

X	Y	x-x'	y-y'	(x-x')²	(x-x') (y-y')
1	2	1 – 3 = –2	2 – 4 = –2	4	TRUE
2	4	2 – 3 = –1	4 – 4 = 0	1	TRUE
3	6	3 – 3 = 0	6 – 4 = 2	0	0 * 2 = 0
4	3	4 – 3 = 1	3 – 4 = –1	1	1 * -1 = –1
5	5	5 – 3 = 2	5 – 4 = 1	4	1 * 2 = 2
				10	5

Now that the calculation is complete and the table is ready with information, it is easy to proceed with the formula toward completing the process. There are some fascinating tips to be followed when constructing the table. The sum of the x-x' and y-y' should always be 0. If non zero, then, there is something wrong in the computation.

$$Y' = b0 + b1 * X'$$

$$b1 = 5 / 10 = 0.5$$

The above is derived through the expression

$$b1 = Summation (x – x') (y – y') / summation (x – x2)$$

We are into the final stage of the computation.

$$Y' = b0 + b1. X' (X' \text{ and } Y' \text{ are the mean } x \text{ and } y \text{ respectively})$$

$$4 = b0 + b1.3$$

$$4 = b0 + 0.5 * 3$$

$$4 = b0 + 1.5$$

$$4 – 1.5 = b0 + 1.5 – 1.5$$

$$b0 = 2.5$$

$$b1 = slope = 0.5$$

$$b0 = y\ intercept = 2.5$$

The time has come for us to learn what exactly is the Logistic regression. The terminologies, Logistic Regression and Linear Regression are very important, and are among the most discussed topics in ML.

3.7 LOGISTIC REGRESSION – A COMPLETE UNDERSTANDING

Logistic regression is a mathematical model that predicts the probability of occurrence of Y given the information of X, a previous event. Given X, logistic regression predicts whether Y will occur or not. Logistic regression is a binary event, which means Y can be either 0 or 1. Y gets the value 1, if the event occurs and Y gets the value 0 if the event does not occur.

Logistic regression is mainly used for classification applications like spam email detection, diabetes detection for a person based on various features provided, and so forth. Popular applications include – Spam Detection, Customer Choice Prediction – that is, whether the customer will click a particular link or not? Will the customer buy the product or not? Also, diabetes/cancer prediction and more.

Linear Regression gives a continuous output, but logistic regression provides a discrete output. Linear Regression has a straight line, but Logistic regression uses a sigmoid function.

To concisely convey,

- Linear Regression is an approach to model relationship between the dependent and independent variables.
- Logistic Regression is more statistical in nature, where the model predicts the outcome, which could be one of the two values.

Learning or implementing Logistic Regression and Linear Regression through codes is beyond the present scope. But the authors have provided a clear video lecture for readers who want to explore the implementation aspect as well.

- Implementation of Linear Regression: *https://youtu.be/i6G94Me9LN0*
- Implementation of Logistic Regression: *https://youtu.be/snr1q_iq-bE*

It is time to understand what classification is about.

3.8   CLASSIFICATION – A MUST-KNOW CONCEPT

The first question normally gets raised this way: What is the difference between Regression and Classification? We explain this point first.

To start with, Regression and Classification both come under Supervised Learning Algorithms! (Yes, Supervised, Labeled). Both have extensive usage in ML, and both use the labeled data set. Then, where are they different? The problems they solve are different and there is the difference.

As discussed, Regression predicts continuous values – salary, marks, age, and so forth. Classification classifies things – male/female, pass/fail, false/true, spam/legitimate, and so forth (It classifies, and that is it). Classification divides the given data set into classes based on the parameters considered. An example can be very helpful.

Gmail is the best example. Gmail classifies email as legitimate or spam. The model is trained with millions of emails and has many parameters in consideration. Whenever new mail pops up, the classification is done as "Inbox, Spam, Promotions or Updates." If spam, it goes to the spam box. If legitimate, it goes to the Inbox. There are many famous and frequently used classification algorithms. They are listed as follows:

- Support Vector Machines
- K-Nearest Neighbors
- Kernel SVM
- Logistic Regression
- Naïve Bayes
- Decision Tree Classification
- Random Forest Classification

It is good to understand and learn all of these. But would it be out of the scope for this book? So, we handpick Support Vector Machines (SVM) and K-Nearest Neighbors for the discussion.

3.8.1   SVM – Support Vector Machines

To start with, SVM is very easy to use and to learn. It is expanded as Support Vector Machine. Data scientists claim that SVM offers better accuracy than other classifiers we work with. SVM is mostly used in email classification, Handwriting recognition and so forth. Readers are introduced to the SVM, explained clearly in this section, followed by the K-NN.

SVM is usable for regression / classification problems. But, most commonly it is used for the Classification problems over Regression. The main aim or target of SVM is about creating an optimum line or a decision boundary. The decision boundary enables segregating the data set into classes. Also, new data is on entry correctly classified – as well in the future.

The appropriate decision boundary is referred to technically as hyperplane. It is very important for readers to understand the terminologies used in SVM. They are presented one after another in a detailed manner.

Hyperplane

This is an important term. It is a plane that separates (i.e., enables grouping) objects that belong to different classes. This line helps in classifying the data points (i.e., the Red Stars and Green Triangles). One can refer to Figure 3.18 to understand the hyperplane concept.

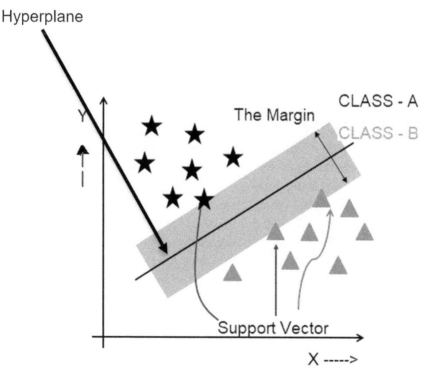

FIGURE 3.18   The SVM: complete picture.

The dimension of a hyperplane is a variable, too. Is it possible that way? Yes, it is. Figure 3.18 has two features and, hence, one straight line is sufficient. If there are three features, then it has to be a two-dimensional plane.

Support Vectors

One should refer to Figure 3.18 again. The Red Stars and Green Triangles are the Support Vectors. These points are very close to the hyperplane. These data points are the ones that affect the position of the hyperplane as well. These points are vectors that have a role in deciding the hyperplane's placement; they are called support vectors.

Margin

This is a gap. If the margin between two classes is larger, then it is a good margin. Otherwise, it is considered a bad margin. In simple terms, margin is a gap between two lines on closer class points. By referring to Figure 3.18 one can understand that the margin can be calculated as the perpendicular distance from the line to the support vectors (Red Stars and Green Triangles).

How SVM Works

Simple, one should group/segregate the data set (i.e., non-classified to classified) in the best possible way.

Readers know what a margin is. Margin is a gap between two lines on closer class points. Now, the task in hand is simple. One has to select/draw a hyperplane with maximum margin between the support vectors from the input data set. The more the margin, the larger the gap. Readers are taken through the process step by step,

One should generate something called a hyperplane. Three such plans are generated. One is brown, followed by blue and red, as could be assumed from Figure 3.19. As anyone can see, brown and blue have failed miserably to classify. This reflects a high error rate. Red is very apt, and it does the separation properly. So, what do we do? The answer is obvious. Choose the best line. The best drawn line is presented as a black line in the right side of the Figure 3.19 (This is line is the bit fit).

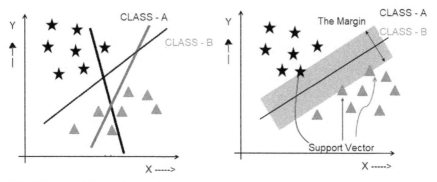

FIGURE 3.19   Hyperplane selection.

That is it. One can now understand that all the Red Stars and Green Triangles are grouped appropriately based on the hyperplane. It is now time for readers to quickly navigate to the next one in the must-know list: K-NN, the K-Nearest Neighbor Algorithm. The complete implementation of SVM and a quick lecture on the same can be found @ *https://youtu.be/ Qd9Aj_EMfk0*

3.8.2   K-NN (K-Nearest Neighbor)

K-NN is one of the easiest and most frequently used approaches; like SVM. K-NN is also based on supervised learning. It is founded on a very simple approach. Based on history, the current case is predicted. That is, when the new data is sent in for classification, based on the similarity of data available in the past, the new data gets classified. That is, the most similar category shall be found, and the new data entry shall be classified into that. In simple words: New data can be classified with ease into a most similar category with K-NN in place.

The next question would be, where can we use K-NN? It has been used for classification and regression. But, like SVM, K-NN has better results when used with classification and, hence, is preferred for classification. K-NN has two very important aspects:

- It is referred to as non-parametric.
- It is also said to be a Lazy Learner algorithm.

It is important to understand what is non-parametric. It means the algorithm does not make any assumption regarding the underlying data.

Next, what is Lazy Learning? Nothing happens immediately in this approach. It means the algorithm does not learn anything from the training set in that instance. But it stores the entire data set during the classification and then does the action on the data set. This means there is no specialized training phase required. It delays the raining until a query for classification is raised.

As ever, an instance could be useful. If someone wants to classify a fruit or vegetable, when the input is sent in, the algorithm works with the similarity concept. Based on the similarity of the features, it would now classify.

In the K-NN, remember, K is the king. Data scientists have preferred K to be an odd number when the classes are even. K could be 1, 3, 5, 7 for the classes being 2. One should also note that when K = 1, It is the nearest neighbor algorithm. It is now the time to approach K-NN step by step.

- Can we select the number, K, of the neighbors? It is the first step.
- One should calculate the Euclidean distance of K number of neighbors.
- Then, take the K nearest neighbors as per the calculated Euclidean distance.
- Start counting. Among these K neighbors, count the number of the data points in each category.
- Assign the new data points to that category for which the number of the neighbors is maximum.
- The model is ready.

An example is very handy and easy to understand in Figure 3.20.

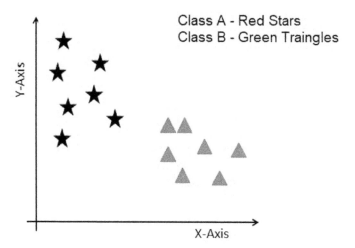

FIGURE 3.20   The assumed scenario.

The problem statement is presented pictorially in Figure 3.21. The new data entry has to be classified as a Red Star or a Green Triangle.

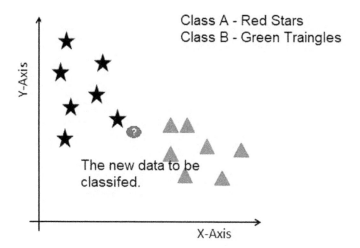

FIGURE 3.21   The assumed scenario: with new entrant.

Case 1 – When K is chosen as 1.

If K is chosen as 1, then the task becomes easier, and is the simplest option. The input data gets classified as Class A. One can with ease understand this from Figure 3.22.

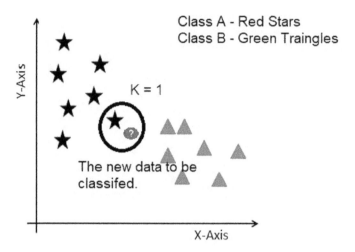

FIGURE 3.22   Case, 1: K = 1.

Case 2 – When K is chosen as 3.

Let us choose the K = 3. One can calculate the Euclidean distance between the data points. The Euclidean distance is the distance between two points (Can be done through other methods, also; Python has inbuilt functions to help the programmers). Figure 3.23 shows how K-NN works with K value chosen as 3.

- Class A = 1 count
- Class B =2 count.
- So, naturally, the new entry is classified as B. (I.e. green triangles)

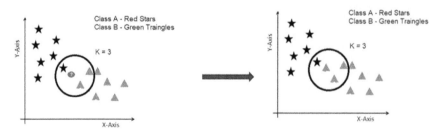

FIGURE 3.23   Case, 2: K = 3.

Case 3 – When K is chosen as 7

Here is the scenario where K is set as 7. One can understand how it works by referring to Figure 3.24.

- Class A = 4 count
- Class B =3 count.
- So, naturally, the new entry is classified as A. (I.e. Red Stars)

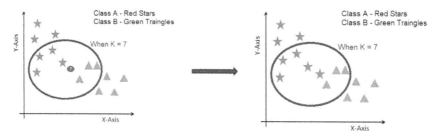

FIGURE 3.24   Case, 2: K = 7.

By now, readers should have understood the way the K-NN works. One must make a note that "Keeping low K values should be avoided, as the prediction would go wrong."

Advantages

- Simple.
- The more the data, the better the classification.

Disadvantages

- Finding the optimum value for K is challenging.

One can receive a brief note from the authors by listening to *https:// youtu.be/nVgZbVUmh50.*

The next topic for discussion is "Clustering." It is one of the very important areas to learn and is interesting as well.

3.9   CLUSTERING – AN INTERESTING CONCEPT TO KNOW

To make it simple, this is a method or technique to group data into clusters. The objects inside a cluster should/must have high similarity. (Example. Medical students – First year is a cluster; second year is a cluster, etc.). A cluster's objects should be definitely dissimilar to the objects from another cluster. (Example. Engineering students – First year is another cluster when compared with a medical student's first year). These two clusters are disjointed. Clustering helps in dividing the complete data to multiple clusters. This is a *non-labeled* approach. So, it can be called an Unsupervised approach. One could understand clustering by referring the Figure 3.25.

Cluster – A (Medical Students – I Year)   Cluster – B (Engineering Students – I Year)

FIGURE 3.25 Clustering.

It is time to understand K-Means clustering, one of the most commonly used techniques.

3.9.1 K-Means Clustering

As discussed, it is a method or technique to group data into clusters. The objects inside a cluster should/must have high similarity. A cluster's objects should be definitely dissimilar to the objects from another cluster. This "similarity" is the metric used! It is the metric, which talks about the relationship between the objects.

Now comes the next question: Why do we need clustering? Simple. Clustering gives you an exploratory view of the data. One gets a better idea about the data with the clustering.

K-Means is actually called a "Centroid Based Clustering." The next question to be answered: What is a centroid? The dictionary says, *Centroid* is the center of mass of a geometric object of uniform density. Well, coming to ML, centroid definition remains the same. It is the data point at the center of a cluster. Centroid need not be a member of the data set considered. (It can as well be)

This clustering approach is iterative in nature. It means the algorithm keeps working until the goal is achieved. One sample data set is taken and is explained step by step. The challenge is to group the eight objects in the data set as two clusters. All the objects have the X, Y and Z coordinates clearly available. How do we select K value? K is nothing but number of clusters. Here, it is 2. So, let us get the K Value set as 2.

Let us have a look at the data set.

TABLE 3.3   The Data Set Considered for Clustering

Objects	X	Y	Z
O1	1	4	1
O2	1	2	2
O3	1	4	2
O4	2	1	2
O5	1	1	1
O6	2	4	2
O7	1	1	2
O8	2	1	1

Initially, we have to take any two centroids.
There can be a question. Why go with 2 centroids? Since the K Value is 2, the number of centroids chosen is also 2. Once chosen, the data points get tagged to any of the clusters, based on the distance. It is time to start with the computation.

- First Centroid = O2 – This shall be cluster 1 (O2 = First Centroid = 1, 2, 2)
- Second Centroid = O6 – This shall be cluster 2. (O6 = Second Centroid = 2, 4, 2)

Can we not choose any other object as centroid? This is a very common question. The answer is that any object can become a centroid. The next question to be answered is: How do we measure distance? There is a formula, and it comes to the rescue.

$$d=|x2-x1|+|y2-y1|+|z2-z1|$$

It is termed *Manhattan distance.*

- d = Yes, as you predicted is the distance between two objects.
- Remember – Any object has X, Y, Z coordinates as per the data set! So, the task is simple.

It is time to reconstruct the table, and one has to use the distance between each object and the centroids chosen.

TABLE 3.4   Distance from C1 and C2

Objects	X	Y	Z	Distance from C1(1,2,2)	Distance from C2(2,4,2)
O1	1	4	1	D= |1-1|+|4-2|+|2-1|= 3	D= |1-1|+|4-2|+|2-1|=2
O2	1	2	2	D= |1-1|+|2-2|+|2-2|=0	D= |2-1|+|4-2|+|2-2|= 3
O3	1	4	2	D= |1-1|+|4-2|+|2-2|=2	D= |2-1|+|4-4|+|2-2|=1
O4	2	1	2	2	3
O5	1	1	1	2	5
O6	2	4	2	3	0
O7	1	1	2	1	4
O8	2	1	1	3	4

Like O1, O2 and O3, the rest of the calculations to find out the distance from C1 and C2 are to be computed. One can refer to Table 3.4 to acquire clearer understanding.

The next step is to go ahead with the clustering. How can that be achieved? Simple. Based on the distance, one can go ahead with clustering. Whichever is shorter: Say C1 is shorter than C2 for an object, the object falls to C1. Hence, the clustering looks like:

TABLE 3.5   Clustering

Objects	X	Y	Z	Distance from C1(1,2,2)	Distance from C2(2,4,2)
O1	1	4	1	D= |1-1|+|4-2|+|2-1|= 3	D= |1-1|+|4-2|+|2-1|=2
O2	1	2	2	D= |1-1|+|2-2|+|2-2|=0	D= |2-1|+|4-2|+|2-2|= 3
O3	1	4	2	D= |1-1|+|4-2|+|2-2|=2	D= |2-1|+|4-4|+|2-2|=1
O4	2	1	2	2	3
O5	1	1	1	2	5
O6	2	4	2	3	0
O7	1	1	2	1	4
O8	2	1	1	3	4

Cluster 1
OB-2 (0 < 3)
OB-4 (2 < 3)
OB-5 (2 < 5)
OB-7 (1 < 4)
OB-8 (3 < 4)

Cluster 1
OB-2 (0 < 3)
OB-4 (2 < 3)
OB-5 (2 < 5)
OB-7 (1 < 4)
OB-8 (3 < 4)

For clearer understanding, the following guidelines have been followed in Table 3.5. Cluster 1 cluster 2 are differentiated by shades in the figure.

To make it clearer, one can refer to Table 3.6 as presented below.

TABLE 3.6   Clusters 1 and 2

Objects	X	Y	Z
01	1	4	1
02	1	2	2
03	1	4	2
04	2	1	2
05	1	1	1
06	2	4	2
07	1	1	2
08	2	1	1

- **Cluster 1:** $((1+2+1+1+2)/5, (2+1+1+1+1)/5, (2+2+1+2+1)/5) = (1.4, 1.2, 1.6)$
- **Cluster 2:** $((1+1+2)/3, (4+4+4)/3, (1+2+2)/3) = (1.33, 4, 1.66)$.

The next round, that is, the next iteration, has to be started.

TABLE 3.7   Reiterated Results

Objects	X	Y	Z	Distance from C1(1.4,1.2,1.6)	Distance from C2(1.33, 4, 1.66)
01	1	4	1	3.8 (1.4 -1 + 4 − 1.2 + 1.6 -1)	1 (1.33 − 1 + 4 − 4 + 1.66 − 1)
02	1	2	2	1.6 (1.4- 1+ 2 − 1.2 + 2 − 1.6)	2.66 (1.33 − 1+ 4 − 2 + 2 − 1.66)
03	1	4	2	3.6	0.66
04	2	1	2	1.2	4
05	1	1	1	1.2	4
06	2	4	2	3.8	1
07	1	1	2	1	3.66
08	2	1	1	1.4	4.33

Hence, the new clusters would be:

So, we can stop here. No updates in the centroids or changes in the cluster grouping has been observed. Hence, this is the correct clustering. This is how the K-Means clustering works.

TABLE 3.8   New Clusters

Cluster 1	Cluster 2
O2	O1
O4	O3
O5	O6
O7	
O8	

One can listen to the lecture by the authors on K-Means clustering from –*https://youtu.be/Fuq9Dw43co0*

One can also understand the way the model has to be developed by listening to – *https://youtu.be/6d6HcLG6lFQ*

We have come to the end of this chapter. This is all the fundamentals, and we request readers to pay attention to these fundamentals to the best of their ability. The video links are helpful as well.

KEY POINTS TO REMEMBER

- If machines can exhibit intelligence and act as we do, it is called Artificial Intelligence.
- Machine Learning will enable the systems to perform a specific task without explicit interventions or inputs.
- In Deep Learning the human brain is imitated in processing data and understanding the same. Solutions also are sought in the way the brain thinks.
- There are four categories of ML algorithms. (Some say there are three, but we make it four for enhanced understanding and clarity)
  - Supervised Learning
  - Unsupervised Learning
  - Reinforced Learning
  - Evolutionary Learning
- In Supervised Learning your data enables examples for each situation. It also specifies outcomes for the same.
- With Supervised Learning, training data is used to build the model; the model will predict the outcome for the new data.
- The Unsupervised Learning approach does not have knowledge of the outcome variable in the data set.
- The Reinforcement algorithm is about feedback-based learning.
- Evolutionary Learning algorithms imitate natural evolution to solve particular problems.
- Machine Learning and Deep Learning require users to install some tools and libraries.
- Seaborn is a Python data visualization library based on matplotlib.

- Regression tries to establish a clear relationship between input and output.
- Ordinary least squares are a type of linear least squares method for estimating the unknown parameters in a Linear Regression model.
- Classification shall classify something like Male/Female, Pass/Fail, False/True, Spam/Legitimate, and so forth. (It classifies, folks).
- The main aim or target of the SVM is about creating an optimum line or a decision boundary.
- Hyperplane is a plane which separates (i.e. enables grouping) objects that belong to different classes.
- K-NN is one of the easiest and most frequently used like SVM.
- Clustering is a method or technique to group data into clusters. The objects inside a cluster should/must have high similarity.

QUIZ

1. Define Machine Learning.
2. Define Deep Learning.
3. Where will one use Deep Learning or Machine Learning?
4. How is regression useful?
5. What is Linear Regression?
6. How is Linear Regression different from Logistic Regression?
7. Differentiate clustering and classification.
8. Explain clearly how SVM works?
9. Explain how K-Means clustering functions.

FURTHER READING

✓ Williams, D., & Hill, J. (2005). *U.S. Patent Application No. 10/939,288.*
✓ Jordan, M.I. and Mitchell, T.M., 2015. "Machine learning: Trends, perspectives, and prospects." *Science*, 349(6245), pp. 255–260.
✓ Goodfellow, I., Bengio, Y. and Courville, A., 2016. "Machine learning basics." *Deep Learning*, 1, pp. 98–164.
✓ Mohri, Mehryar, Afshin Rostamizadeh, and Ameet Talwalkar. *Foundations of Machine Learning.* MIT Press, 2018.

✓ Sammut, Claude, and Geoffrey I. Webb, eds. *Encyclopedia of Machine Learning*. Springer Science & Business Media, 2011.

✓ Burkov, Andriy. *The Hundred-page Machine Learning Book*. Vol. 1. Canada: Andriy Burkov, 2019.

✓ Zhang, Xian-Da. "Machine learning." In *A Matrix Algebra Approach to Artificial Intelligence*, pp. 223–440. Springer, Singapore, 2020.

✓ Shalev-Shwartz, Shai, and Shai Ben-David. *Understanding Machine Learning: From theory to algorithms*. Cambridge University Press, 2014.

✓ Goldberg, D.E. and Holland, J.H. "Genetic algorithms and machine learning." 1988.

## CHAPTER 4

The Deep Learning Framework

LEARNING OBJECTIVES

After this chapter, the reader shall be able to understand the following:

- Various layers in Artificial Neural Networks.
- What is a Perceptron and a Multilayer Perceptron and advanced MLP?
- Various terminologies like Optimization, weight initialization, cost function, dropout, and hyper parameters.

4.1 INTRODUCTION

Artificial Intelligence (AI) has become an indispensable part of human life. We have smart phones, smart TV, smart water heaters, and smart air conditioning, even a complete smart home. Everything around us is smart after the advent of AI. In the previous chapters, we have already talked about what exactly AI is and how it differs from Machine Learning and Deep Learning.

Deep Learning helps the machine to learn adaptively and respond to an unprecedented scenario, as how a human being responds. This capability is brought to a machine by building and training various models. These models are capable of having various abstracted layers. These layers help in extracting the required features for the decision-making layer to correctly classify and predict the most effective output.

DOI: 10.1201/9781003185635-4

4.2 ARTIFICIAL NEURON

It is a universal rule in computer science that anything should follow an input – output process model. It is the same case for Deep Learning. Why does Deep Learning have layers? Yes, we have already talked about this in an earlier scenario. We need Deep Learning to help machines to deal with unprecedented scenarios as human beings do. That is great, but have we ever thought about how a human brain works? Is that so simple that anyone and everyone can understand? Definitely, no, which is why we have serious research work still going on, and neuroscientists are trying to unveil the process inside a human brain. If we need the machines to work like human brains, it has something to do with neurons and its structure. Yes, now we understand Deep Learning has neural networks inside.

4.2.1 Biological Neuron

The human brain is filled with neurons. Say, a human is passing through a colorful garden of pretty flowers, and that sight triggers the neurons to enjoy their beauty. He or she smells the fragrance that is triggered by the neurons in the brain and thus humans are able to enjoy the fragrance. According to the inputs, the right response is activated by the brain (Figure 4.1).

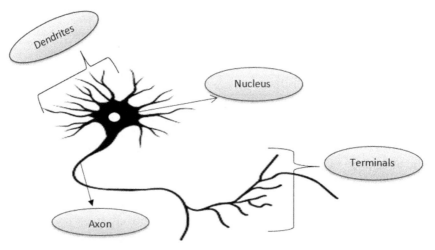

FIGURE 4.1   Biological neuron.

A biological neuron has dendrites to collect the data from other neurons, and the data is processed by the nucleus. The processed information is passed through the transmission channel axon to the terminals for passing the information to the next neuron, and the chain continues. This is how a biological neuron works. Deep Learning is trying to imitate the structure of a neuron in our brain. This is why a simple neural network could be depicted as in the Figure 4.2.

This picture could be mapped to a simple neural network as simple as having one set of inputs, one hidden layer and one output layer. For your initial understanding, the hidden layer is where the processing happens. The hidden layers are the abstractive layers, which help in performing the extraction of features. We will learn about this in detail in upcoming chapters.

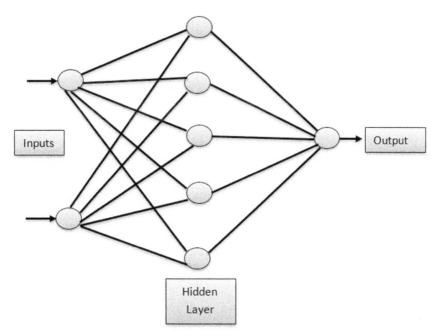

FIGURE 4.2   Simple neural network: an artificial neuron.

This is how a biological neuron is mapped to an artificial neuron.

4.2.2   Perceptron

A neuron is the basic element in any artificial neural networks. Here, it is important to talk about the term *perceptron*, is coined by Frank Rosenblatt in the year 1957. Perceptron is the unit in the artificial neural network that acts as the computational unit for extracting features. This unit also acts as the major business logic to classify or predict from the input data fed to the system. This can be depicted as in Figure 4.3.

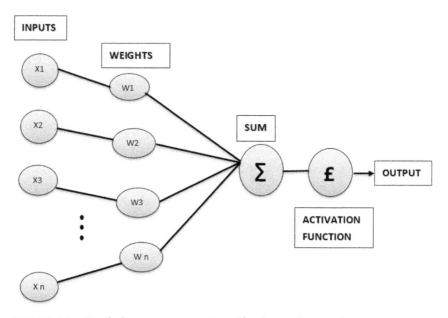

FIGURE 4.3   Single-layer perceptron in artificial neural network.

The perceptron uses Supervised Learning to classify or predict the output. Supervised Learning is a Machine-learning algorithm that learns the data by dividing the data into training and testing data. The data used in Supervised Learning would be associated with a label. A single layer perceptron helps to classify the data by drawing a decision boundary using a linearly separable line. There is another kind of perceptron called a multi-level perceptron, or MLP. This uses feed forward networks with more than one hidden layer apart from the input layer and one output layer. This has more classification capabilities than a single layer perceptron. A single layer perceptron could be used for a binary classification problem.

4.2.2.1   How a Perceptron Works?

A perceptron helps to learn the weight for the input data in order to classify or predict the desired output. This is achieved by the perceptron following a certain rule. This rule states that the algorithm automatically learns the weights associated with all input data. The learned weight has to be the most optimal one for the input data. The inputs are multiplied with the associated optimal weights. The products of input and associated weights are combined, and then passed through a function.

$$w_1 x_1 + w_2 x_2 + \cdots + w_n x_n$$

This is called an activation function, which classifies or predicts the output. Activation functions help to draw the decision boundary of the data mapping them to a certain range of values.

4.2.3 Activation Functions

For any function, say:

$$F(X) = Y$$

X is the input value, which is applied on a function F, and it transforms the domain value X to a range Y, to be precise, a mapping from X to Y by the application of the function F.

There are various activation functions available as linear activation functions and non-linear activation functions. The most commonly used non-linear activation functions are RELU (Rectified linear unit), Sigmoid, Softmax, and TanH. All these will make the value fall within a boundary according to the input data and applications. They are capable of working with high dimensional and complex data such as audio, video, images, and so forth.

The simplest and most commonly used activation function is the Sigmoid function as shown in Figure 4.4.

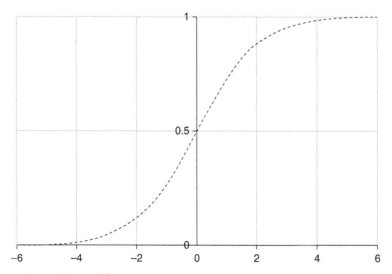

FIGURE 4.4   Sigmoid function.

TanH is another function, which is used often. They are the simplest activation functions. Refer to Figure 4.5 to understand TanH.

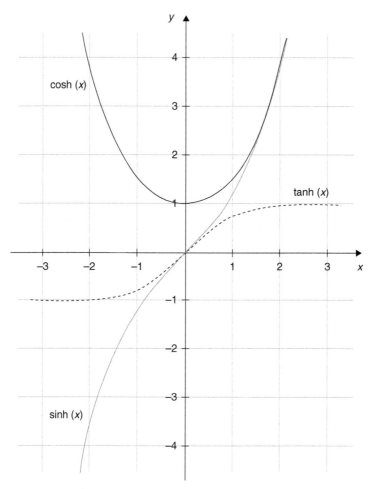

FIGURE 4.5   TanH function.

The most commonly used non-linear activation function is the Rectified Linear Unit (ReLU). This helps the model built to converge faster than other activation functions. It converts the negative values mapped to zero and brings non-linearity to the solution, as shown in Figure 4.6.

$$F(x) = \max(0, x)$$

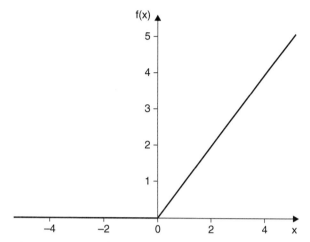

FIGURE 4.6 ReLU activation function.

Softmax is normally used when the probability of the output is important. It is mainly used along with the last layers of neural networks to understand the probability of categorization to each of the classes used in the system. One can refer to Figure 4.7 to understand Softmax functions.

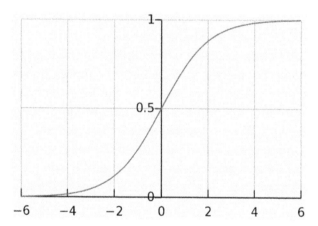

FIGURE 4.7 Softmax function.

Now, as we know how activation functions help neural network to learn, it is also important to know about the threshold value, which decides whether the neuron has to be fired or not. This is part of the perceptron rule. In addition, if there is an error associated with the perceptron, which is given as a feedback to improve the performance, this error is actually the derivative of an activation function. These are called gradients.

Back propagation is the method normally used in training the neural networks to adjust weights. This algorithm gives feedback from the output obtained from the model and updates the weight coefficients for the betterment of the model. This operation helps the model to classify or predict efficiently, as it modifies to optimal weights. Selection of best activation function for the model follows an experiential process and needs to try different activation functions to identify which one is important for the application.

Few of the activation functions deal with problems such as Vanishing Gradient and dead ReLU. The vanishing gradient problem is commonly raised by a few of the activation functions. This is seen in the backpropagation, and due to vanishing of gradients it makes it difficult for the system to learn and tune the parameters of the earlier layers in the network. The vanishing gradient problem worsens when the number of layers is higher in the neural network. This is commonly seen in a Sigmoid activation function and be eliminated by using a ReLU activation function.

But ReLU deals with "dying relu" issue, where the function starts to output zero for all the inputs. This happens because the neuron becomes inactive and will not recover. This issue can be overcome by using Leaky ReLU. It has a slight slope with some minor negative values instead of zero, which speeds up the whole training process.:

Advanced Machine Learning uses multilayer perceptron for classification or prediction of output from the obtained inputs. Inputs are passed through multiple hidden layers where the feature extraction takes place. The activation functions help the neural network to obtain the optimal decision boundary. When compared with the ground truth image, a feedback error is propagated for fixing the optimal weights for the network. These optimal weights are fixed from continuous learning and tuning of parameters through multiple rounds. Finally, the desired output is ready.

4.2.4 Parameters

In any Deep Learning neural network there are two different types of parameters: One type is the model parameter and other one the hyper parameter. Model parameters are those parameters in the model that are identified automatically by the system from training data. Hyper parameters are those parameters that are adjustable and have to be tuned for obtaining the best performance of the built model. Hyper parameters guard the whole neural network process. Some of the hyper parameters include the number of hidden layers that determine the network structure. The learning rate is a hyper parameter that helps to understand how the network is trained. Selection of optimal hyper parameters plays a significant role in the whole process. If the learning rate is too slow, then the network consumes lot of time in training to reach the global optimum. On the other hand, if the learning rate is too fast, then it diverges, and the global optimum is hardly reached. So, what is learning rate? A learning rate is a tuning parameter in an optimization function wherein the size of each step decides how fast or slow the network converges to a global optimum. Why do we need an optimization function in Deep Learning, and what is the use of it? In addition, what exactly do we mean by global optimum?

An optimization function is used in a neural network to reduce losses. Optimizers tune the parameters such as weights and learning rates in such a way that the model built is accurate with less loss. Optimization algorithms help to fine-tune the learning rate in a neural network to reach a global optimum. Global optima could be considered as the best possible solutions by an optimization function from among multiple local optima as shown in Figure 4.8.

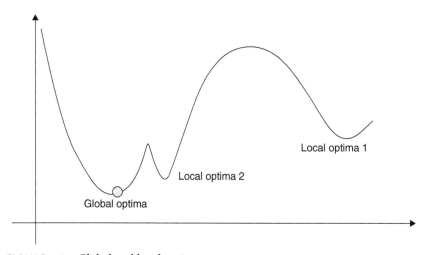

FIGURE 4.8   Global and local optimas.

Cost function is another term that is important in an optimization function in Deep Learning. The cost function helps to understand how well the built model performs. Loss functions are mainly used in the context of parameter estimation and cost function in the context of the optimization function. The major aim is to reduce the value of loss function and cost function. There is mathematical explanation for each of these.

4.2.5 Overfitting

So, what is overfitting of data? When the model is tested elaborately with a quantum of datasets, the model will start including every point, thus resulting in overfitting. This mainly happens when the model is unable to differentiate and learns even the noise in the training data, which in turn has a negative impact in overall training. Overfitting is presented in Figure 4.9. The model is trained many numbers of times as it tries to fit most of the data. This affects the efficiency of the model in an adverse manner, giving many false positives. Regression is prone to overfitting.

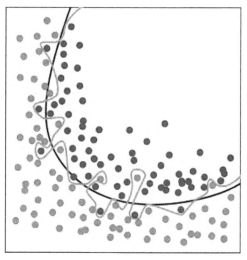

FIGURE 4.9   Overfitting.

Therefore, can we prevent overfitting in some way while training neural networks? Yes, of course, by introducing the concept of dropouts in the model. Dropout is a significant term in Deep Learning, one which is used to prevent overfitting. Dropouts help to work on dropping out some random samples while training and, hence, prevent the overfitting of data.

Early stopping is another way to prevent overfitting. In this, it guides the model when to stop training so that overfitting is prevented. This acts like a rule to be followed all through the training to identify a number of epochs and decide on stopping the process when it crosses a certain threshold value. This threshold is the generalization error on the validation dataset. The main idea is that, when the performance of the system does not show any major improvements, then the system has to stop training. This can be achieved by using call-backs, which is a set of functions. These functions help to identify and stop training when the model starts giving a certain accuracy. This acts as a checkpoint to adjust the learning rates after each epoch. This helps the model from overfitting.

4.3 A FEW MORE TERMS

It is important to know the difference between other terminologies that will be used frequently in the rest of the present volume's chapters. Batch size, training step, and epoch are such terms.

Batch size could be explained with an example: Consider our dataset as being too big – say 1 million image data. It is extremely hard for the computing system to train all the 1 million data at one go. Therefore, the entire data could be divided into various chunks so that the processing done by systems using CPU, GPU, or TPU would go well. Say a batch size of 25,000 at one go will make it easier to process each step faster. This explains the significance of batch size. Batch size will not affect the time taken for training; instead, it has a positive impact on model performance. A training step is the processing of one batch size that in the above example, 25,000 images are processed all at once. This updates the gradient of the model simultaneously after the complete process. This is also called as an iteration.

For example, if the dataset contains 1 million data and if the batch size is 25,000 images, then the number of steps to complete the processing of data is given to be 1 million/25,000 which is 40 steps. So, 1 epoch is the number of steps a model takes to complete the processing of whole dataset at once. Relating batch size, number of steps, and epochs, we can formulate as follows:

$$Number\ of\ steps\ per\ EPOCH = \frac{No\ of\ samples\ in\ data\ set}{Batch\ size}$$

4.4 OPTIMIZERS

It is time to examine optimization algorithms, which iterate many times, fine-tuning the various parameters to bring out the best using the model developed. There are various optimization algorithms. The evolution of optimization algorithms in Deep Learning has emerged in a beautiful manner. Optimizers define how neural networks learn. They help to adjust the values of parameters such that the loss function is at its minimum as shown in Figure 4.10.

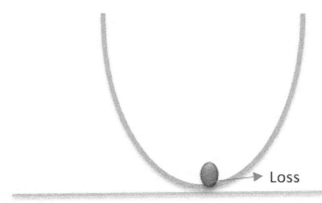

FIGURE 4.10   Loss function at its minimum.

The simplest optimization algorithm used in Deep Learning is Gradient Descent. In this method, the learning rates are updated such that the data points try to converge to the optimum, where the loss function is lowest. Loss function is the error for the single training example whereas cost function is the error for the entire training dataset.

However, the issue here is that the weights are updated after only one epoch. Therefore, the gradient here is large, which makes bigger hops and difficult for the data points to converge to the optimum value.

For every epoch,

$$\theta = \theta - \alpha.\nabla_\theta J(\theta)$$

Where θ is the current position and in formula above indicates the negative direction; α indicates the step size (learning rate), ∇_θ gradient at current position and, finally, $J(\theta)$ is the cost function, which has to be minimum.

In order to overcome the issue in gradient descent, the only solution is to update the parameters more frequently. How can we do that? It is possible by an improvised model of gradient descent algorithm named the Stochastic Gradient Descent Algorithm. Let us see what happens here.

For every epoch,

For every data point in a sample,

$$\theta = \theta - \alpha.\nabla_\theta J(\theta)$$

This tries to update the weights considering each sample, which makes things worse as it is biased by every single sample. Therefore, came the next model of optimization algorithm, called Mini Batch Gradient Descent, which does not look upon every sample, but instead on a batch of samples in the dataset.

For every epoch,

For every N data point in a sample,

$$\theta = \theta - \alpha.\nabla_{\theta} J(\theta)$$

Improvisation to this is done by adding momentum, which calculates the weighted average of gradients and then uses them. However, the major drawback here is that it learns too much faster and becomes too difficult to converge. So, another variant of SGD came where both momentum and acceleration are added. This acceleration is self-adjusting as it slows down the learning rate when needed. This helps to reach the global optimum in a faster speed.

There are various adaptive learning rate optimizers like Autograd, which updates the weights for each parameter in an epoch. However, here lies an issue where, after some epochs, the parameter stops learning by itself. In order to deal with such an issue, came the next method, Ada delta, where the parameter does not tend toward zero. There comes ADAM, one of the most commonly used optimization functions, which is a variant of Adadelta combined with the momentum, which requires slow learning initially and gains momentum and reaches global optimum faster. Therefore, Adam can take different size steps for different parameters, thus leading to a faster convergence. There is yet another optimization function, called RMS prop. All these optimization functions help to reach a faster convergence, reducing the loss and cost functions.

In the previous chapter, readers were introduced to Regression and Classification terminologies, and this chapter has introduced the Deep Learning terminologies.

YouTube Session on Deep Learning Applications: *https://youtu.be/h4Vvuc2mXKc*

KEY POINTS TO REMEMBER

- Artificial Neural Networks try to imitate a human brain with help of Deep Learning.
- Perceptron, Multilevel perceptron uses feed forward and backpropagation techniques.

- Activation functions help to identify the decision boundary of a data point mapping from a domain to a range value.
- There are various terminologies, such as epoch, step per epoch, batch size, and so forth.
- Overfitting influences the output in a disgraceful manner.
- Optimization functions are significant in the neural networks, and the various optimization functions help for a faster convergence to a global optimum reducing the loss and cost function.

QUIZ

1. Define ANN.
2. Explain Perceptron.
3. What is the need of activation functions?
4. Which activation function deals with the issue of dead ReLU?
5. What is the Vanishing Gradient Problem? How can we overcome it?
6. What is an optimization function?
7. What are your thoughts about selecting the right optimization function?
8. Define the terms epoch and batch size.
9. What is the major problem that Regression analysis suffers from?
10. Differentiate Linear Regression and Logistic Regression.

FURTHER READING

✓ Grigorescu Saxe, Andrew, Stephanie Nelli, and Christopher Summerfield. "If Deep Learning is the answer, what is the question?" *Nature Reviews Neuroscience*, 22.1 (2021): 5567.

✓ Wang, Xiaoyu, and Martin Benning. "Generalised Perceptron Learning." *arXiv preprint arXiv:2012.03642 (2020)*.

✓ Jagtap, Ameya D., Kenji Kawaguchi, and George Em Karniadakis. "Adaptive activation functions accelerate convergence in deep and physics-informed neural networks." *Journal of Computational Physics* 404 (2020): 109136.

✓ Bingham, Garrett, William Macke, and Risto Miikkulainen. "Evolutionary optimization of Deep Learning activation functions." *arXiv preprint arXiv:2002.07224 (2020)*.

✓ Yan, Yan, et al. "Optimal Epoch Stochastic Gradient Descent Ascent Methods for Min-Max Optimization." *Advances in Neural Information Processing Systems* 33 (2020).

✓ Hussain, Sadiq, et al. "Regression analysis of student academic performance using Deep Learning." *Education and Information Technologies* (2020): 1–16.

✓ Redd, Douglas, Joseph Goulet, and Qing Zeng-Treitler. "Using Explainable Deep Learning and Logistic Regression to Evaluate Complementary and Integrative Health Treatments in Patients with Musculoskeletal Disorders." *Proceedings of the 53rd Hawaii International Conference on System Sciences.* 2020.

## CHAPTER 5

CNN – Convolutional Neural Networks: A Complete Understanding

LEARNING OBJECTIVES

After this chapter, the reader shall be able to understand the following:

- Overfitting, Underfitting and Appropriate fitting.
- Bias and Variance.
- Fundamentals of Convolutional Neural Networks.
- The workings of Convolution.
- Zero padding.
- How is max pooling performed?
- The role of activation function?
- What are Sigmoid and ReLU?
- Building the CNN model.

DOI: 10.1201/9781003185635-5

5.1 INTRODUCTION

When someone claims they know Deep Learning concepts, the first and foremost question would be from CNN – Convolutional Neural Networks. Yes, it is so very important and acts as the foundation for the rest of the concepts, which are dealt in the subsequent sections. It is easier to learn all these concepts if there is fundamental image processing knowledge. However, the authors have explained these concepts well, and step by step. All the codes presented in this chapter are coded and tested with Anaconda, through Jupyter. Readers are requested to follow the instructions and guidelines presented in Chapter 2 to install the required software tools. All of them are open source, and the reader need not buy anything.

5.2 WHAT IS UNDERFITTING, OVERFITTING AND APPROPRIATE FITTING?

Before getting into the core concepts with CNN it is important to learn some fundamentals and terminology that will repeatedly be used in this chapter and beyond. One such term is *fitting*.

What is underfitting? The line does not cover all the points shown in Figure 5.1, presented below. This is called underfitting. Some also refer it as "High Bias".

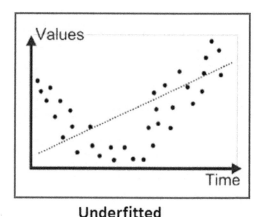

Underfitted

FIGURE 5.1   Underfitting.

What is overfitting? – The graph shows the predicted line covers all the points in the graph. Is this not perfect and okay to go? No. It is ideally not possible. It covers all the points. This means it could as well miss the noise and outliers. So, this is not a good approach. This model certainly will give poor results. Avoiding this is mandatory! This is a "high variance" approach. Refer to Figure 5.2 to understand the same.

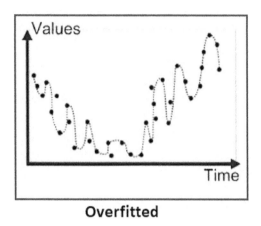

Overfitted

FIGURE 5.2   Overfitting.

What is correct fit? – The name says it all! It is the perfect fit. This will not have High Bias/Variance. This covers a majority of the points. The plot shown in Figure 5.3 presents the correct fit representation.

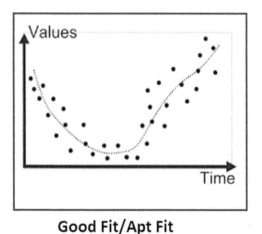

Good Fit/Apt Fit

FIGURE 5.3   Appropriate fitting.

Whenever a model is developed, it is important to provide an apt fitting. Overfitting or underfitting may lead to results that are not accurate.

One could make a note of the term *bias* in the above explanation. Yes, correctly observed. The next topics for discussion are *bias* and *variance*.

5.3 BIAS/VARIANCE – A QUICK LEARNING

Bias is how far are the predicted values from the actual values. If the average predicted values are far off the actual values, then the bias is high. This is what is seen with the underfitting, this is to be avoided!

What is the results of High Bias? The model is said to be too simple and will not capture all the complexity of the data. This will lead to underfitting.

Variance occurs when the model performs very well with the trained dataset, but does not do well on a dataset that it is not trained on, like a test dataset or validation dataset. Variance tells us how far out is the predicted value from the actual value.

What is the result? Noise/outliers would be included and will be regarded as overfitting which should also be avoided.

Having understood the fundamental terminology, it is important to navigate promptly to the Convolutional Neural Networks.

5.4 CONVOLUTIONAL NEURAL NETWORKS

CNN is an ANN – Artificial Neural Network. A prominent application for CNN is in image analysis. Yes, it is so very perfect and useful there in that area. As conveyed earlier, it is better if the reader possesses image processing knowledge, but if not, matrix multiplication knowledge is sufficient.

CNN can be seen as an ANN, has some specialization, and detects patterns in the images. CNN has hidden layers called convolutional layers. There can be one or more hidden layers. It has non-convolutional layers, too. But the basis is convolutional layers. It does the operation.

Like any other neural network architectures, CNN also has multiple hidden layers; these are called convolutional layers (some of them could be non-convolutional as well). One can study the pictorial representation in Figure 5.4 to understand the aforesaid explanation.

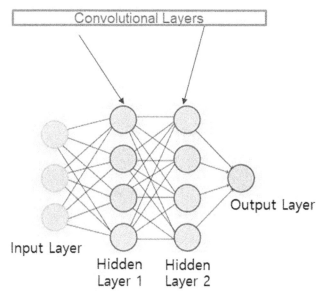

FIGURE 5.4   Convolutional layers – CNN.

It is time to define what convolution is. It is all mathematical. In mathematics (in particular, functional analysis), convolution is a mathematical operation on two functions (f and g) that produces a third function expressing how the shape of one is modified by the other. CNN is all about finding patterns. This is fundamentally connected with the number of filters, which help in detecting the patterns.]

Can we understand this a little better? Refer to Figure 5.5. What do you think is inside this image that can be filtered? The answer: Edges, Objects, Shapes, Texture, and so forth. All these can be detected using the filters.

FIGURE 5.5   An image – a deeper view.

When the edges are detected (filtered), we term it edge detection filtering. Similarly, we can detect the squares, rectangles, corners, and so forth, and all through filters. Smoothing, sharpening, and so forth, all also come under this category. We shall see the simple example below in Figure 5.6. The input image has been operated with filters and the respective results are provided below. The deeper the networks, the more sophisticated the filters should be. The more sophisticated it becomes, the better the detection and results. For instance, from the image presented one can even detect the IC, cable, battery, and so forth.

Detected Edges

Gaussian Blur operated image

Input Image

FIGURE 5.6 An image – filter operations.

5.4.1   How Convolution Works

The first hidden layer in the CNN is a convolution layer, and one should specify the filter. A filter is nothing but a matrix and can be selected based on various factors. A table is presented as annexure in the last section of this book with details of the filters and their dimensions. But, for now understand that filters are nothing but Matrix with rows and columns.
One can have a 3 * 3 filter like the one shown below:

The filter below (Figure 5.7) slides over the input block (matrix). Sliding is called convolving. The filter is going to convolve and is the crux of the entire explanation.

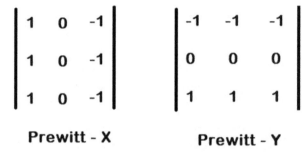

FIGURE 5.7   Filter – 3 x 3 filter.

Can we take an example for the same? – 5 * 5 input matrix to be convolved with the filter chosen. An example is handy, and we can do it now.

The input image (as a matrix) assumed is presented below (Figure 5.8) as a 5 x 5 matrix.

1	1	1	0	1
0	1	0	0	1
1	1	1	0	1
0	1	0	1	0
0	0	0	1	0

FIGURE 5.8   Input image as a 5 x 5 matrix.

The filter chosen for the convolution process is presented below in Figure 5.9. Now, the convolution should be performed, step by step.

$$\begin{vmatrix} 1 & 0 & -1 \\ 1 & 0 & -1 \\ 1 & 0 & -1 \end{vmatrix} \qquad \begin{vmatrix} -1 & -1 & -1 \\ 0 & 0 & 0 \\ 1 & 1 & 1 \end{vmatrix}$$

Prewitt - X   **Prewitt - Y**

FIGURE 5.9   The 3 x 3 filter.

Step 1

One can see from the below math that (Figure 5.10), the filter has convolved (hovered) over the input image and, during the first step, that is, the first stretch of convolution, the result "0" has been updated in the resultant matrix shown on the right side of the image. Similar convolving will happen across the entire input image matrix, and the resulting cells will be updated consequently. One can better understand the same by having a look at Step 2.

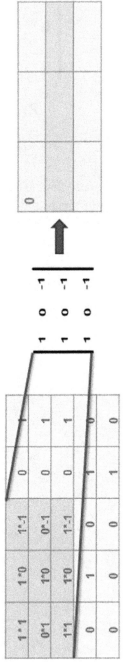

FIGURE 5.10   The 3 x 3 filter convolving over 5 x 5 input image.

Steps 2 and 3

Readers can look at Figure 5.11 to understand the next step in the convolution process. Readers need to visualize the movement of the filter to the right side in the input image by a pixel (i.e., by a cell). Again, matrix multiplication has to be carried out, and the result is to be updated on the result matrix as shown in the right side of the figure below. Similarly, the filter has to move further as shown in Figure 5.12.

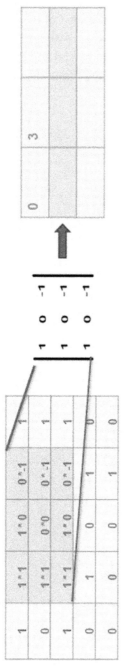

FIGURE 5.11 The 3 x 3 filter convolving over 5 x 5 input image – second step.

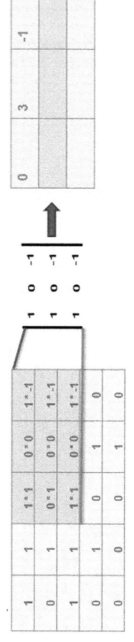

FIGURE 5.12 The 3 x 3 filter convolving over 5 x 5 input image – Third step.

Now one can observe that the first row is completed, and the edges are met in the matrix. That is, there cannot be any movement on the right side of the input matrix. Similarly, the next row will be processed, and one can understand the entire flow for the second row by referring to Figure 5.13.

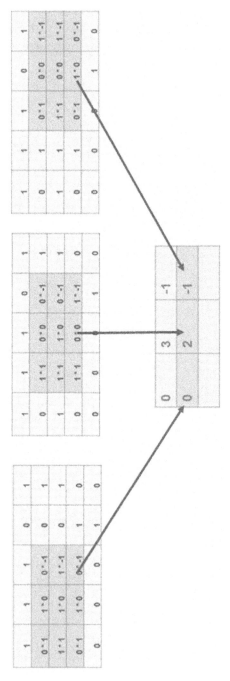

FIGURE 5.13   The 3 x 3 filter convolving over 5 x 5 input image – second row.

Step 4

Finally, the last set of the convolution happens. Like the previous two steps, convolution goes on here, and the final resultant matrix is obtained (Figure 5.14).

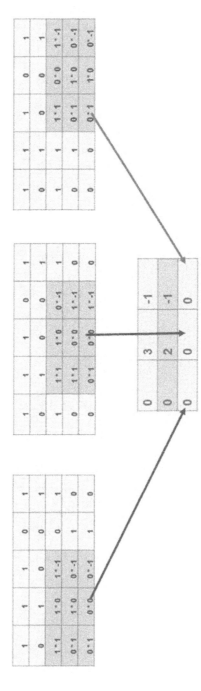

FIGURE 5.14   The final row of convolution operation.

This filtered matrix may undergo one more round of convolution. A number of hidden layers and convolving will get one final convolved matrix. The above explained process is referred to as the convolution and is one of the most important topics to be learned and understood in the Deep Learning.

YouTube Link for Convolution Fundamentals: https://youtu.be/ GKmCw03o6JQ

5.4.2 How Zero Padding Works

The parameters that decide the size of the image:

- Zero Padding
- Stride
- Depth

We shall learn about zero padding in this section followed by stride and depth in successive sections. The reader can recollect the above process we carried out with the convolution section. The input matrix became convolved with the filter and finally, the convolved result arrived as shown in Figure 5.15.

FIGURE 5.15   The convolved results.

The input image becomes convolved with the filter and is getting us output as shown in Figure 5.15. The input is the matrix of 5 * 5, which gets convolved with a 3 * 3 filter here. One can see that the dimension of the input image gets reduced to 3 * 3 after convolving. There is a definite shrink happening, and why is this? Yes, a 3 * 3 filter can fit only 3 * 3 positions in the input image, and this can be understood clearly with the following Figure 5.16.

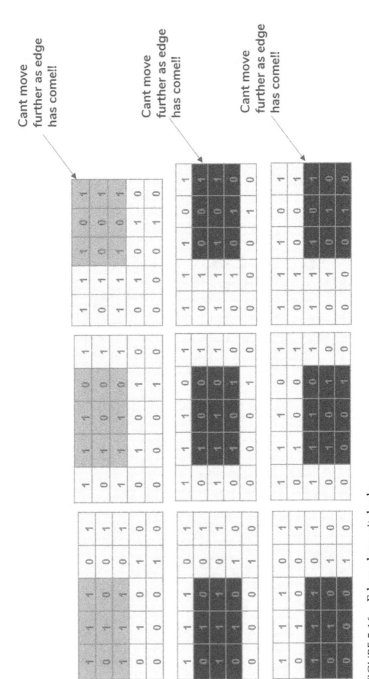

FIGURE 5.16   Edges play a vital role.

As a result, we get 3 * 3 from a 5 * 5 input. But what is the problem? Understand that no data or information from the input image will be lost if the needed information is only in the center! If meaningful information is on the edges? It results in the loss of the information! 5 * 5 becoming 3 * 3 comes with a price. One more question: This is the case we considered for just one filter. When there are many filters, many hidden layers, the shrinking rate would be more. Hence, this is a problem. Can we calculate the dimension of the convolved results before mathematically doing the same?

$$O/P\ Size = (n - f + 1) * (n - f + 1)$$

Where

- $n * n$ – input size
- $f * f$ – Filter size

Here in the case,

- 5 * 5 – Input Size
- 3 * 3 – Filet Size

So, the output size = (5 – 3 + 1) * (5 – 3 + 1). So, 3 * 3 is the resultant image size!

If the input image size is 20 * 20 this shrinking may be okay. But assume the case we have considered here. The input image size is only 5 x 5 and if we have multiple filters, and many convolutions need to happen, imagine the size of the final image and the amount of information we could have lost on the edges?

More filters – Deeper and Deeper – Output shall be smaller and smaller – hence, we end up with meaningless results. So, what is the solution? Zero Padding is the solution. This is explained technically below for easier understanding. The input image matrix, when padded with zero (one layer of zeros is chosen for the example), as shown below in Figure 5.17, it is referred to as zero padding.

0	0	0	0	0	0	0
0	1	1	1	0	1	0
0	0	1	0	0	1	0
0	1	1	1	0	1	0
0	0	1	0	1	0	0
0	0	0	0	1	0	0
0	0	0	0	0	0	0

FIGURE 5.17   Zero padding.

It is important to understand how zero padding works. The below mathematical calculation enables the reader to understand this. Let us consider the same formula as discussed earlier.

$$O/P\ Size = (n - f + 1) * (n - f + 1)$$

Where

- $n * n$ – input size
- $f * f$ – Filter size

Considering the input matrix as shown in Figure 5.17 with the filter size 3 x 3, the result would be

- $7 * 7$ – Input Size
- $3 * 3$ – FilterSize

So, the output size = $(7 - 3 + 1) * (7 - 3 + 1)$. So, $5 * 5$ is the resultant image size! Hence, we retained the size (dimension of the image).

This is how the size, that is, the dimension of the image can be retained through zero padding. To bring better understanding, the complete convolution with the zero padded input matrix is presented below. The filter to be used for convolution is 3 x 3 filter as presented below (Figure 5.18):

$$\begin{vmatrix} 1 & 0 & -1 \\ 1 & 0 & -1 \\ 1 & 0 & -1 \end{vmatrix}$$

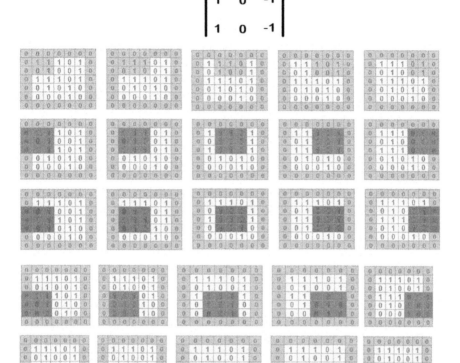

FIGURE 5.18   Zero padding – convolution with 3x3 filter.

On completing the calculation, the resultant matrix would be a 5 x 5, thereby retaining the original input dimensions. This is the impact created by zero padding. The layers of zeros (we had one) can be increased as well, based on the requirement. The same can be practically tested with code. One can try the below code with Keras to understand the use of zero padding.

First, without zero padding, means the dimensions get reduced on the convolution being implemented.

YouTube link for Zero Padding Session – https://youtu.be/rNkSCs4_k8w

```
import keras
from keras.models import Sequential
from keras.layers import Activation
from keras.layers.core import Dense, Flatten
from keras.layers.convolutional import *
# All the above shall be explained with the code for CNN, Shortly.

model = Sequential([
    Dense(16, input_shape=(30,30,3), activation='relu'),
    Conv2D(32, kernel_size=(4,4), activation='relu', padding='valid'),
    Conv2D(64, kernel_size=(5,5), activation='relu', padding='valid'),
    Conv2D(128, kernel_size=(6,6), activation='relu', padding='valid'),
    Flatten(),
    Dense(2, activation='softmax')
])

# Remember this, Valid as the option for padding, the size will shrink. No padding happens with Valid.
# with same for padding, zero padding happens and dimension gets retained.
model.summary()
```

CODE 5.1   Without zero padding.

The above code snippet carries out the convolution with the specified filter size, and when the padding option is set to valid, no padding happens, and the dimensions will certainly be reduced, that is, shrinking happens. One can run the same code in the Jupyter with all installations properly done. The result on running the above code snippet is presented below (Figure 5.19), where the dimensions are reduced and is circled.

Layer (type)	Output Shape	Param #
dense_1 (Dense)	(None, 30, 30, 16)	64
conv2d_1 (Conv2D)	(None, 27, 27, 32)	8224
conv2d_2 (Conv2D)	(None, 23, 23, 64)	51264
conv2d_3 (Conv2D)	(None, 18, 18, 128)	295040
flatten_1 (Flatten)	(None, 41472)	0
dense_2 (Dense)	(None, 2)	82946

FIGURE 5.19   Output for Code 5.1 – the shrink is visual.

Having seen this option, the next step is to find if the zero padding works well when enabled with the code.

```
import keras
from keras.models import Sequential
from keras.layers import Activation
from keras.layers.core import Dense, Flatten
from keras.layers.convolutional import *
# All the above shall be explained with the code for CNN, Shortly.

model = Sequential([
    Dense(16, input_shape=(30,30,3), activation='relu'),
    Conv2D(32, kernel_size=(4,4), activation='relu', padding='same'),
    Conv2D(64, kernel_size=(5,5), activation='relu', padding='same'),
    Conv2D(128, kernel_size=(6,6), activation='relu', padding='same'),
    Flatten(),
    Dense(2, activation='softmax')
])

# Remember this, 'valid' as the option for padding, the size will shrink.
# with 'same' for padding, zero padding happens and dimension gets retained.
model.summary()
```

CODE 5.2   Zero padding.

One could notice that padding is set to *same*, which means the padding is enabled, and dimensions should be retained. The below output can make this understanding clearer (Figure 5.20). The dimensions remain consistent, and no change is reported.

Layer (type)	Output Shape	Param #
dense_22 (Dense)	(None, 30, 30, 16)	64
conv2d_28 (Conv2D)	(None, 30, 30, 32)	8224
conv2d_29 (Conv2D)	(None, 30, 30, 64)	51264
conv2d_30 (Conv2D)	(None, 30, 30, 128)	295040
flatten_10 (Flatten)	(None, 115200)	0
dense_23 (Dense)	(None, 2)	230402

FIGURE 5.20   Output for Code 5.2 – no shrink.

YouTube Link for Zero Padding and Max Pooling implementation: https:// youtu.be/mh_yYOpdBLc

Depth – As conveyed earlier, depth is fundamentally based on the number of filters used. When someone uses n different filters, the depth of the feature map is also n.

Stride – We moved the matrix over the input image, right? That sliding is important here. Moving one pixel at a time corresponds to Stride 1. An example: One can refer to Figure 5.21 to understand the striding concept.

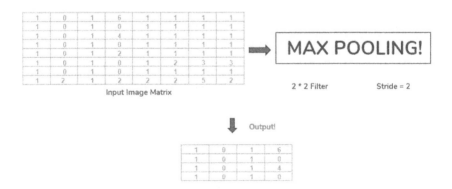

- Stride = 1   - Stride = 2

FIGURE 5.21   Striding 1 and 2.

5.4.3   How Max Pooling Works

It is generally a practice to add max pooling after every convolutional layer in the CNN. But why do we need it?

It is purely math and, after the max pooling process, the dimensions of the image (i.e., the result) will be reduced. The number of pixels become reduced when comparing with the previous stage.

It reduces the number of pixels. We shall understand the process and then can understand the need for max pooling and other types of pooling as well.

The entire idea is presented as a pictorial representation in Figure 5.22. one can understand that the 8 x 8 matrix, after max pooling with 2 x 2 filter with a stride of 2, gets reduced to 4 x 4. The math behind this is explained.

FIGURE 5.22   Max Pooling: a big picture.

A scaled-down example with input of 4 x 4 matrix is taken for max pooling with filter size 2x2; stride 2 is shown below. The entire process of max pooling is diagrammatically represented and is definitely easier to understand (Figures 5.23 and 5.24).

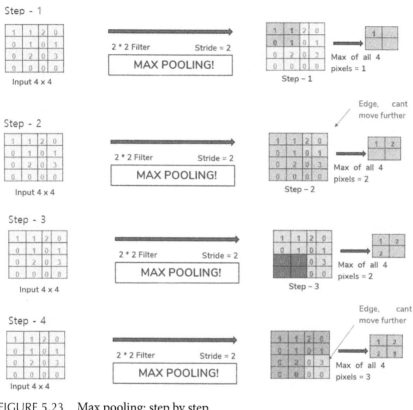

FIGURE 5.23   Max pooling: step by step.

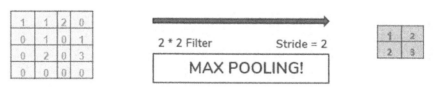

FIGURE 5.24   Max pooling: summary.

One can understand the complete flow from Figure 5.22 as in how max pooling works; The 4 x 4 matrix has been reduced to 2 x 2 through the max pooling process. This definitely reduces the computational load. (The fewer pixels to handle, the easier the computation.) This also helps in avoiding overfitting. There are two more types of pooling. They are Average Pooling and Sum Pooling. A brief note on this is presented below.

Average Pooling – This is like the max pooling, but with a slight deviation in the approach. Instead of taking the maximum values from the identified region, it is now the average of all the values in the region. Thus came the name average pooling. This is not preferred over the max pooling as it fails with the detection of sharp edges and other complex features.

Sum Pooling – This again is a variation of the max pooling. Here, instead of average or max value, the sum of all the pixels in the chosen region is calculated. Sum pooling also is preferred next to the max pooling in applications.

YouTube link for Max Pooling – https://youtu.be/0uwStkFys-I

A Simple python code with Keras is presented below as a code snippet, and the corresponding output is presented. One can understand the way max pooling has halved the size of the input dimension.

```python
import keras
from keras.models import Sequential
from keras.layers import Activation
from keras.layers.core import Dense, Flatten
from keras.layers.convolutional import *
# All the above shall be explained with the code for CNN, Shortly.

model = Sequential([
    Dense(16, input_shape=(30,30,3), activation='relu'),
    Conv2D(32, kernel_size=(4,4), activation='relu', padding='valid'),
    MaxPooling2D(pool_size=(2, 2), strides=2, padding='valid'),
    Dense(2, activation='softmax')
])

# Remember this, 'valid' as the option for padding, the size will shrink.
# with 'same' for padding, zero padding happens and dimension gets retained.
# Max pooling is with size 2x2, striding of 3.

model.summary()
```

CODE 5.3   Max pooling.

```
Layer (type)                  Output Shape           Param #
=================================================================
dense_3 (Dense)               (None, 30, 30, 16)     64
_____
conv2d_2 (Conv2D)             (None, 27, 27, 32)     8224
_____
max_pooling2d_2 (MaxPooling2  (None, 13, 13, 32)     0
_____
dense_4 (Dense)               (None, 13, 13, 2)      66
=================================================================
Total params: 8,354
Trainable params: 8,354
Non-trainable params: 0
```

FIGURE 5.25   Output for Code 5.3: the pooling effect.

One can see from the above execution result that the size is reduced by half (Figure 5.25).

5.4.4   The CNN Stack – Architecture

To understand CNN stack, that is, the layers one can refer to the below explanation and Figure 5.26. The layers in the CNN stack are explained below, step by step.

Convolutional layer –This is the core process. Here, a filter will pass over (convolve) over the input image, scanning the pixels and then creating a feature map. Each feature belongs to some class. The filter essentially goes over the input image and this process is called the convolving (We have to include activation functions in this layer, too, which shall be discussed shortly).

Pooling layer (down sampling/sub sampling)–It is the process of reducing the number of pixels (i.e., down sampling) while not losing the important information. One method we discussed in detail was max pooling where we could retain the strongest of the pixels while ignoring the weaker ones. One should note that there can be many rounds of convolution and pooling!

Flattening – Yes, this flattens. Output from the previous layers are flattened to a single vector so that they can be input to the next level. Before handing over the results to the fully connected layers after the convolution, it is important to flatten the same so that can be processed by the fully connected layers.

The first fully connected layer – This layer takes the inputs from the feature analysis and applies weights to predict the correct label.

Fully connected output layer – This gets us the final probabilities for each label. Here is where one can get the final output.

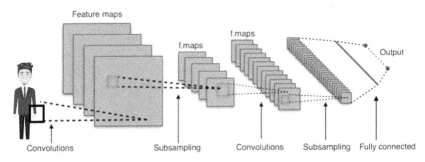

FIGURE 5.26   CNN layers.

YouTube link for CNN architecture explanation – *https://youtu.be/ R9CSbcGxKzo*

5.4.5   What Is the Activation Function?

In ANN the activation function of a neuron defines output of the neuron given a set of inputs. The activation function operates on the value that can be then transformed to anything between a lower limit and an upper limit (Say 0 and 1). This is referred as firing, technically.

How our brain works? Simple. In the same way as the activation function works. When we cross a garden that has lot of nice fragrant flowers, we tend to react positively. It is through some neurons becoming activated and firing. Similarly, when cross a dirty place where there is dust, and the smell is bad, certain other neurons get activated and fire. One can refer to firing as one and no firing as zero.

Readers will be introduced to two of the activation functions at this stage. They are Sigmoid and ReLU.

5.4.5.1   *Sigmoid Activation Function*

Sigmoid is the simplest of the activation functions that can be understood with ease. For Sigmoid, zero is the lower limit, and one is the upper limit. The transformation is also simple to understand. If the input is negative, Sigmoid transforms this number close to 0. If input is positive, Sigmoid transforms this number close to 1. If the input is close to 0, then, Sigmoid transforms this number close to 0 and 1.One can understand the transition by referring to the graph in Figure 5.27.

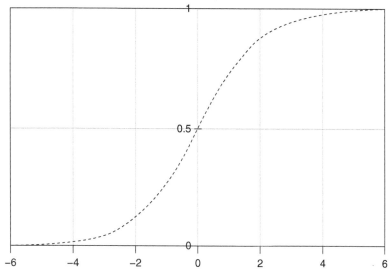

FIGURE 5.27   Sigmoid.

5.4.5.2   ReLU – Rectified Linear Unit

Try answering this question: Is it a rule that activation function should always transform the input to be between 0 or 1? Not necessarily. ReLU is different and is an example of breaking the traditional myth. It is known as a Rectified Linear Unit. It does activations differently. It actually transforms the input to 0 or Input value itself. When the input value is negative (i.e., less than 0 or equal to 0), it will make it as 0 and 0 is the output. If the input is greater than 0, then the output will be nothing other than the given input.

If (x<=0)
{
return 0;
}else   *{f(x) = max(0,x)}*
return x;   }

YouTube Session on Activation Functions: https://youtu.be/ja5CRR-wY30

5.4.6   CNN – Model Building – Step by Step

The main section has come. It is going to be very interesting in this section to develop a CNN model to classify a given input image as a cat or dog.

Readers can try this out, step by step in their machines and visualize the output as well.

Prerequisites for the code to be run:

- One must have installed Keras Libraries properly. (*pip install keras or conda install keras* in the conda prompt are to be issued).

- While running the code one may get the following error:

  Import Error: Could not find '**nvcuda.dll**'

  This can be rectified by visiting www.dll-files.com/nvcuda.dll.html where one can download the .dll file and save it in the directory –**C:\ Windows\System32**

- One should also install the following as they are to be used in future. Entire model is to be run over the tensor flow and, hence, it is to be installed as well. The commands are presented for ready reference.

  pip install protobuf.

  pip install tensor flow

The dataset

Whenever a model is built, it is to be tested with an appropriate dataset for its functioning. The CNN model to be developed is first to be used to classify the input image as a cat or dog. The dataset collected is stored appropriately in the local drive of your choice (Figure 5.28). One can see the test_set, training_set directories shown below. Also, cat_or_dog_1, cat_or_dog_2 are used as the input images to be classified by the CNN model developed.

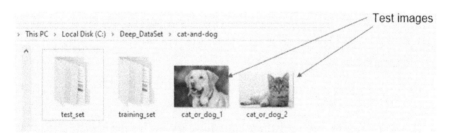

FIGURE 5.28   The dataset and its location.

It can be seen that test_set and training_set are present in the dataset location. One should understand the fundamental idea of having the test and training images. Below Figures 5.29 and 5.30 reveal the content inside both the directories. The amount of training images is generally expected to be more than the testing images. Normally, 70 percent of the images will be used as training images while 30 percent will be used as testing images. However, there is no hard and fast rule for this 70–30 ratio.

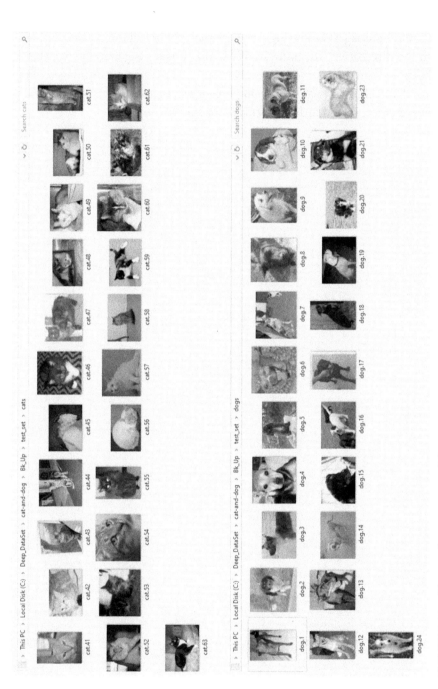

FIGURE 5.29   The test dataset: cats and dogs.

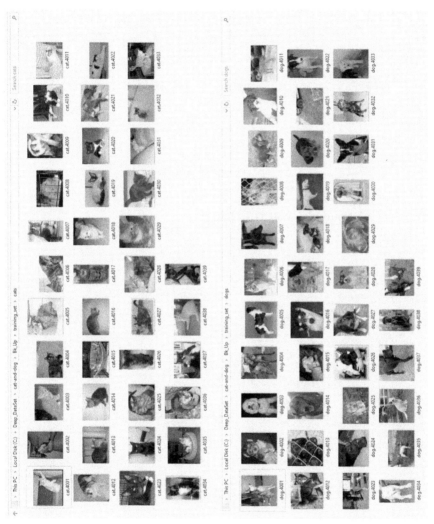

FIGURE 5.30   The training dataset: cats and dogs.

The code is presented as step by step in a modularized manner so that it will be easier for the reader to understand. Each line of the code is provided with apt comment lines so that it is easier to grasp the purpose of each line of code written. The entire code is presented also in the GitHub link in the annexure, which would enable the readers to download / clone the code to test its functioning locally.

```
######## Section - 1, Setup ############
from keras.models import Sequential
#  Sequential from keras.models, This gets our neural network as Sequential network.
#  As we know, it can be sequential layers or graph

from keras.layers import Conv2D
# We are working with images. All the images are basically 2D.
# One can go with the 3D if working with videos.

from keras.layers import MaxPooling2D
# Average Pooling, Sum Pooling and Max Pooling are there.
# We choose Max pooling. Re collect all what I taught you.

from keras.layers import Flatten
# Well, we must flatten. It is the process of converting all the resultant 2D arrays as single long continuous linear vector.
# This is mandatory, folks.

from keras.layers import Dense
# This is the last step! Yes, full connection of the neural network is performed with this Dense.

from keras.preprocessing.image import ImageDataGenerator
# We are going to use ImageDataGenerator from Keras and hence import it as well!
```

CODE 5.4   CNN model: Section 1 – setup.

```
# Section 2 - Convolution/Pooling/Flattening/Dense
classifier = Sequential()
# Can we initialize the CNN and start the real coding?

classifier.add(Conv2D(32, (3, 3), input_shape = (64, 64, 3), activation = 'relu'))
# We need 2D Convolution. It is 2D image we are dealing with.
# WE have four arguments to be passed, you know that.
# First is the number of filters, We have chosen 32 here. You are free to change the same.
# Shape of the filter chosen 3 X 3 is mentioned as the second argument.
# Third argument talks about the input image type, We have RGB (It can be BW also. ) 64 x 64 resolution, 3 refers to RGB
# 4th is the activation function and yes, we stay with ReLU.

classifier.add(MaxPooling2D(pool_size = (2, 2)))
# As taught, we have chosen Max Pooling with pool size 2 x 2
classifier.add(Flatten())
# Here, what we are basically doing here is taking the 2-D array,
# i.e pooled image pixels and converting them to a one dimensional single vector.

classifier.add(Dense(units = 128, activation = 'relu'))
# Real fun starts here, we need to create fully connected layer.
# We have many nodes available after flattening and these nodes shall serve as input to the fully connected layers.
# This layer is present between the input layer and output layer, we can refer to it a hidden layer.
# 'units' is number of nodes that should be present in this hidden layer,

classifier.add(Dense(units = 1, activation = 'sigmoid'))
# Here, it can be reLu as well.
# This is the output and contain only one node, as it is binary classification
# We chose sigmoid function.

classifier.compile(optimizer = 'adam', loss = 'binary_crossentropy', metrics = ['accuracy'])
# Compiling the CNN.
# It is time to compile, Yes we specify the following before the same.
# Optimizer = stochastic gradient descent algorithm.
# Loss function to be chosen .
# Metrics remain Accuracy
```

CODE 5.5   CNN model: Section 2.

```
###### Section - 3, Fitting images with CNN ###########
# Can we do some preprocessing, which is done with keras.preprocessing library
# Remember, it is very structred approach with Keras, all the images in the directory Dogs are considered dogs by KERAS
# Dont worry too much, we do flipping, rotating, blurring in the part as preprocessing steps.
train_datagen = ImageDataGenerator(rescale = 1./255,
shear_range = 0.2,
zoom_range = 0.2,
horizontal_flip = True)
test_datagen = ImageDataGenerator(rescale = 1./255)

training_set = train_datagen.flow_from_directory('C:/Deep_DataSet/cat-and-dog/training_set',
target_size = (64, 64),
batch_size = 32,
class_mode = 'binary')

test_set = test_datagen.flow_from_directory('C:/Deep_DataSet/cat-and-dog/test_set',
target_size = (64, 64),
batch_size = 32,
class_mode = 'binary')

classifier.fit_generator(training_set,
steps_per_epoch = 80,
epochs = 10,
validation_data = test_set,
validation_steps = 46)

# Here is the most important thing to be learnt!
# Epochs - What is it? Simple, Epoch is once all the images are proocessed one time individually
# both forward and backward to the network.
# Epoch number can be determined by the Trail and Error. More the epoch, better the accuracy, but, it could be overfitting too.
# Remember -'steps_per_epoch' holds the number of training images, i.e the number of images the training_set folder contains.
```

CODE 5.6   CNN model: Section 3.

```
###### Section - 4, The classification with CNN ############
# We are going to test now! Let us send, cat_or_dog_1.jpg as input to see what the result is.
import numpy as np
from keras.preprocessing import image
test_image = image.load_img('C:/Deep_DataSet/cat-and-dog/cat_or_dog_1.jpg', target_size = (64, 64))
test_image = image.img_to_array(test_image)
test_image = np.expand_dims(test_image, axis = 0)
result= classifier.predict(test_image)
training_set.class_indices

if result[0][0] == 1:
    prediction = 'dog'
else:
    prediction = 'cat'
print(prediction)


# We are going to test now! # Let us send, cat_or_dog_2.jpg as input to see what the result is.
import numpy as np
from keras.preprocessing import image
test_image = image.load_img('C:/Deep_DataSet/cat-and-dog/cat_or_dog_2.jpg', target_size = (64, 64))
test_image = image.img_to_array(test_image)
test_image = np.expand_dims(test_image, axis = 0)
result= classifier.predict(test_image)
training_set.class_indices

if result[0][0] == 1:
    prediction = 'dog'
else:
    prediction = 'cat'
print(prediction)
```

CODE 5.7   CNN model: Section 4.

On seeing the above code snippet, one can connect the fundamental concepts learned clearly in the previous sections. The CNN architecture can be visualized from the code as well. This code can be run on a PC with a reasonable configuration such as Intel I5 with minimum of 4 GB RAM. The dataset is collected from various resources and is made available for readers' ready reference in the GitHub link. On running the above developed CNN model successfully, one could get the below result clearly on screen with classification done (Figure 5.31).

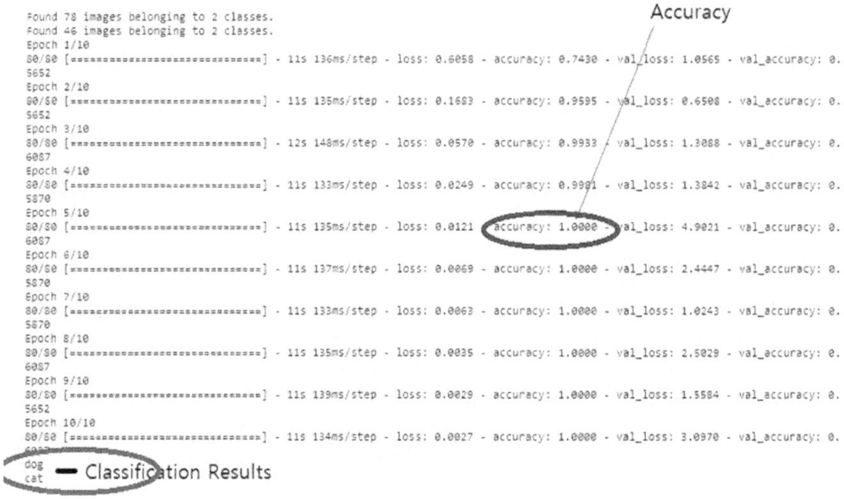

FIGURE 5.31   Output for Code 5.4, 5.5, 5.6, 5.7: CNN model.

One can understand from the above screenshot that the system itself started giving 100 percent accuracy at the 5th epoch. Hence, once the accuracy is found consistent – that is, if is found stable with epoch 7 or 8 – then, one can stop with 8 epochs. All these are trial-and-error based findings and, once the code runs, one can tune the parameters to understand all these clearly.

YouTube link for complete CNN Implementation: https://youtu.be/ lN-1m7pPVkY

KEY POINTS TO REMEMBER

- One should know that a mode's result should not reflect underfitting or overfitting; it should be apt fitting.
- Underfitting leads to high bias, overfitting leads to high variance.
- Bias is how far are the predicted values from the actual values.
- Variance occurs when the model performs very well with the trained dataset but, on the other hand, does not do well on a dataset that it is not trained on, like a test dataset or validation dataset.
- CNN, Convolutional Neural Network is an ANN – Artificial Neural Network.

- Prominent application for CNN is in image analysis.
- The parameters which decide the size of the image:
  - Depth
  - Stride
  - Zero Padding
- Zero padding ensures the maintaining of the dimensions without any change.
- Depth fundamentally is based on number of filters used. When someone uses n different filters, the depth of the feature map is also n.
- Moving one pixel at a time corresponds to Stride 1. This concept of moving is referred to as striding.
- Before handing over the results to the fully connected layers after the convolution, it is important to flatten the same so that can be processed by the fully connected layers.

QUIZ

1. Definite convolution.
2. What is the role of filters in convolution?
3. Why and how is zero padding important?
4. How is max pooling achieved?
5. What is the major difference between max pooling and average pooling?
6. What are the layers in CNN architecture?
7. What is the need to flatten before the fully connected layer in CNN?
8. Explain clearly the term *striding*.

FURTHER READING

✓ Ma, N., Zhang, X., Zheng, H.T., and Sun, J., 2018. "Shufflenet v2: Practical guidelines for efficient CNN architecture design." In *Proceedings of the European Conference on Computer Vision (ECCV)* (pp. 116–131).
✓ Luo, R., Tian, F., Qin, T., Chen, E., and Liu, T.Y., 2018. "Neural architecture optimization." In *Advances in Neural Information Processing Systems* (pp. 7816–7827).

✓ Dumoulin, V. and Visin, F., 2016. "A guide to convolution arithmetic for Deep Learning." *arXiv preprint arXiv:1603.07285.*

✓ Liu, G., Shih, K.J., Wang, T.C., Reda, F.A., Sapra, K., Yu, Z., Tao, A. and Catanzaro, B., 2018. "Partial convolution-based padding." *arXiv preprint arXiv:1811.11718.*

✓ Tolias, G., Sicre, R. and Jégou, H., 2015. "Particular object retrieval with integral max-pooling of CNN activations." *arXiv preprint arXiv:1511.05879.*

✓ Wang, S.H., Phillips, P., Sui, Y., Liu, B., Yang, M. and Cheng, H., 2018. "Classification of Alzheimer's Disease based on eight-layer convolutional neural network with leaky rectified linear unit and max pooling." *Journal of Medical Systems*, 42(5), p. 85.

## CHAPTER 6

CNN Architectures: An Evolution

LEARNING OBJECTIVES

After this chapter, the reader will be able to understand the following:

- Variants of CNN architectures
- Clear architectural details of LeNET
- Practical implementation of LeNET
- Clear architectural details of VGGNet
- Practical implementation of VGGNet
- Architectural aspects of AlexNet and Skeleton design
- A brief note on other prevailing architectures.

6.1   INTRODUCTION

One should understand a point: CNN is a beginning for a revolution. CNN has laid the foundation for many innovations in the field of Deep Learning. Many architectures have evolved based on the CNN, and learning these architectures will eventually help the reader to select the appropriate architecture for the application. Let us first know the names of the available architectures:

DOI: 10.1201/9781003185635-6

- LeNet
- VGGNet
- AlexNet
- ResNet
- ZFNet
- GoogleNet

Implementing the first three architectures is carried out step by step in this chapter. The rest of the three are briefly analyzed. Authors will be introduced to LeNet first, followed by VGGNet. It is expected that readers try developing the rest of the models with the clear inputs and guidelines provided in the models developed here.

6.2 LENET CNN ARCHITECTURE

Although CNN is believed to detect the patterns in the image and is believed to be the only application area, actually, this is not so. More than just patterns, it can be used for applications in real-time object detection, OCR – Optical character recognition, hand writing recognition, and so forth. CNN architectures mentioned in the introduction are similar in basic aspects, but they could vary in the number of layers or types of layers being deployed. One can understand this clearly as we deal with the models, one by one.

It all started in the year 1998. LeCun et al. suggested LeNet architecture in their research article was primarily meant for OCR. It is believed that they tried to recognize the handwriting on the cheque. The LeNet model that was developed is run with Intel I7 8th Gen CPU and is found to provide good performance. So, the author's observation is that CPU can be sufficient.

The original LeNet architecture proposed by the creators is presented below:

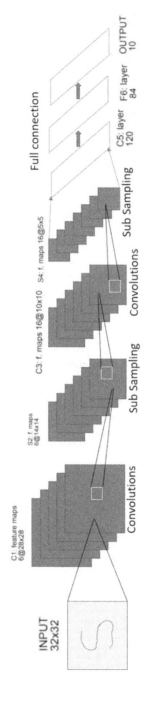

FIGURE 6.1   LeNet architecture.

(Source LeCun et al, 1998).

The architecture is explained step by step (Figure 6.1).

Step 1

Input for this model is a 32 x 32 grayscale image. This goes into the convolution layer (First convolution layer – C1). LeNet has 6 feature maps, with filter size 5 x 5, striding set as 1. The input sample becomes reduced (convolved) to 28 x 28 with 6 feature maps.

Table 6.1 will be expanded step by step to enable easier and complete understanding for readers.

TABLE 6.1   The Layers for LeNet – Step by Step

Layer	Layer Type	Feature Map count	Size (Dimension)	Kernel Size	Stride	Activation
Input Layer	Grayscale Images	1	32 x 32	NA	NA	NA
C1	Convolution layer 1	6	28 x 28	5 x 5	1	tanh

Step 2

So, what would be the next step? The implementation takes up down sampling/sub-sampling as the next step. How can this be achieved? Readers were introduced in Chapter 5 to average pooling. Average pooling is to be deployed in this stage with filter size 2 x 2, striding set to 2. As one can understand, the average pooling will reduce the dimensions by half. Hence, as expected, the size of the image will get reduced to 14 x 14, retaining 6 feature maps. Max pooling will not have any impact on the feature maps and hence it is retained.

Readers should look at the expanded Table 6.1, which is presented as Table 6.2 below.

TABLE 6.2   First Average Pooling Included

Layer	Layer Type	Feature Map count	Size (Dimension)	Kernel Size	Stride	Activation
Input Layer	Grayscale Images	1	32 x 32	NA	NA	NA
C1	Convolution layer 1	6	28 x 28	5 x 5	1	tanh
S2	Average Pooling	6	14 x 14	2 x 2	2	tanh

It is time to move on to the next step.

Note: The feature maps of a CNN capture the result of applying the filters to an input image. That is at each layer; the feature map is the output of that layer.

Step 3

It is time to for the convolution again. The more the number of convolution layers, the deeper the network. The convolution happens with a filter size of 5 x 5, and the output dimensions will be 10 x 10 with 16 feature maps. The striding rule is set to 1, and the activation function deployed is tanh. For easier understanding, Table 6.2 gets restructured as Table 6.3 and one can refer to the same.

TABLE 6.3   Second Convolution

Layer	Layer Type	Feature Map count	Size (Dimension)	Kernel Size	Stride	Activation
Input Layer	Grayscale Images	1	32 x 32	NA	NA	NA
C1	Convolution layer 1	6	28 x 28	5 x 5	1	tanh
S2	Average Pooling	6	14 x 14	2 x 2	2	tanh
C3	Convolution layer 2	16	10 x 10	2 x 2	1	Tanh

Step 4

This layer is again the down sampling or subsampling layer. One should use Average Pooling in this layer. The filter size preferred is 2 x 2 with striding of 2. Naturally, the down sampling will reduce the size of the image by half and 10 x 10 image gets reduced to 5 x 5 with retaining 16 feature maps. Table 6.3 is updated as Table 6.4 and presented below for ready reference.

TABLE 6.4 Second Round of Average Pooling

Layer	Layer Type	Feature Map count	Size (Dimension)	Kernel Size	Stride	Activation
Input Layer	Grayscale Images	1	32 x 32	NA	NA	NA
C1	Convolution layer 1	6	28 x 28	5 x 5	1	tanh
S2	Average Pooling	6	14 x 14	2 x 2	2	tanh
C3	Convolution layer 2	16	10 x 10	5 x 5	1	tanh
S4	Average Pooling	16	5 x 5	2 x 2	2	tanh

It is time for the final round of the convolution process.

Step 5

One can see from the architecture that the C5 layer is the convolutional layer with 120 feature maps each, sized 1 x 1. The filter dimension is 5 x 5 with striding set to 1. The activation function remains tanh, like the previous layers. The table has to be updated again and is presented as Table 6.5.

TABLE. 6.5 Convolution Layer

Layer	Layer Type	Feature Map count	Size (Dimension)	Kernel Size	Stride	Activation
Input Layer	Grayscale Images	1	32 x 32	NA	NA	NA
C1	Convolution layer 1	6	28 x 28	5 x 5	1	tanh
S2	Average Pooling	6	14 x 14	2 x 2	2	tanh
C3	Convolution layer 2	16	10 x 10	5 x 5	1	tanh
S4	Average Pooling	16	5 x 5	2 x 2	2	tanh
C5	Convolution layer	120	1 x 1	5 x 5	1	tanh

We are nearing the end. Yes, only a few more layers left.

Step 6

The sixth layer is a fully connected layer (F6) with 84 units.

Step 7

Fully connected softmax output layer with 10 possible values as the classi-fication result.

The table in its final form is presented below as Table 6.6.

TABLE 6.6   Layers in LeNet

Layer	Layer Type	Feature Map count	Size (Dimension)	Kernel Size	Stride	Activation
Input Layer	Grayscale Images	1	32 x 32	NA	NA	NA
C1	Convolution layer 1	6	28 x 28	5 x 5	1	tanh
S2	Average Pooling	6	14 x 14	2 x 2	2	tanh
C3	Convolution layer 2	16	10 x 10	5 x 5	1	tanh
S4	Average Pooling	16	5 x 5	2 x 2	2	tanh
C5	Convolution layer	120	1 x 1	5 x 5	1	tanh
F6	Fully Connected Layer	-	84	-	-	tanh
Output	Fully Connected Layer	-	10	-	-	softmax

Well, the model can be built now. Before getting into the process of model building, it is important to connect the model with what it is going to be used for. Here, we are going to use it for character recognition, that is, handwriting character recognition. There are many handwriting datasets available for usage, and the reader can themselves prepare one, too. But the most common and most frequently used dataset is MNIST (Modified National Institute of Standards and Technology) dataset. We will first understand the dataset and navigate to the next stage, where we build the model, step by step.

The Dataset – MNIST

One can find the MNIST dataset for download at the website http://yann.lecun.com/exdb/mnist/.

This webpage has a lot of data. Really, a lot. The MNIST database has a collection of handwritten digits. The dataset has 60,000 images for training and 10,000 images for testing. It is a larger count and certainly found to be very handy. This MNIST dataset originated from the NIST (National Institute of Standards and Technology) dataset. One good aspect of the MNIST dataset is that all the digits have been properly size normalized and positioned centrally in the image, which makes the life of the programmer easier. Also, the same dataset is made open in many GitHub links. The following Figure 6.2 presents sample images from the dataset to establish a quicker understanding for the readers about the dataset.

FIGURE 6.2   The MNIST dataset.

Having learned the fundamentals of the dataset, it is important to start the coding. We will start building the model, step by step, with clear comments for each line of the code. The same can be tried in PCs having an I5 or above processor with a minimum of 4GB RAM. Authors have tested the same and is found to be fully functional. The code will start with the initialization, and Keras is used for the implementation

```
import matplotlib.pyplot as plt
# Here is where we import the matplotlib as plt. Henceforth, it is plt.

import tensorflow as tf
# We run with Tensforflow. So, import it folks.

import numpy as np
# We got to import numpy as well.

mnist = tf.keras.datasets.mnist
(x_train, y_train), (x_test, y_test) = mnist.load_data()
# Here you go, we are using the most common and prominet dataset MNIST
# many sources are tehre and here, we take it direct and we load that too as test and training data.

rows, cols = 28, 28
# See the architecture, first set 28 x 28 is the number of rows and columns!!

x_train = x_train.reshape(x_train.shape[0], rows, cols, 1)
x_test = x_test.reshape(x_test.shape[0], rows, cols, 1)

input_shape = (rows, cols, 1)
```

CODE 6.1   LeNET – import.

```
# Here, we normalize it.
x_train = x_train.astype('float32')
x_test = x_test.astype('float32')
x_train = x_train / 255.0
x_test = x_test / 255.0

# one-hot encode the labels
y_train = tf.keras.utils.to_categorical(y_train, 10)
y_test = tf.keras.utils.to_categorical(y_test, 10)
```

CODE 6.2   LeNET – normalize.

```
def build_lenet(input_shape):
  # sequentail API
  model = tf.keras.Sequential()
  # Convolution #1. Filters as we know, is 6. Filter size is 5 x 5, tanh is the activation function. 28 x 28 is the dimension.
  model.add(tf.keras.layers.Conv2D(filters=6,
                      kernel_size=(5, 5),
                      strides=(1, 1),
                      activation='tanh',
                      input_shape=input_shape))

  # SubSampling #1. Input = 28x28x6. Output = 14x14x6. SubSampling is simply Average Pooling so we use avg_pool
  model.add(tf.keras.layers.AveragePooling2D(pool_size=(2, 2),
                            strides=(2, 2)))

  # Convolution #2. Input = 14x14x6. Output = 10x10x16 conv2d
  model.add(tf.keras.layers.Conv2D(filters=16,
                      kernel_size=(5, 5),
                      strides=(1, 1),
                      activation='tanh'))

  # SubSampling #2. Input = 28x28x6. Output = 14x14x6. SubSampling is simply Average Pooling so we use avg_pool
  model.add(tf.keras.layers.AveragePooling2D(pool_size=(2, 2), strides=(2, 2)))

  model.add(tf.keras.layers.Flatten())
  # We must flatten for the further steps to happen.
  # It is the process of converting all the resultant 2D arrays as single long continuous linear vector
  model.add(tf.keras.layers.Dense(units=120, activation='tanh'))
  #Fully Connected #1. Input = 5x5x16. Output = 120

  model.add(tf.keras.layers.Flatten())
  # Flattening here. It is the process of converting all the resultant 2D arrays as single long continuous linear vector

  model.add(tf.keras.layers.Dense(units=84, activation='tanh'))
  #Fully Connected #2. Input = 120. Output = 84

  # output layer
  model.add(tf.keras.layers.Dense(units=10, activation='softmax'))
  # Final, output and activation through softmax.

  model.compile(loss='categorical_crossentropy',optimizer=tf.keras.optimizers.SGD(lr=0.1, momentum=0.0, decay=0.0),
            metrics=['accuracy'])
  # Arguments passed are like the past, nothing to worry!! :)

  return model

lenet = build_lenet(input_shape)
# We built it!
```

CODE 6.3   LeNET – build.

```
# number of epochs
epochs = 10
# Can we train the model?
history = lenet.fit(x_train, y_train,
                         epochs=epochs,
                         batch_size=128,
                         verbose=1)
loss, acc = lenet.evaluate(x_test, y_test)
print('ACCURACY: ', acc)

# Here is the most important thing to be learnt!
# Epochs - What is it? Simple, Epoch is once all the images are proocessed one time individually
# both forward and backward to the network.
# Epoch number can be determined by the Trail and Error.


#Transformation / Reshape into 28x 28 pixel
x_train=x_train.reshape(x_train.shape[0], 28,28)
print("Training Data",x_train.shape,y_train.shape)

x_test=x_test.reshape(x_test.shape[0], 28,28)
print("Test Data",x_test.shape,y_test.shape)

#Example 1 image @index 4444 (9 is the number in the dataset)
image_index = 4444
plt.imshow(x_test[image_index].reshape(28, 28),cmap='Greys')

pred = lenet.predict(x_test[image_index].reshape(1, rows, cols, 1))
print(pred.argmax())

# Example : 2 to visualize a single image at the index 8888 (6 is in the dataset)
image_index = 8888.
plt.imshow(x_test[image_index].reshape(28, 28),cmap='Greys')

#To predict the output using the Lenet model built
pred = lenet.predict(x_test[image_index].reshape(1, rows, cols, 1))
print(pred.argmax())
```

CODE 6.4   LeNET – epochs.

One can go through the below result screenshots (Figure 6.3 and 6.4) to understand the accuracy achieved with this model in classifying the handwritten digits from the MNIST dataset with the identification result considered for two instances in the code.

Results for index – 4444 (9 in the dataset)

```
Epoch 1/10
60000/60000 [==============================] - 6s 100us/sample - loss: 0.4229 - acc: 0.8820
Epoch 2/10
60000/60000 [==============================] - 6s 98us/sample - loss: 0.1755 - acc: 0.94841s - los
Epoch 3/10
60000/60000 [==============================] - 6s 98us/sample - loss: 0.1178 - acc: 0.9651
Epoch 4/10
60000/60000 [==============================] - 6s 100us/sample - loss: 0.0888 - acc: 0.9735
Epoch 5/10
60000/60000 [==============================] - 6s 98us/sample - loss: 0.0718 - acc: 0.9786
Epoch 6/10
60000/60000 [==============================] - 6s 98us/sample - loss: 0.0607 - acc: 0.9816
Epoch 7/10
60000/60000 [==============================] - 6s 98us/sample - loss: 0.0528 - acc: 0.9840
Epoch 8/10
60000/60000 [==============================] - 6s 98us/sample - loss: 0.0467 - acc: 0.98642s - loss: 0.0480 - ac
Epoch 9/10
60000/60000 [==============================] - 6s 98us/sample - loss: 0.0421 - acc: 0.9874
Epoch 10/10
60000/60000 [==============================] - 6s 98us/sample - loss: 0.0380 - acc: 0.9887
10000/10000 [==============================] - 1s 64us/sample - loss: 0.0399 - acc: 0.9863
ACCURACY:  0.9863
Training Data (60000, 28, 28) (60000, 10)
Test Data (10000, 28, 28) (10000, 10)
9
```

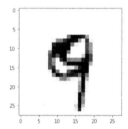

FIGURE 6.3   Output for Code 6.1, 6.2, 6.3, 6.4 – MNIST dataset recognition for digit 9.

Results for Index – 8888 (6 in the Dataset)

```
Epoch 1/10
60000/60000 [==============================] - 6s 102us/sample - loss: 0.4223 - acc: 0.8821
Epoch 2/10
60000/60000 [==============================] - 6s 100us/sample - loss: 0.1698 - acc: 0.9495
Epoch 3/10
60000/60000 [==============================] - 6s 100us/sample - loss: 0.1159 - acc: 0.9656
Epoch 4/10
60000/60000 [==============================] - 6s 101us/sample - loss: 0.0882 - acc: 0.9732
Epoch 5/10
60000/60000 [==============================] - 6s 107us/sample - loss: 0.0714 - acc: 0.9788s - loss: 0.0724 -
Epoch 6/10
60000/60000 [==============================] - 6s 105us/sample - loss: 0.0607 - acc: 0.9823
Epoch 7/10
60000/60000 [==============================] - 6s 107us/sample - loss: 0.0523 - acc: 0.9844
Epoch 8/10
60000/60000 [==============================] - 6s 103us/sample - loss: 0.0465 - acc: 0.9862
Epoch 9/10
60000/60000 [==============================] - 6s 107us/sample - loss: 0.0420 - acc: 0.9876
Epoch 10/10
60000/60000 [==============================] - 6s 103us/sample - loss: 0.0382 - acc: 0.9884
10000/10000 [==============================] - 1s 68us/sample - loss: 0.0474 - acc: 0.9840
ACCURACY  0.984
Training Data (60000, 28, 28) (60000, 10)
Test Data (10000, 28, 28) (10000, 10)
6
```

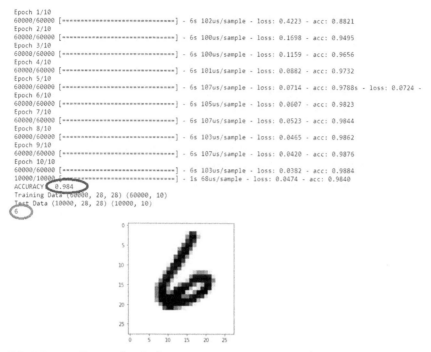

FIGURE 6.4   Output for Code 6.1, 6.2, 6.3, 6.4 – MNIST dataset recognition for digit 6.

YouTube Session and Implementation for the LeNet – https://youtu.be/ PiF0l6xif-k

One should not just stop with this. Many modifications in the parameters can be tried and can derive even better results. The code for the same is made available in the GitHub. On to the next architecture – VGG16.

6.3   VGG16 CNN ARCHITECTURE

This is one of the most preferred CNN architectures in the recent past. It had been developed by Simonyan and Zisserman by 2014. It has 16 convolutional layers. One can see the complexity increasing gradually comparing the initial versions of CNN architectures like LeNET. VGG 16 is preferred as it has a very uniform architecture. Initially, it may look tougher, but it is not as complicated as it appears. It is simple provided we establish a correct understanding. The only point to worry about regarding VGG 16 is the huge number of parameters it has. That is, it has 138 million parameters, which is certainly difficult to handle. Also, the authors wish to make an important note here: Please do not try this model deployment in your machine if it has a low end configuration. Certainly, the machine will be slowed down and it may even crash. Authors have developed this model with an I7, 8th Gen, 16 GB RAM machine in place.

The VGG16 architecture is presented as simple pictorial representation as shown in Figure 6.5, which is then established as a detailed diagram immediately as shown in Figure 6.6. This figure can tell you the way VGG 16 is structured. It has 16 convolution layers.

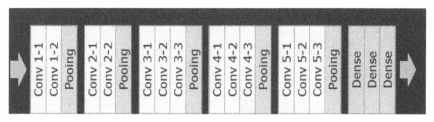

FIGURE 6.5   The VGG 16 architecture – simplified view.

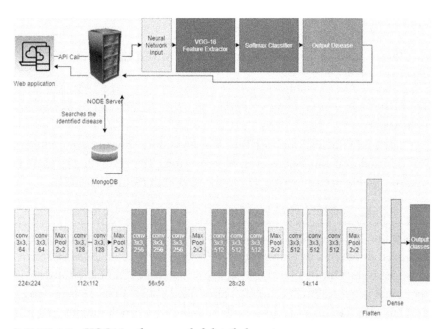

FIGURE 6.6   VGG16 – the expanded detailed version.

Since the number of layers is very high, it is better to explain the details of layers through a table that has the complete information embedded in it. One can refer to the Table 6.7 to understand the details.

TABLE 6.7   The Complete Information of VGG16 Configuration

Layer	Convolution Details	Output Dimensions	Pooling	Output Dimension
Layer 1 and 2	Convolution layer, 64 feature maps, 3x3 kernel with padding 1, stride 1	224x224x64	Max pooling Stride=2, Dimension = 2x2	112x112x64
Layer 3 and 4	Convolution layer, 128 feature maps, 3x3 kernel with padding 1, stride 1	112x112x128	Max pool Stride=2, Dimension = 2x2	56x56x128
Layer 5,6, and 7	Convolution layer of 256 feature maps, 3x3 kernel with padding 1, stride 1	56x56x256	Max pool Stride=2, Dimension = 2x2	28x28x256
Layer 8, 9, and 10	Convolution layer of 512 feature maps, 3x3 kernel with padding 1, stride 1	28x28x512	Max pool, Stride=2, Dimension = 2x2	14x14x512
Layer 11, 12, and 13	Convolution layer of 512 feature maps, 3x3 kernel with padding 1, stride 1	14x14x512	Max pool, Stride=2, Dimension = 2x2	7x7x512
Layer 14	Dense Layer	4096 Units	-	-
Layer 15	Dense Layer	4096 Units	-	-
Layer 16	Dense Layer	2 Units		

One can understand the above table better after going through the implementation. Details of the activation functions used is also clearly mentioned in the code for easier reference.

The Model Development and Deployment

The Dataset

Whenever a model is built, it is to be tested with an apt dataset for its functioning. The VGG16 model to be developed is first used to classify the input image as a cat or dog. The dataset collected is stored appropriately in the local drive of your choice. One can see the test_set, training_set directories shown below. Also, cat_or_dog_1, cat_or_dog_2 are used as the input images to be classified by the CNN model developed.

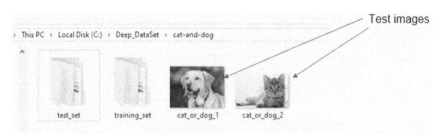

FIGURE 6.7   The dataset and its location.

It can be seen that test_set and training_set are present in the dataset location (Figure 6.7). One should understand the fundamental idea of having the test and training images. Figures 6.8 and 6.9 reveal the content inside both directories. The amount of training images is generally expected to be more than the testing images. Normally, 70 percent of the images will be used as training images while 30 percent will be used as testing images. However, there is no hard and fast rule for this 70–30 ratio.

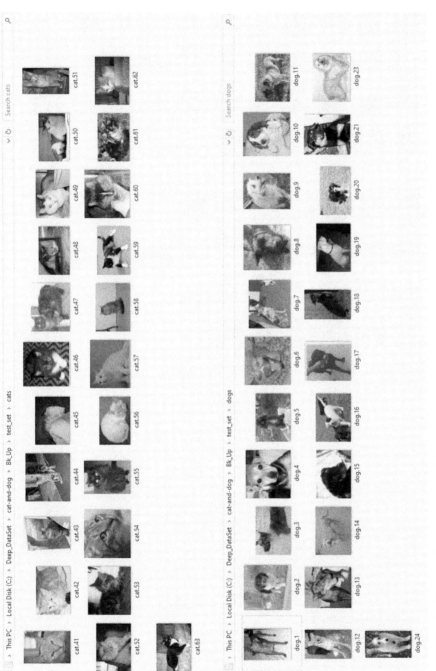

FIGURE 6.8   The test dataset – cats and dogs.

FIGURE 6.9   The training dataset – cats and dogs.

```
import keras,os
from keras.models import Sequential
# Sequential from keras.models, This gets our neural network as Sequential network.
# As we know, it can be sequential layers or graph

from keras.layers import Conv2D
# We are working with images. All the images are basically 2D.
# One can go with the 3D if working with videos.

from keras.layers import MaxPool2D
# Average Pooling, Sum Pooling and Max Pooling are there.
# We choose Max pooling. Re collect all what I tought you. from keras.layers import

from keras.layers import Flatten
# Well, we must flatten. It is the process of converting all the resultant 2D arrays as single long continuous linear vector.
# This is mandatory, folks.

from keras.layers import Dense
# This is the last step! Yes, full connection of the neural network is performed with this Dense.

from keras.preprocessing.image import ImageDataGenerator
# We are going to use ImageDataGenerator from Keras and hence import it as well! It helps in rescale, rotate, zoom, flip etc.

import numpy as np
# Yes, Numpy matters too!
trdata = ImageDataGenerator()
traindata = trdata.flow_from_directory(directory="C:/Deep_DataSet/cat-and-dog/training_set",target_size=(224,224))
tsdata = ImageDataGenerator()
testdata = tsdata.flow_from_directory(directory="C:/Deep_DataSet/cat-and-dog/test_set", target_size=(224,224))
# Can we assign the test and training images. As usual, we can take 70/30
```

CODE 6.5   VGG16 model – import.

```
                              # Section 2 - Convolution/Pooling/Flattening/Dense
model = Sequential()
# Can we initialize the CNN and start the real coding?

model.add(Conv2D(input_shape=(224,224,3),filters=64,kernel_size=(3,3),padding="same", activation="relu"))
model.add(Conv2D(filters=64,kernel_size=(3,3),padding="same", activation="relu"))
model.add(MaxPool2D(pool_size=(2,2),strides=(2,2)))
# We need 2D Convolution. It is 2D image we are dealing with. (All these are specs you need to follow - No other go!)
# We have four arguments to be passed, you know that.
# Specify input shape (224, 224, 3), Number of filters, Filter size and activation function.
# Remember this, filter == kernel. Number of filters is specified along with dimension.

model.add(Conv2D(filters=128, kernel_size=(3,3), padding="same", activation="relu"))
model.add(Conv2D(filters=128, kernel_size=(3,3), padding="same", activation="relu"))
model.add(MaxPool2D(pool_size=(2,2),strides=(2,2)))
# Follow the same procedure

model.add(Conv2D(filters=256, kernel_size=(3,3), padding="same", activation="relu"))
model.add(Conv2D(filters=256, kernel_size=(3,3), padding="same", activation="relu"))
model.add(Conv2D(filters=256, kernel_size=(3,3), padding="same", activation="relu"))
model.add(MaxPool2D(pool_size=(2,2),strides=(2,2)))
# Follow the same procedure

model.add(Conv2D(filters=512, kernel_size=(3,3), padding="same", activation="relu"))
model.add(Conv2D(filters=512, kernel_size=(3,3), padding="same", activation="relu"))
model.add(Conv2D(filters=512, kernel_size=(3,3), padding="same", activation="relu"))
model.add(MaxPool2D(pool_size=(2,2),strides=(2,2)))
# Follow the same procedure
model.add(Conv2D(filters=512, kernel_size=(3,3), padding="same", activation="relu"))
model.add(Conv2D(filters=512, kernel_size=(3,3), padding="same", activation="relu"))
model.add(Conv2D(filters=512, kernel_size=(3,3), padding="same", activation="relu"))
model.add(MaxPool2D(pool_size=(2,2),strides=(2,2)))
# Follow the same procedure
```

CODE 6.6   VGG16 model – convolution.

```
model.load_weights('vggweights.h5')
for layer in model.layers:
    layer.trainable=False
model.add(Flatten())
# Remember, loading the weights here and is a very important process.
# This saves a lot of time and we need not do everything from scratch as we have pretrained weights available.
# Here, What we are basically doing here is taking the 2-D array,
# i.e pooled image pixels and converting them to a one dimensional single vector.

model.add(Dense(units=256,activation="relu"))
model.add(Dense(units=256,activation="relu"))
model.add(Dense(units=2, activation="softmax"))
# We have 1 x Dense Layer of 4096 units
# We have 1 x Dense Layer of 4096 units
# We have 1 x Dense Softmax Layer of 2 units

model.compile(optimizer='adam', loss=keras.losses.categorical_crossentropy, metrics=['accuracy'])
# Can we compile??
# Specify all the arugyments, metrics clearly.
model.summary()
# We get a summary out here. It is a table, folks!
hist = model.fit_generator(steps_per_epoch=100,generator=traindata, validation_data= testdata, validation_steps=10,epochs=5)
model.save('weights1')
```

CODE 6.7   VGG16 model – add weights.

```
# We can test with first input image - It is dog!
from keras.preprocessing import image
img = image.load_img("C:/Deep_DataSet/cat-and-dog/cat_or_dog_1.jpg",target_size=(224,224))
img = np.asarray(img)
plt.imshow(img)
img = np.expand_dims(img, axis=0)
from keras.models import load_model
saved_model = load_model("weights1")
output = saved_model.predict(img)
if output[0][0] > output[0][1]:
    print("cat")
else:
    print('dog')
```

CODE 6.8   VGG16 model – test.

On compiling this code (one should make sure that all the prerequisites are installed) the following result will be presented (Figure 6.10). The image tested 'cat_or_dog_1' has a dog, and the same is classified appropriately in the results. One can also see the details of accuracy and other parameters.

Layer (type)	Output Shape	Param #
conv2d_144 (Conv2D)	(None, 224, 224, 64)	1792
conv2d_145 (Conv2D)	(None, 224, 224, 64)	36928
max_pooling2d_56 (MaxPooling	(None, 112, 112, 64)	0
conv2d_146 (Conv2D)	(None, 112, 112, 128)	73856
conv2d_147 (Conv2D)	(None, 112, 112, 128)	147584
max_pooling2d_57 (MaxPooling	(None, 56, 56, 128)	0
conv2d_148 (Conv2D)	(None, 56, 56, 256)	295168
conv2d_149 (Conv2D)	(None, 56, 56, 256)	590080
conv2d_150 (Conv2D)	(None, 56, 56, 256)	590080
max_pooling2d_58 (MaxPooling	(None, 28, 28, 256)	0
conv2d_151 (Conv2D)	(None, 28, 28, 512)	1180160
conv2d_152 (Conv2D)	(None, 28, 28, 512)	2359808
conv2d_153 (Conv2D)	(None, 28, 28, 512)	2359808
max_pooling2d_59 (MaxPooling	(None, 14, 14, 512)	0
conv2d_154 (Conv2D)	(None, 14, 14, 512)	2359808
conv2d_155 (Conv2D)	(None, 14, 14, 512)	2359808
conv2d_156 (Conv2D)	(None, 14, 14, 512)	2359808
max_pooling2d_60 (MaxPooling	(None, 7, 7, 512)	0
flatten_3 (Flatten)	(None, 25088)	0
dense_7 (Dense)	(None, 256)	6422784
dense_8 (Dense)	(None, 256)	65792
dense_9 (Dense)	(None, 2)	514

FIGURE 6.10 Values.

```
Epoch 1/5
100/100 [==============================] - 276s 3s/step - loss: 0.8944 - accuracy: 0.9789 - val_loss: 0.0000e+00 - val_accurac
y: 1.0000
Epoch 2/5
100/100 [==============================] - 277s 3s/step - loss: 3.9357e-10 - accuracy: 1.0000 - val_loss: 0.0000e+00 - val_accu
racy: 1.0000
Epoch 3/5
100/100 [==============================] - 278s 3s/step - loss: 0.0000e+00 - accuracy: 1.0000 - val_loss: 0.0000e+00 - val_accu
racy: 1.0000
Epoch 4/5
100/100 [==============================] - 278s 3s/step - loss: 0.0000e+00 - accuracy: 1.0000 - val_loss: 0.0000e+00 - val_accu
racy: 1.0000
Epoch 5/5
100/100 [==============================] - 275s 3s/step - loss: 0.0000e+00 - accuracy: 1.0000 - val_loss: 0.0000e+00 - val_accu
racy: 1.0000
dog
```

FIGURE 6.11   Output for Code 6.5, 6.6, 6.7 – cat or dog classification with the VGG 16 dataset.

One can see that the model is performing well and is giving the correctly classified output (Figure 6.11). Once again, it is important for the readers to tweak the parameters to try something different to understand the complete behavior of the model.

Complete Demo and Description of VGG – 16 in YouTube: https://youtu.be/ bEsRLXY7GCo

The time has come to understand one more model, which is believed to be a trendsetter in this field. AlexNet is the next one to be understood and learned!

Disclaimer: The reader should understand that the number of images considered for the model implementation should be higher. For the want of illustrations and understanding, the number of images considered in these implementations could be limited. It is strongly encouraged to have as many images in the training and testing dataset to increase accuracy and to eliminate overfitting problems.

6.4   ALEXNET CNN ARCHITECTURE

Disclaimer: Readers should not try this model in a lower configuration machine, and it would certainly make the system frozen. This is computationally intense model and should be developed with proper configuration machine.

The AlexNet architecture was proposed by Alex Krizhevsky, Ilya Sutskever, and Geoffrey E. Hinton, and the research paper written based on this architecture is "ImageNet Classification with Deep Convolutional Neural Networks." It is strongly recommended that one should go through this paper to understand the views of the authors who built it and created it from scratch. One can understand the impact AlexNet has created is a result of its winning the famous ILSVRC-2012 competition. The Deep Learning enthusiasts celebrated the success of this model as this has achieved a whopping top-5 test error rate of 15.3 percent, compared to 26.2 percent achieved by the second-best entry. (10 percent almost comparing the second entry in the contest).

The architecture has:

- Five convolution layers;
- Three fully connected layers (The final layer is softmax).

One can see a lot of similarity for AlexNet with LeNET. Remember, there were many convolution layers in the LeNET architecture. This is called a deep neural network, and **60 Million Parameters** are there, which makes it very challenging. A significant difference, or development, one can see from AlexNet is the depth. It is much deeper with having more filters per layer. Also, the number of convolution layers are more. This can be called a deep neural network without any doubt! A **Dropout** feature is added to ensure overfitting is avoided. **Data Augmentation** (Mirroring image, to increase the training volume) is also done. With the advent of GPUs and Storage, AlexNet is found to be one of the best and, undoubtedly, it has set a new trend.

The original architecture proposed by the authors of the architecture is presented as Figure 6.12. It is eventually difficult for any beginner to understand the architecture, and we realized the same. The revised, simpler version for easier understanding is presented as Figure 6.13.

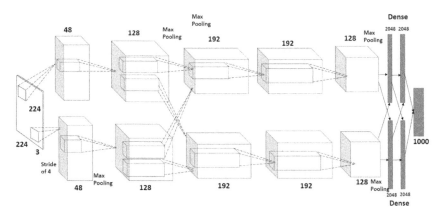

FIGURE 6.12   The AlexNet architecture.

(Source: ImageNet Classification with Deep Convolutional Neural Networks, by Alex Krizhevsky, Ilya Sutskever, and Geoffrey E. Hinton).

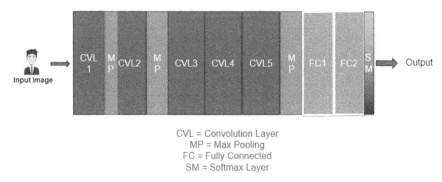

FIGURE 6.13   The simpler AlexNet architecture.

In this architecture, the input size is RGB 224 x 224 x 3 (Actually 227 x 227, this mistake has been pointed out by many experts). The code developed by us goes with 227 x 227 and can be observed from the code. The architecture has 5 convolution layers, 2 fully connected layers, followed by one softmax layer (output). One can understand that after the first convolution, max pooling is carried out. After the second convolution, max pooling is again carried out. Then the third and the fourth convolutions are carried out respectively. After the fifth convolution, again max pooling is carried out. Entirely in this architecture up until the final layer, it is the ReLU activation function being used, and the final layer is the softmax layer.

The dimensions, filter details, and striding information for the convolution layers and the max pooling are presented as a table below with a brief note for each layer, which will enable the reader to build the model with ease.

Layer 1, Followed by Max Pooling.

As discussed, the input image is of the dimension 227 x 227 and is fed to the convolution layer. The convolution layer generates the resultant image with 96 feature maps, the dimensions being 55 x 55 with filter size 11 x 11. The striding is set to 4. ReLu activation function is used in this layer. One can go through Table 6.8 to understand the aforementioned details. This is followed by the max pooling layer with the kernel size 3 x 3 and striding of 2. The dimensions are reduced by half after max pooling and become 27 x 27 x 96. Feature maps never get altered through pooling operations and hence there is no change.

TABLE 6.8   Input Layer and First Convolution Layer

Layer	Layer Type	Feature Map count	Size (Dimension)	Kernel Size	Stride	Activation
Input Layer	RGB	1	227 x 227 x 3	NA	NA	NA
C1	Convolution layer 1	96	55 x 55 x 96	11x11	4	ReLu
Sub Sampling	Max Pooling	96	27 x 27 x 96	3 x 3	2	ReLu

Layer 2

The next round of convolution is carried out: 256 feature maps and a kernel size of 5 x 5 with striding 1 gets the size as 1. Followed by this, there has to be a max pooling carried out with the kernel size 3 x 3 and stride 2. This certainly again halves the pixel count and brings it down. Table 6.8 is updated as Table 6.9 and is presented below for quick reference.

TABLE 6.9   updated Table with Layer 2 Dimensions

Layer	Layer Type	Feature Map count	Size (Dimension)	Kernel Size	Stride	Activation
Input Layer	RGB	1	227 x227 x3	NA	NA	NA
C1	Convolution layer 1	96	55 x 55 x 96	11x11	4	ReLu
Sub Sampling	Max Pooling	96	27 x 27 x 96	3 x 3	2	ReLu
C2	Convolution layer 2	256	27 x 27 x 256	5 x 5	1	ReLU
Sub Sampling	Max Pooling	256	13 x 13 x 256	3 x 3	2	ReLu

Layers 3, 4, and 5 Followed by Max Pooling
The layers 3, 4, and 5 are convolution layers with feature maps 384, 384, and 256 respectively. The filter size is consistent throughout 3, 4 and 5 convolution layers as 3 x 3 with striding set to 1. ReLU activation is used for all these layers. After the 5th convolution, the results are to be handed over to fully connected layers after a max pooling operation with 3 x 3 filter and stride set to 2. One can go through the table below to understand the dimensions clearly (Table 6.10).

TABLE 6.10   All the Layers Updated with Dimensions

Layer	Layer Type	Feature Map count	Size (Dimension)	Kernel Size	Stride	Activation
Input Layer	RGB	1	227 x227 x3	NA	NA	NA
C1	Convolution layer 1	96	55 x 55 x 96	11x11	4	ReLu
Sub Sampling	Max Pooling	96	27 x 27 x 96	3 x 3	2	ReLu
C2	Convolution layer 2	256	27 x 27 x 256	5 x 5	1	ReLU
Sub Sampling	Max Pooling	256	13 x 13 x 256	3 x 3	2	ReLu
C3	Convolution	384	13 x13x 384	3 x3	1	ReLu
C4	Convolution	384	13 x13x 384	3 x3	1	ReLu
C5	Convolution	256	13 x 13 x 256	3 x 3	1	ReLu
Sub Sampling	Max Pooling	256	6 x 6 x 256	3 x 3	2	ReLu

Finally, comes the fully connected layers and two fully connected layers with 4096 neurons and ReLu activation are carried out. The final output layer is with 1000 neurons, and softmax activation is used to fire the output classification. Final Table 6.11 is presented below for a complete and comprehensive understanding by the readers.

TABLE 6.11   The Complete AlexNet Architecture

Layer	Layer Type	Feature Map count	Size (Dimension)	Kernel Size	Stride
Input Layer	RGB	1	227 x227 x3	NA	NA
C1	Convolution layer 1	96	55 x 55 x 96	11x11	4
Sub Sampling	Max Pooling	96	27 x 27 x 96	3 x 3	2
C2	Convolution layer 2	256	27 x 27 x 256	5 x 5	1
Sub Sampling	Max Pooling	256	13 x 13 x 256	3 x 3	2
C3	Convolution	384	13 x13x 384	3 x3	1
C4	Convolution	384	13 x13x 384	3 x3	1
C5	Convolution	256	13 x 13 x 256	3 x 3	1
Subsampling	Max Pooling	256	6 x 6 x 256	3 x 3	2
Fully Connected	NA	4096	NA	NA	NA
Fully Connected	NA	4096	NA	NA	NA
Fully Connected Output Layer	NA	1000	NA	NA	NA

Having understood the math and the dimensions, it is important to build the model. It is coding time for the readers.

```
import keras

from keras.models import Sequential
#  Sequential from keras.models,  This gets our neural network as Sequential network.
#  As we know, it can be sequential layers or graph

from keras.layers import Dense, Activation, Dropout, Flatten, Conv2D, MaxPooling2D
# Importing, Dense, Activation, Flatten, Activation, Dropout, Conv2D and Maxpooling.
# Dropout is a technique used to prevent a model from overfitting.

from keras.layers.normalization import BatchNormalization
# For normalization.

import numpy as np

image_shape = (227,227,3)
# Many code this as 224x224, actual dimension is 227x227.
np.random.seed(1000)

model = Sequential()
# It starts here. The neural network is sequential.
```

CODE 6.9   AlexNet architecture – import.

```
# 1st Convolutional Layer
model.add(Conv2D(filters=96, input_shape=image_shape, kernel_size=(11,11), strides=(4,4), padding='valid'))
model.add(Activation('relu'))
# First layer has 96 Filters, the input shape is 227 x 227 x 3
# Kernel Size is 11 x 11, Striding 4 x 4, ReLu is the activation function.

# Max Pooling
model.add(MaxPooling2D(pool_size=(3,3), strides=(2,2), padding='valid'))

# 2nd Convolutional Layer
model.add(Conv2D(filters=256, kernel_size=(5,5), strides=(1,1), padding='valid'))
model.add(Activation('relu'))
# Max Pooling
model.add(MaxPooling2D(pool_size=(3,3), strides=(2,2), padding='valid'))

# 3rd Convolutional Layer
model.add(Conv2D(filters=384, kernel_size=(3,3), strides=(1,1), padding='valid'))
model.add(Activation('relu'))

# 4th Convolutional Layer
model.add(Conv2D(filters=384, kernel_size=(3,3), strides=(1,1), padding='valid'))
model.add(Activation('relu'))

# 5th Convolutional Layer
model.add(Conv2D(filters=256, kernel_size=(3,3), strides=(1,1), padding='valid'))
model.add(Activation('relu'))
# Max Pooling
model.add(MaxPooling2D(pool_size=(3,3), strides=(2,2), padding='valid'))

# Passing it to a Fully Connected Layer, Here we do flatten!
model.add(Flatten())
```

CODE 6.10   AlexNet architecture – convolutional layers.

```
# 1st Fully Connected Layer has 4096 neurons
model.add(Dense(4096, input_shape=(227*227*3,)))
model.add(Activation('relu'))
# Add Dropout to prevent overfitting
model.add(Dropout(0.4))

# 2nd Fully Connected Layer
model.add(Dense(4096))
model.add(Activation('relu'))
# Add Dropout
model.add(Dropout(0.4))

# Output Layer
model.add(Dense(1000))
model.add(Activation('softmax'))

model.summary()

# Compile the model
model.compile(loss=keras.losses.categorical_crossentropy, optimizer='adam', metrics=["accuracy"])
```

CODE 6.11   AlexNet architecture – fully connected layers.

The model developed is compiled for its functioning and the results are presented below for ready reference (Figure 6.14). Readers can try training the model with training dataset, test set and see if they derive a successful classification as result.

```
Layer (type)                    Output Shape              Param #
=================================================================
conv2d_51 (Conv2D)              (None, 55, 55, 96)        34944
_____
activation_90 (Activation)      (None, 55, 55, 96)        0
_____
max_pooling2d_31 (MaxPooling    (None, 27, 27, 96)        0
_____
conv2d_52 (Conv2D)              (None, 23, 23, 256)       614656
_____
activation_91 (Activation)      (None, 23, 23, 256)       0
_____
max_pooling2d_32 (MaxPooling    (None, 11, 11, 256)       0
_____
conv2d_53 (Conv2D)              (None, 9, 9, 384)         885120
_____
activation_92 (Activation)      (None, 9, 9, 384)         0
_____
conv2d_54 (Conv2D)              (None, 7, 7, 384)         1327488
_____
activation_93 (Activation)      (None, 7, 7, 384)         0
_____
conv2d_55 (Conv2D)              (None, 5, 5, 256)         884992
_____
activation_94 (Activation)      (None, 5, 5, 256)         0
_____
max_pooling2d_33 (MaxPooling    (None, 2, 2, 256)         0
_____
flatten_11 (Flatten)            (None, 1024)              0
_____
dense_40 (Dense)                (None, 4096)              4198400
_____
activation_95 (Activation)      (None, 4096)              0
_____
dropout_30 (Dropout)            (None, 4096)              0
_____
dense_41 (Dense)                (None, 4096)              16781312
_____
activation_96 (Activation)      (None, 4096)              0
_____
dropout_31 (Dropout)            (None, 4096)              0
_____
dense_42 (Dense)                (None, 1000)              4097000
_____
activation_97 (Activation)      (None, 1000)              0
_____
Total params: 28,823,912
Trainable params: 28,823,912
Non-trainable params: 0
```

FIGURE 6.14   Output for Code 6.9, 6.10, 6.11 – compilation results for AlexNet architecture.

YouTube Session on AlexNet: https://youtu.be/8GheVe2UmUM

There are many other architectures drafted by many Deep Learning innovators worldwide. Dealing with all of them in one text book is very difficult. Hence, the best three models have been chosen and implemented.

The next section gives a brief note on the rest of the architectures. With the given inputs until now, one can easily implement any CNN architecture.

6.5 OTHER CNN ARCHITECTURES AT A GLANCE

1. GoogleNet – After the evolution of VGG16, multiple other models have started coming out and many innovations appeared. Out of all those models that came out in 2014, the one that gained attention is GoogleNet. It is famously regarded as an *inception*. This model also emerged as the winner of the famous and challenging ImageNet contest. The model actually introduced a new module known as inception modules. Inception modules used image distortion, batch normalization, and RMSProp, which is a gradient-based optimization technique. Batch normalization is an appreciable technique that is deployed in GoogleNet for improving speed, performance, and stability, as it is used in many other ANN applications. This module (inception) is fundamentally built with many small convolutions so as to bring down the number of parameters. As promised, the number of parameters is brought to 4 million from a whopping 60 million presented by AlexNet. This architecture is also deep and has 22 layers. One can have a look at how the architecture looks from Figure 6.15.

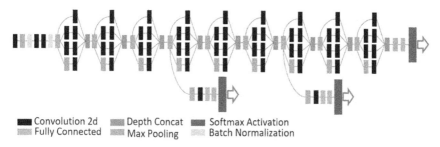

■ Convolution 2d	■ Depth Concat	■ Softmax Activation
▦ Fully Connected	▦ Max Pooling	Batch Normalization

FIGURE 6.15 GoogleNet architecture – as proposed by the authors.

(Source: Szegedy, C., Liu, W., Jia, Y., Sermanet, P., Reed, S., Anguelov, D., Erhan, D., Vanhoucke, V. and Rabinovich, A., 2015. "Going deeper with convolutions." In *Proceedings of the IEEE conference on computer vision and pattern recognition*; pp. 1–9).

2. ZFNet – This is one of the architectures that gained a lot of attention during the ILSVRC 2013 contest and is the winner of that contest, too. It has achieved a stunning error rate of 14.8 percent. By then, in 2013, it was seen as a great improvement over the AlexNet architecture, which was seen as the best architecture until that time. Technically

speaking, ZFNet is a modification of the AlexNet. The major difference one could spot in the architecture is that the ZFNet used 7 x 7
filters whereas, in the AlexNet, it was 11 x 11 filters. This change has
proven effective and has improved accuracy. One can refer to the
architecture proposed by authors of ZFNet presented in Figure 6.16.

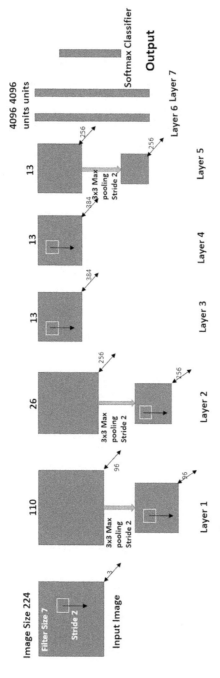

FIGURE 6.16   ZFNet architecture.

(Source: Zeiler, M.D. and Fergus, R., 2014, September. "Visualizing and understanding convolutional networks." In *European Conference on Computer Vision*; pp. 818–833. Springer, Cham).

3. ResNet – Kaiming and his team take the credit for building ResNet. The research team from Microsoft is the first to introduce the term Skipping Connections while not compromising quality when building very deep neural networks. The skipping actually enabled skipping one or more layers. It is certainly seen as innovative to design such a deep network with up to 152 layers without any quality compromise. Also, ResNet is one of the first to adapt Batch Normalization. Use of residual blocks also avoided the vanishing gradient to a very large extent. One can have a look at the architecture of ResNet in Figure 6.17.

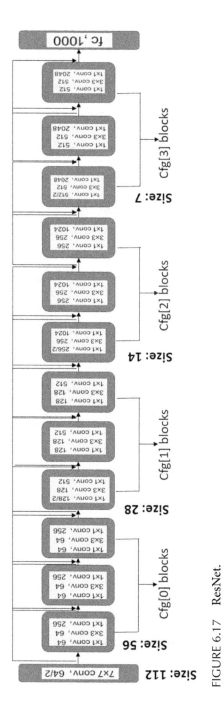

FIGURE 6.17   ResNet.

(Source: He, K., Zhang, X., Ren, S. and Sun, J., 2016. "Deep residual learning for image recognition." In *Proceedings of the IEEE conference on computer vision and pattern recognition*; pp. 770–778).

YouTube Session on Architecture Comparison: https://youtu.be/5yyjTxeJy-s

KEY POINTS TO REMEMBER

- Many architectures have evolved based on the CNN, and learning these architectures will eventually help the reader to select the appropriate architecture for the applications.
- The feature maps of the CNN capture the result of applying the filters to an input image. That is, at each layer, the feature map is the output of that layer.
- LeNet is most commonly used for OCR applications.
- LeNet suggested using 3 level convolutions.
- VGG16 architecture has 16 convolutional layers and is found to be successful model classification.
- One significant difference or development one could see with AlexNet is the depth. Yes, it is much deeper with having more filters per layer. Also, the number of convolution layers are more in AlexNet.
- Data Augmentation is one of the techniques whereby image mirroring is carried out to increase the training images' volume.
- As promised, the number of parameters is brought to 4 million in GoogleNet from 60 million presented by AlexNet.
- The more the number of images used for training and testing dataset, the better the results will be.
- One should make sure the model developed is not leading to overfitting or underfitting issues.
- Choosing the appropriate dataset is a challenge and is to be done appropriately.
- Without correct hardware/software configuration, the developed models may crash.

QUIZ

1. Mention the layers used in the LeNET architecture.
2. What are the important aspects of VGG16 architecture?
3. Where can someone use VGG 16 over other applications?
4. Draw the simple version of AlexNet architecture and explain the important terminologies in the AlexNet architecture.

5. Define the term Inception.

6. What is RMSProp? Explain.

7. Highlight the complexities faced in ZFNet.

8. Mention and highlight the features of ResNet.

FURTHER READING

✓ Mollahosseini, A., Chan, D. and Mahoor, M.H., 2016, March. "Going deeper in facial expression recognition using deep neural networks." In *2016 IEEE Winter Conference on Applications of Computer Vision (WACV)* (pp. 1–10). IEEE.

✓ Christian, S., Wei, L., Yangqing, J., Pierre, S., Scott, R., Dragomir, A., Dumitru, E., Vincent, V. and Andrew, R., 2015, June. Going deeper with convolutions. In *Proceedings of the IEEE Conference on Computer Vision and Pattern Recognition* (pp. 1–9).

✓ Szegedy, C., Liu, W., Jia, Y., Sermanet, P., Reed, S., Anguelov, D., Erhan, D., Vanhoucke, V. and Rabinovich, A., 2015. "Going deeper with convolutions." In *Proceedings of the IEEE Conference on Computer Vision and Pattern Recognition* (pp. 1–9).

✓ Zeiler, M.D. and Fergus, R., 2014, September. "Visualizing and understanding convolutional networks." In *European Conference on Computer Vision* (pp. 818–833). Springer, Cham.

✓ Simonyan, K. and Zisserman, A., 2014. "Very deep convolutional networks for large-scale image recognition." *arXiv preprint arXiv:1409.1556.*

✓ Herath, S., Harandi, M. and Porikli, F., 2017. "Going deeper into action recognition: A survey." *Image and Vision Computing, 60,* pp.4–21.

✓ Lee, H. and Kwon, H., 2017. "Going deeper with contextual CNN for hyperspectral image classification." *IEEE Transactions on Image Processing, 26*(10), pp. 4843–4855.

## CHAPTER 7

Recurrent Neural Networks

LEARNING OBJECTIVES

After this chapter, the reader will be able to understand the following:

- What is RNN?
- Challenges in the Basic RNN.
- Functioning of LSTM function.
- What is GRU?

7.1 INTRODUCTION

This chapter focuses on the new term, Recurrent Neural Networks (RNN). It is interesting and challenging, too. The Readers are requested to read the contents of this chapter thoroughly and, in case of queries, one could look into the video lecture links provided at appropriate places.

RNN is married to both Machine Learning and Deep Learning. Yes, it is married to Artificial Intelligence (AI). Recurrent Neural Networks have a variety of applications, which is unavoidable. Many of us are unwittingly using some applications that could have deployed RNN. If you have used speech recognition, language translators, or market stock predictor applications, RNN is a regular customer. It is even very handy for image recognition (Figure 7.1).

DOI: 10.1201/9781003185635-7

Speech Recognition | Language Translation | Stock Market Prediction | Image Recognition

FIGURE 7.1   RNN applications.

Needless to say, RNN is one of the types of ANN. Here in RNN, the output of the previous step is fed in as the input (i.e., feedback) to the current step. It is definitely different from the traditional approach or even from CNN, which we dealt with in the previous chapters. There, traditionally, the input and output are certainly independent of each other. Remember, in CNN, we never remembered the previous state fully to get to further layers.

But RNN is not that. It remembers. Means, it has memory like humans and animals. Coming to the applications of Natural Language Processing (NLP), like the prediction of words in a sentence, it is always important to remember the words in the past. Then the memory comes into the picture.

So, RNN came into the picture this way! The appreciable feature came in with RNN is the "hidden state." Hidden state is nothing but the memory, which remembers some information. Figure 7.2 helps understand the difference between traditional neural networks and recurrent neural networks.

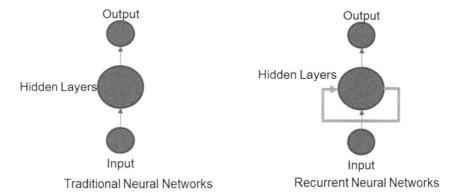

FIGURE 7.2   Traditional neural networks vs. RNN.

Giving the France example is quite common when someone discusses RNN.

"I had a good time in France. I also learned to speak some _____."
If someone asks you to predict what would be the word that fits in in the
blank space, how would you answer? Simple, you will remember the previous phrase. The previous phrase says it was France. So, the prediction
would be "French." One needs memory to calculate the next word. It is the
same with RNN. It has Memory, and it helps in prediction. Previous stage
output plays a role in deriving the current output.

RNN is all about sequential memory. One can easily write the alphabet!

A   l   p   h   a   b   e   t   s

But, if asked to write the reverse of the alphabet as the same speed as one
could write the sequence, it would be tough. Sequential Memory is easy for
the brain. RNN follows the same approach.

We are going to take an example. Yes, Chabot is the example. It has to
clearly classify the intentions of the user and predict through the input text
fed in already. When a person feeds in "How is the climate outside right
today?" the RNN approach would proceed as follows (Figure 7.3).

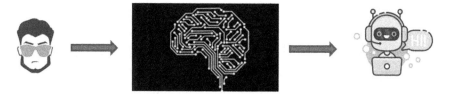

FIGURE 7.3   The Chabot experience.

How is the climate outside right today? How this could be processed is
presented step by step as shown.

- The first step is to feed "How" into the RNN. The RNN encodes
  "How" and produces an output.
- Next, the word "is" should be fed. RNN now has the information
  "How" and "is." This stage gets OP2.
- Next stage, "the" would be fed. RNN now has the information from
  the previous stages. So, in total it would be. How, is, the. This process
  goes on until the end, and this is the fundamental idea. One can refer
  to Figure 7.4 to understand the entire flow.

OP1

How is the climate outside right today?

OP1 OP2 OP3

How is the climate outside right today?

OP1 OP2 OP3   OP8

How is the climate outside right today?

FIGURE 7.4 The RNN process.

One should understand this point: The final output is derived through the complete sequence. So, the final output, that is, OP8 in the example above, can be passed to the feed forward layer and get the result!

One can listen to the lecture: "RNN: How It Works?" – *https://youtu.be/Gir8xDkEB8s*.

7.2 CNN VS. RNN: A QUICK UNDERSTANDING

CNN is a feed forward neural network that finds lot of its applications in the Image Recognition and Object Recognition sectors. RNN is fundamentally based on the feedback, that is, the output of the current layer is dependent on the previous layer as well. CNN worries only about the current input and, as discussed, RNN has concern for previous output. RNN is memory driven. It has memory. CNN is normally constructed with four layers: the convolution layer, activation layer, pooling layer and fully connected layer. The major task carried out by each layer is to extract features and to find out patterns in the input image. RNN is all about input/hidden and output layers. The hidden layers do the looping and have the memory to store the previous results.

CNN is most suitable for images, whereas RNN is suitable for sequential data. CNN has a finite set of input and generates only the finite set of predicted values based on the input. RNN is not so. It allows arbitrary input length. CNN is found to be too good for image- and video-related projects, whereas RNN is always found to be good with time series information. Such as, what can be the next word in the sequence, and so forth. One can understand the difference between RNN and CNN by referring to Figure 7.5.

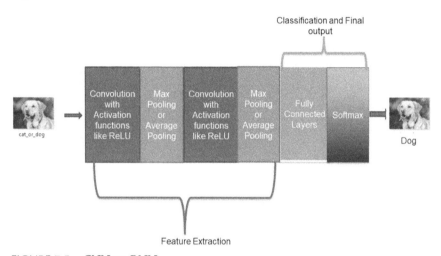

FIGURE 7.5 CNN vs. RNN.

7.3 RNN VS. FEEDFORWARD NEURAL NETWORKS: A QUICK UNDERSTANDING

When it comes to Feedforward Neural Networks (FFN), the data navigates from the input layer to the output layer, that is, from left to right. The data moves through the hidden layers, which are structured in between. The information, that is, the flow of the data, will be received only from left to right, that is, no looking back.

Also, remember, never, ever does information reach a particular node twice in the full cycle. A particular node receives input, and it is the only time it can receive and never can it receive again. This will not be suitable for applications like stock forecasting, market predictions and so forth, as there is no knowledge of history. Any prediction needs history. One has to agree to this point. History can be remembered only when there is memory. No memory, no history in place. So, to conclude: feedforward networks have memory loss (No memory at all!). FFN can remember only the current input and the training instructions. RNN is different in this aspect.

When it comes to RNN, we should remember there is a loop. The information goes through the loop, and memory comes in. The decision on the data is arrived at through the current state input and the previous outputs. That is, prediction of markets will be done through the consideration of current and historical data. Only then, is it prediction. One can understand the concept better with the following Figure 7.6.

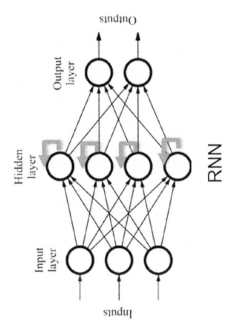

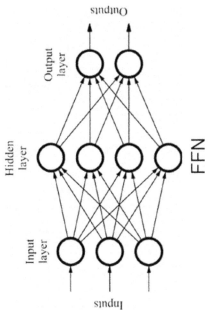

FIGURE 7.6   FFN vs. RNN.

One can listen to the lectures on the above topic by referring below the links:

- CNN Vs. RNN: https://youtu.be/EvaDbW92gGg
- Feed forward neural networks vs. RNN: *https://youtu.be/BJz2QAz0YzM*

7.4 SIMPLE RNN

All these started with something called Elman Network, built by Jeffrey Elman in 1990. It was the inspiration for everything we have now as RNNs. Elman followed a simple strategy. He proposed to have the input layer, hidden layer, and context layer along with the recurrent feedback concept. To see what is was like, one can look at Figure 7.7.

Here, as one can see, there are connections from hidden layer to context layer. (Feedback is to be seen as well, it provides data of the past). Also, there is a connection from input to hidden layer, too.

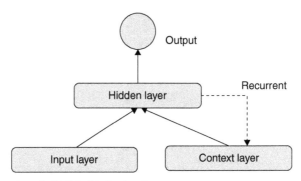

FIGURE 7.7   Simple RNN: this is simple.

There are three important things to be remembered:

- We are concerned with the time, t (The present).
- We are also concerned with the time, t-1 (The recent past).
- The current output is determined by the present + recent past together.

It is now time to go with some mathematics.

new_state @ time t = Recursive_Function
(Old_state@ time $_{t-1}$, input @ time $_t$)

State $_t$ = fn (State $_{t-1}$ + X$_t$)

X$_t$ = Input at time t.

The function we use is recursive and is tanh. Also, weights are to be multiplied appropriately. So,

State $_t$ = fn (State $_{t-1}$, X$_t$) becomes State $_t$ = tanh(Wq * State $_{t-1}$ + W$_p$ * X$_t$)

Hence, the output is

$$Y_t = W_r * State_t$$

State t = St
Finally,

$$Y_t = S_t * W_r \text{ is the result}$$

One should remember:

- Wp = Weights for X, that is, input state.
- Wq = Weights for previous state.
- Wr = Weights for output.

One can look at Figure 7.8 to understand the concept even better.

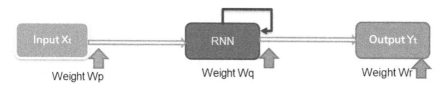

FIGURE 7.8   The simple RNN.

The unrolled version is presented below, which helps readers to better understand the concept (Figure 7.9).

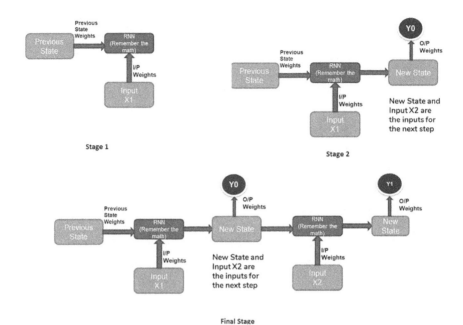

FIGURE 7.9   The unrolled RNN.

One can refer to the lectures @

- Simple RNN: *https://youtu.be/EN60ZmxmSyA*
- LSTM explained: *https://youtu.be/XsFkGGlocc4*
- LSTM with Keras: *https://youtu.be/QfZEmY6tl5M*

The time has come for the reader to understand the next concept, LSTM. It is easier and interesting, too.

7.5   LSTM: LONG SHORT-TERM MEMORY

We need to go step by step in LSTM. LSTM is expanded as Long Short-Term Memory. Readers will be taken through the entire process in small steps, one after another, so that learning is effective and easier. One has to use three gates and something called the cell state throughout this section. The three gates are,

- Forget Gate
- Input Gate
- Output Gate

The cell states are,

- Intermediate Cell State
- Cell State

Readers will be introduced to the gates one after another in succession.

Forget Gate

Forget Gate is represented as ft. It is computed through

Sigmoid (Weights.forgetgate * St-1 + Weights.forgetgate * xt)

Mathematically,

$$ft = \sigma \, (Wf * St\text{-}1 + Wf * Xt)$$

Where, σ = Sigmoid function,
- W_f = Weights for Forget Gate
- S_{t-1} = old state
- X_t = Input

Why is Forget Gate required? What does it do? The first Sigmoid activation function in the network is the Forget Gate. As the name says, this gate will decide which information has to be retained or dropped. The information from the previous hidden state and the current input gets through the Sigmoid function, and the output arrives. It is between 0 and 1. So, the closer the value to 0, it is to be forgotten; the closer it to 1, it is to be remembered. The next to be learned is the Input Gate.

Input Gate

The input gate is represented as i_t and computed through

Sigmoid (Weights.inputgate * St-1 + Weights.inputgate * xt)

Mathematically

$$i_t = \sigma \, (Wi * St\text{-}1 + Wi * Xt)$$

Where, σ = Sigmoid function
- W_i = Weights for Input Gate
- S_{t-1} = Old state
- X_t = Input

Why is the Input gate required and what does it do? This is the second Sigmoid function and first tanh activation function. This decides which information should be saved to the cell State and which should be dropped. Finally, one has to learn what the Output Gate is.

Output Gate

Output Gate is represented as Ot. It is computed through

Sigmoid (Weights.outputgate * S$_{t-1}$ + Weights.output * x$_t$).

Mathematically,

$$O_t = \sigma (W_o * S_{t-1} + W_o * X_t)$$

Where, σ = Sigmoid function
- W_o = Weights for Input Gate
- S_{t-1} = Old state
- X_t = Input

Why do we need Output Gate? What does it do? It highlights which information should be going to the next hidden state.

Intermediate Cell State $C_{t'} = tanh (W_c * S_{t-1} + W_c * X_t)$

Cell State $C_t = (It * C_{t'}) + (F_t * C_{t-1})$

The new State $= O_t * tanh (C_t)$

The new state is the new hidden state formed. One could go diagrammatic now to understand the entire flow in a better way. One has to remember that

- f_t = Forget Gate
- o_t = Output Gate
- i_t = Input Gate
- C_t = Cell State
- $C_{t'}$ = Intermediate Cell State

Also, it is important to recollect the following

- $f_t = \sigma\,(W_f * S_{t-1} + W_f * X_t)$
- $i_t = \sigma\,(W_i * S_{t-1} + W_i * X_t)$
- $O_t = \sigma\,(W_o * S_{t-1} + W_o * X_t)$
- *Intermediate Cell State* $C_{t'} = tanh\,(W_c * S_{t-1} + W_c * X_t)$
- *Cell State* $C_t = (It * C_{t'}) + (F_t * C_{t-1})$

The entire functioning is clearly represented as figures from stage 1 to stage 6 as follows.

Stage 1
We have the previous state c_0, Old State S_0, and input X_1 with us. One can understand the same by referring Figure 7.10.

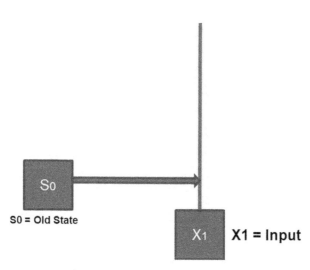

FIGURE 7.10   Stage 1 of LSTM.

Stage 2
There are weights available to be visualized as presented below.

C0 = Previous Cell state

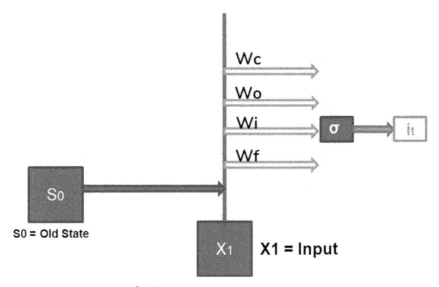

FIGURE 7.11   Stage 2 of LSTM.

One can compute the Input Gate through the Sigmoid function.

Stage 3

Next, one should compute the $C_{t'}$ through tanh and with which W_c can be computed; the same is presented below.

C0 = Previous Cell state

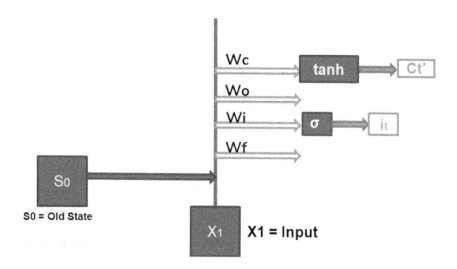

S0 = Old State

X1 = Input

FIGURE 7.12   Stage 3 of LSTM.

Stage 4

One should multiply the results as shown below (Figure 7.13). It should be multiplied with C_t. Also, f_t is to be computed with Sigmoid function. Then multiplication should happen as shown above with C_0.

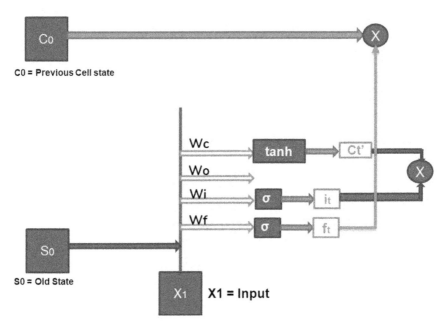

FIGURE 7.13   Stage 4 of LSTM.

Stage 5

Finally, with adder being used, one could get the C_1 from the previous results. Cell State is updated at this point. Next is to compute O_t through the usage of tanh, and is presented above. One can understand the same by referring Figure 7.14.

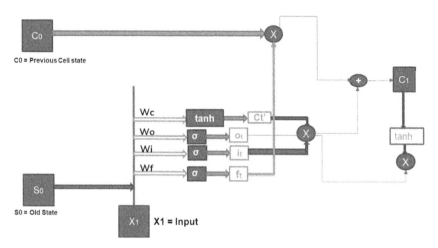

FIGURE 7.14   Stage 5 of LSTM.

Stage 6

Here is the final result (Figure 7.15), and LSTM is completed.

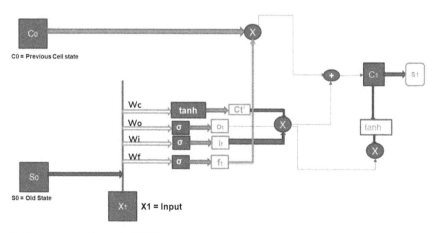

FIGURE 7.15   Stage 6 of LSTM.

One can understand the complete flow by also referring to the link: *https://youtu.be/XsFkGGlocc4*

The next step is to implement the same with Keras. It is interesting and easier, too. One can use LSTM to carry out the sentiment analysis from the IMDB dataset. The complete code is presented with clear comments for each of the lines.

```
#SENTIMENT ANALYSIS OF REVIEWS FROM IMDB Using LSTM
# Used IMDB database which comes with Keras.
# This program will classify reviews from IMDB based on sentiment, positive or negative.
# The reviews are already preprocessed ones.
# So we dont use any encoding explicitly here
# They have given score as 2 for popular word and 3 for the third most popular word etc.

from keras.preprocessing import sequence

from keras.models import Sequential
# As usual, you could see we imported Sequential - Seq. neural networks.

from keras.layers import Dense, Embedding, LSTM
# The purpose of Embeddeding - The Embedding layer is used to create word vectors for incoming words.
# It sits between the input and the LSTM layer, i.e. the output of the Embedding layer is the input to the LSTM Layer
# LSTM is also imported.

from keras.callbacks import EarlyStopping
# Early stopping is basically stopping the training once your loss starts to increase
# or in other words validation accuracy starts to decrease

from keras.datasets import imdb
# Dataset IMDB is imported from keras.
# The OS module in Python provides a way of using operating system dependent functionality.
# The functions that the OS module provides allows you to interface with the underlying operating system
# that Python is running on - be that Windows, Mac or Linux.
import os
os.environ['TF_CPP_MIN_LOG_LEVEL'] = '3'
# We are suppressing the log and informational/warning messages.
# We should set the parameters.
NUM_WORDS = 6000         # Considering the top most n frequent words
SKIP_TOP = 2             # Skipping the top most words that are likely (the, and, a)
MAX_REVIEW_LEN = 100     # maximum number of words in reviews

# Load pre-processed sentiment classified review data from IMDB Database
# First time it will download and load the data
(x_train, y_train), (x_test, y_test) = imdb.load_data(num_words = NUM_WORDS,
                       skip_top=SKIP_TOP)
# Printing a sample data to have an understanding of dataset
# This returns word index vector (ex. [2, 4, 2, 2, 33, 2804, ...]) and class (0 or 1)
print("encoded word sequence:", x_train[3], "class:", y_train[3])
print("encoded word sequence:", x_train[2], "class:", y_train[2])
# Padding and truncating the review word sequences so that they are all the same length
x_train = sequence.pad_sequences(x_train, maxlen = MAX_REVIEW_LEN)
x_test = sequence.pad_sequences(x_test, maxlen = MAX_REVIEW_LEN)

print('x_train.shape:', x_train.shape, 'x_test.shape:', x_test.shape)
```

CODE 7.1   LSTM: Section 1.

```
#   The LSTM Model - The core section
model = Sequential()
model.add(Embedding(NUM_WORDS, 64 ))
model.add(LSTM(64, dropout=0.3, recurrent_dropout=0.3))
model.add(Dense(1, activation='sigmoid'))

#   Compile the LSTM model
model.compile(loss='binary_crossentropy',
          optimizer='adam',
          metrics=['accuracy'])
| . .
EarlyStopping:
Too many epochs can lead to overfitting of the training dataset, whereas too few may result in an underfit model.
Early stopping is a method that allows you to specify an arbitrary large number of training epochs and
stop training once the model performance stops improving on a hold out validation dataset.
. . .
#   Train
BATCH_SIZE = 24
EPOCHS = 5
cbk_early_stopping = EarlyStopping(monitor='val_acc', patience=2, mode='max')
model.fit(x_train, y_train, BATCH_SIZE, epochs=EPOCHS,
          validation_data=(x_test, y_test),
          callbacks=[cbk_early_stopping] )
 #Print the test score and Accuracy obtained by model

 score, acc = model.evaluate(x_test, y_test,
                             batch_size=BATCH_SIZE)
 print('test score:', score, ' test accuracy:', acc)
```

CODE 7.2   LSTM: core module.

The output is presented below (Figure 7.16) for a quicker reference.

```
encoded word sequence: [2, 4, 2, 2, 33, 2804, 4, 2040, 432, 111, 153, 103, 4, 1494, 13, 70, 131, 67, 11, 61, 2, 744, 35, 3715,
761, 61, 5766, 452, 2, 4, 905, 7, 2, 59, 166, 4, 105, 216, 1239, 41, 1797, 9, 15, 7, 35, 744, 2413, 31, 8, 4, 687, 23, 4, 2, 2,
6, 3693, 42, 38, 39, 121, 59, 456, 10, 10, 7, 265, 12, 575, 111, 153, 159, 59, 16, 1447, 21, 25, 586, 482, 39, 4, 96, 59, 716,
12, 4, 172, 65, 9, 579, 11, 2, 4, 1615, 5, 2, 7, 5168, 17, 13, 2, 12, 19, 6, 464, 31, 314, 11, 2, 6, 719, 605, 11, 8, 202, 27,
310, 4, 3772, 3501, 8, 2722, 58, 10, 10, 537, 2116, 180, 40, 14, 413, 173, 7, 263, 112, 37, 152, 377, 4, 537, 263, 846, 579, 17
8, 54, 75, 71, 476, 36, 413, 263, 2504, 182, 5, 17, 75, 2306, 922, 36, 279, 131, 2895, 17, 2867, 42, 17, 35, 921, 2, 192, 5, 12
19, 3890, 19, 2, 217, 4122, 1710, 537, 2, 1236, 5, 736, 10, 10, 61, 403, 9, 2, 40, 61, 4494, 5, 27, 4494, 159, 90, 263, 2311, 4
319, 309, 8, 178, 5, 82, 4319, 4, 65, 15, 2, 145, 143, 5122, 12, 2, 537, 746, 537, 537, 15, 2, 4, 2, 594, 7, 5168, 94, 2, 3987,
2, 11, 2, 4, 538, 7, 1795, 246, 2, 9, 2, 11, 635, 14, 9, 51, 408, 12, 94, 318, 1382, 12, 47, 6, 2683, 936, 5, 2, 2, 19, 49, 7,
4, 1885, 2, 1118, 25, 30, 126, 842, 10, 10, 2, 2, 4726, 27, 4494, 11, 1550, 3633, 159, 27, 341, 29, 2733, 19, 4185, 173, 7, 90,
2, 8, 30, 11, 4, 1784, 86, 1117, 8, 3261, 46, 11, 2, 21, 29, 9, 2841, 23, 4, 1010, 2, 793, 6, 2, 1386, 1830, 10, 10, 246, 50,
9, 6, 2750, 1944, 746, 90, 29, 2, 8, 124, 4, 882, 4, 882, 496, 27, 2, 2213, 537, 121, 127, 1219, 130, 5, 29, 494, 8, 124, 4, 88
2, 496, 4, 341, 7, 27, 846, 10, 10, 29, 9, 1906, 8, 97, 6, 236, 2, 1311, 8, 4, 2, 7, 31, 7, 2, 91, 2, 3987, 70, 4, 882, 30, 57
9, 42, 9, 12, 32, 11, 537, 10, 10, 11, 14, 65, 44, 537, 75, 2, 1775, 3353, 2, 1846, 4, 2, 7, 154, 5, 4, 518, 53, 2, 2, 7, 3211,
882, 11, 399, 38, 75, 257, 3807, 19, 2, 17, 29, 456, 4, 65, 7, 27, 205, 113, 10, 10, 2, 4, 2, 2, 9, 242, 4, 91, 1202, 2, 5, 207
0, 307, 22, 7, 5168, 126, 93, 40, 2, 13, 188, 1076, 3222, 19, 4, 2, 7, 2348, 537, 23, 53, 537, 21, 82, 40, 2, 13, 2, 14, 280, 1
3, 219, 4, 2, 431, 758, 859, 4, 953, 1052, 2, 7, 5991, 5, 94, 40, 25, 238, 60, 2, 4, 2, 804, 2, 7, 4, 2, 132, 8, 67, 6, 22, 15,
9, 283, 8, 5168, 14, 31, 9, 242, 955, 48, 25, 279, 2, 23, 12, 1685, 195, 25, 238, 60, 796, 2, 4, 671, 7, 2804, 5, 4, 559, 154,
888, 7, 726, 50, 26, 49, 2, 15, 566, 30, 579, 21, 64, 2574] class: 1
encoded word sequence: [2, 14, 47, 8, 30, 31, 7, 4, 249, 108, 7, 4, 5974, 54, 61, 369, 13, 71, 149, 14, 22, 112, 4, 2401, 311,
12, 16, 3711, 33, 75, 43, 1829, 296, 4, 86, 320, 35, 534, 19, 263, 4821, 1301, 4, 1873, 33, 89, 78, 12, 66, 16, 4, 360, 7, 4, 5
8, 316, 334, 11, 4, 1716, 43, 645, 662, 8, 257, 85, 1200, 42, 1228, 2576, 83, 68, 3912, 15, 36, 165, 1539, 278, 36, 69, 2, 780,
8, 106, 14, 2, 1338, 18, 6, 22, 12, 215, 28, 610, 40, 6, 87, 326, 23, 2300, 21, 23, 22, 12, 272, 40, 57, 31, 11, 4, 22, 47, 6,
2307, 51, 9, 170, 23, 595, 116, 595, 1352, 13, 191, 79, 638, 89, 2, 14, 9, 8, 106, 607, 624, 35, 534, 6, 227, 7, 129, 113] clas
s: 0
x_train.shape: (25000, 100) x_test.shape: (25000, 100)
Train on 25000 samples, validate on 25000 samples
Epoch 1/5
25000/25000 [==============================] - 47s 2ms/step - loss: 0.4885 - accuracy: 0.7677 - val_loss: 0.4642 - val_accurac
y: 0.7913
Epoch 2/5
   72/25000 [..............................] - ETA: 40s - loss: 0.4972 - accuracy: 0.777

C:\ana\lib\site-packages\keras\callbacks\callbacks.py:846: RuntimeWarning: Early stopping conditioned on metric `val_acc` which
is not available. Available metrics are: val_loss,val_accuracy,loss,accuracy
 (self.monitor, ','.join(list(logs.keys())))), RuntimeWarning

25000/25000 [==============================] - 49s 2ms/step - loss: 0.3784 - accuracy: 0.8352 - val_loss: 0.3962 - val_accurac
y: 0.8264
Epoch 3/5
25000/25000 [==============================] - 48s 2ms/step - loss: 0.3350 - accuracy: 0.8605 - val_loss: 0.3768 - val_accurac
y: 0.8370
Epoch 4/5
25000/25000 [==============================] - 48s 2ms/step - loss: 0.3036 - accuracy: 0.8742 - val_loss: 0.3934 - val_accurac
y: 0.8333
Epoch 5/5
25000/25000 [==============================] - 48s 2ms/step - loss: 0.2696 - accuracy: 0.8902 - val_loss: 0.3819 - val_accurac
y: 0.8401
25000/25000 [==============================] - 10s 382us/step
test score: 0.38190252447605133  test accuracy: 0.8401200175285339
```

FIGURE 7.16   Output of Code 7.1, 7.2: LSTM.

The demo is explained clearly in the YouTube link: *https://youtu.be/ QfZEmY6tl5M*

7.6 GATED RECURRENT UNIT

The next topic queued up is Gated Recurrent Unit (GRU). This is one of the recent innovations, and it is just six years old. It was invented in 2014 by K. Cho. (LSTM was created by 1997). GRU is very closely related to the LSTM and, in fact, can be regarded as a family member of LSTM. When someone says they are related, they share many good features with the newer generation getting better over the previous one. GRUs can effectively address the vanishing gradient problem just like LSTM. In addition to it, GRU appears simpler comparing LSTM.

As seen in the LSTM, GRU also utilizes the gating mechanisms (remember the gates used in LSTM: Forget, Input, and Output) to manage and as well to control the flow of the information between the cells in the neural network.

One has to understand the differences between LSTM and GRU in the architectural perspective as well as the functioning. The subsequent sections will focus on the same.

GRUs do not have the Cell State, and the hidden states are used. The gates are named as Reset Gate and Update Gate. The idea is much the same. The gates help in determining what to be retained/passed or dropped. The gates will get the value between 0 and 1 as we have seen earlier. A 0 from the gate is revealing that the data is unimportant. 1 says it is important (If closer to 0, it is unimportant; closer to 1 it is important).

Again, it is important to remember this point: GRUs do not have the Cell State. A simple representation is presented below as Figure 7.17.

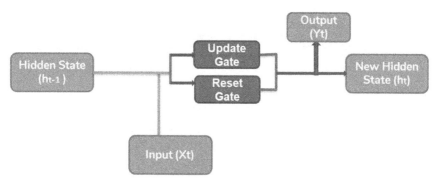

FIGURE 7.17   GRU: representation.

The unrolled version will give reader a better idea and the same is presented in Figure 7.18.

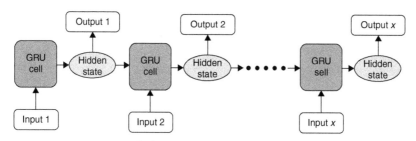

FIGURE 7.18   GRU: unrolled representation.

Update Gate (z)

The major task of this gate is to tell the model, "How much of the past information needs to be maintained, that is, to be passed along to the future."

Update gate is represented by Z_t. Input represented by X_t, Previous h_{t-1} State information multiplied with respective weights as the parameters. (Notations differ, nothing to worry as long as one can understand that respective weights are to be used appropriately.) Sigmoid activation is used to derive Z_t. The same is diagrammatically represented as shown in Figure 7.19.

$$z_t = \sigma\left(W^{(z)}x_t + U^{(z)}h_{t-1}\right)$$

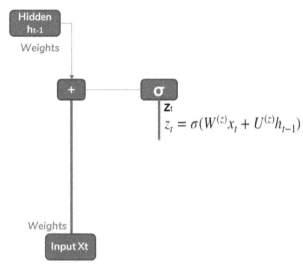

$$z_t = \sigma(W^{(z)}x_t + U^{(z)}h_{t-1})$$

FIGURE 7.19   GRU: update gate.

Reset Gate (r)
This gate is used from the model to decide how much of the past information to forget; as usual there are weights associated with every stage and they have to be remembered.

Reset gate is represented by r_t. Input represented by X_t, Previous h_{t-1} State information multiplied with respective weights as the parameters. Sigmoid activation is used to derive r_t and the same diagrammatically represented below in the Figure 7.20.

$$r_t = \sigma\left(W^{(r)}x_t + U^{(r)}h_{t-1}\right)$$

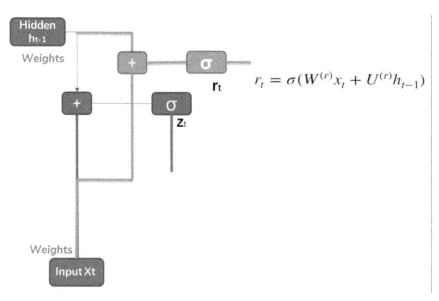

$$r_t = \sigma(W^{(r)}x_t + U^{(r)}h_{t-1})$$

FIGURE 7.20   GRU: reset gate.

A New Component is introduced now, a memory component that will use the reset gate to get the relevant information stored from the past.

If someone is asked to review a movie, initially one will start with "the movie is directed by X, it has featured Y, Music by Z, and so forth. After about ten lines, you say, the movie, I think is a bad one for the money I paid." So, which is the actual review? Ideally, the final line. So, the neural network should not remember the past sentences and instead focus on the last sentence to get to the crux of the matter. It is what is enabled here.

Here, r_t will be assigned 0 until the final phrase is analyzed so as to drop the unfocussed items. Then comes the tanh activation and one gets h_t.

$$h_t' = \tanh\left(Wx_t + r_t \odot Uh_{t-1}\right)$$

The complete architecture is presented below as Figure 7.21.

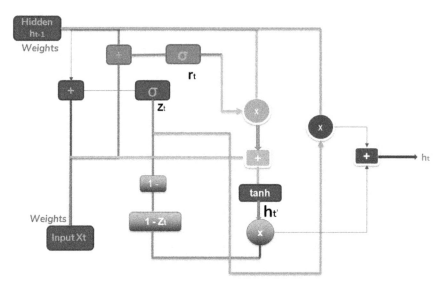

FIGURE 7.21   GRU functioning.

One can try the following a piece of code to understand the practical functioning of the GRU through Keras.

```
# Complete Code
from keras.datasets import imdb
from keras.models import Sequential
from keras.layers import Dense, GRU, Flatten, LSTM
from keras.layers.embeddings import Embedding
# The purpose of Embeddeding - The Embedding layer is used to create word vectors for incoming words.

# load the dataset but only keep the top n words, zero the rest
top_words = 5000
(X_train, y_train), (X_test, y_test) = imdb.load_data(num_words=top_words)

# only take 500 words per review
max_words = 500
X_train = sequence.pad_sequences(X_train, maxlen=max_words)
X_test = sequence.pad_sequences(X_test, maxlen=max_words)

model = Sequential()
model.add(Embedding(top_words, 100, input_length=max_words))
model.add(GRU(100))
model.add(Dense(1, activation='sigmoid'))
model.compile(loss='binary_crossentropy', optimizer='adam', metrics=['accuracy'])
print(model.summary())

# Train
model.fit(X_train, y_train, epochs=3, batch_size=64)

# Final evaluation of the model
scores = model.evaluate(X_test, y_test, verbose=0)
print("fff")
print("Accuracy: %.2f%%" % (scores[1]*100))

# Predict the label for test data
y_predict = model.predict(X_test)
print(y_predict)
```

CODE 7.3   GRU.

The output is presented below as Figure 7.22:

```
Model: "sequential_1"

Layer (type)                  Output Shape              Param #
=================================================================
embedding_1 (Embedding)       (None, 500, 100)          500000

gru_1 (GRU)                   (None, 100)               60300

dense_1 (Dense)               (None, 1)                 101
=================================================================
Total params: 560,401
Trainable params: 560,401
Non-trainable params: 0
```

FIGURE 7.22   Output of Code 7.3: GRU.

One can have a look at

- GRU: *https://youtu.be/xLKSMaYp2oQ*
- GRU Implementation: *https://youtu.be/QtcxL-gd8Ok*

KEY POINTS TO REMEMBER

- Recurrent Neural Networks have a variety of applications.
- In RNN, the output of the previous step is fed as the input (i.e., feedback) to the current step.
- The appreciable feature came in with RNN is the hidden state. Hidden state is no more than the memory, which remembers some information.
- CNN is a feed forward neural network which finds a lot of its applications in the Image Recognition and Object recognition sectors. RNN is fundamentally based on the feedback, that is, the output of the current layer is dependent on the previous layer.
- CNN is most suitable for images, whereas RNN is suitable for sequential data.
- CNN has a finite set of input and generates only the finite set of predicted values and based on the input. RNN is not so.
- LSTM is expanded as Long Short-Term Memory.
- The three gates used in LSTM are,
  - Forget Gate
  - Input Gate
  - Output Gate
- The cell states used in LSTM are
  - Intermediate Cell State
  - Cell State
- GRUs do not have the Cell State.
- GRUs closely resemble LSTM.

QUIZ

1. How is CNN different from RNN?
2. Where could one choose RNN over CNN?
3. What is LSTM, and how does it function?
4. Mention the three gates used in the LSTM.
5. What are the cell states one should be aware of with LSTM?
6. Mention clearly the technical differences between LSTM and GRU.

FURTHER READING

✓ Zaremba, Wojciech, Ilya Sutskever, and Oriol Vinyals. "Recurrent neural network regularization." *arXiv preprint arXiv:1409.2329* (2014).

✓ Medsker, Larry R., and L. C. Jain. "Recurrent neural networks." *Design and Applications* 5 (2001).

✓ Mikolov, Tomáš, Stefan Kombrink, Lukáš Burget, Jan Černocký, and Sanjeev Khudanpur. "Extensions of recurrent neural network language model." In *2011 IEEE International Conference on Acoustics, Speech and Signal Processing (ICASSP)*, pp. 5528–5531. IEEE, 2011.

✓ Rodriguez, Paul, Janet Wiles, and Jeffrey L. Elman. "A recurrent neural network that learns to count." *Connection Science* 11, no. 1 (1999): 5–40.

✓ Gregor, Karol, Ivo Danihelka, Alex Graves, Danilo Rezende, and Daan Wierstra. "Draw: A recurrent neural network for image generation." In *International Conference on Machine Learning*, pp. 1462–1471. PMLR, 2015.

✓ Greff, Klaus, Rupesh K. Srivastava, Jan Koutník, Bas R. Steunebrink, and Jürgen Schmidhuber. "LSTM: A search space odyssey." *IEEE Transactions on Neural Networks and Learning Systems* 28, no. 10 (2016): 2222–2232.

✓ Sundermeyer, Martin, Ralf Schlüter, and Hermann Ney. "LSTM neural networks for language modeling." In *Thirteenth Annual Conference of the International Speech Communication Association*. 2012.

✓ Wen, T.H., Gasic, M., Mrksic, N., Su, P.H., Vandyke, D. and Young, S., 2015. "Semantically conditioned lstm-based natural language generation for spoken dialogue systems." *arXiv preprint arXiv:1508.01745*.

## CHAPTER 8

Autoencoders

LEARNING OBJECTIVES

After this chapter, the reader will be able to understand the following:

- What is an autoencoder?
- Applications of an autoencoder.
- Types of autoencoder and complete implementation of convolutional autoencoder.

8.1 INTRODUCTION

In the previous chapters we have come across CNN, RNN architectures and their applications. They follow Supervised Learning. Do you remember Supervised and Unsupervised Learning techniques? Supervised Learning is a Machine-learning technique that helps to work with the dataset split into training and test data. The training data will be associated with labels; the algorithm has to learn with the training dataset, and the user employs test or validation data to analyze the accuracy of the model created by using the algorithm. On the other hand, with Unsupervised Learning, we have only data with no labels associated with it. Now we are going to see a neural network architecture, called an autoencoder, which has two neural networks, encoder and decoder, working in an unsupervised fashion. Autoencoders are mainly used as transformer-based models that have an encoder part, which extracts the features, say from an image, and reconstructs the same image from the features extracted, but with a low dimensionality.

DOI: 10.1201/9781003185635-8

8.2   WHAT IS AN AUTOENCODER?

An autoencoder is a simple ML algorithm that acquires input image, and it will reconstruct the same. That is, the image is compressed. A dimensionally reduced image is produced as the output image. The dimensionality reduction certainly is used in the data pre-processing (we reduce/compress). Sometimes, we might not require all the attributes that are there in the dataset. So, what can we do? We could apply dimensionality reduction to find out the most similar attributes, if it does not have an impact after removing them on the dataset, and then they could be taken out. Therefore, it helps to retain those features that are useful for the analysis of the dataset. This seriously reduces the dimensionality of the dataset. Autoencoders use dimensionality reduction for the reconstruction of the output image from the input image fed into the neural network (Figure 8.1).

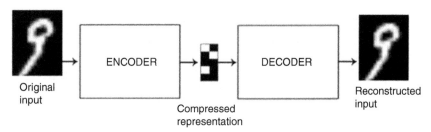

FIGURE 8.1   How an autoencoder works.

In fact, Principal Component Analysis is a dimensionality reduction technique that is commonly used for dimensionality reduction. It is a linear transformation method that helps to reduce the number of dimensions in the dataset in an unsupervised manner. Then why do we need autoencoders. A simple answer is that autoencoders allow us to use both linear transformation and nonlinear transformation, depending on the activation function they use for processing. However, for the time being, let us further understand: Autoencoders have more flexibility in deciding the kind of transformation it can use based on some factors.

8.2.1   How Autoencoders Work

Autoencoders are feed forward networks. We have already discussed feed forward networks in Chapter 4 while explaining Multilayer Perceptron. As explained, feed forward networks use more than one hidden layer according to the processing. Hence, it has more classification and prediction capabilities. Relating this to an autoencoder, it acts as a feed forward network with inputs processed through multiple hidden layers and producing some outputs. However, the major aim is not to predict or classify output, say Y given an input X, but instead to reconstruct a dimensionally reduced X. Here you could also understand the importance of autoencoders being an unsupervised model, as they do not require any label associated with input data. Now let us take a deeper dive into the architecture of autoencoders. Basically, it has three layers:

- Encoder (Input)
- Code (Hidden)
- Decoder (Output)

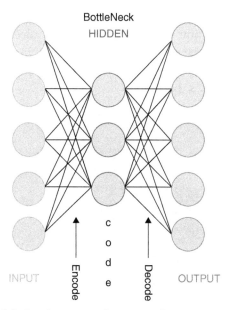

FIGURE 8.2   Simplified architecture of autoencoder.

Here, as given in Figure 8.2, there is an input layer, also called an encoder, which moves on to a hidden layer also called a code or bottleneck, where the necessary features are extracted and, finally, on to the decoder, which reconstructs a compressed image from code or bottleneck feature (Figure 8.3). The final output would be a compressed image than the original one.

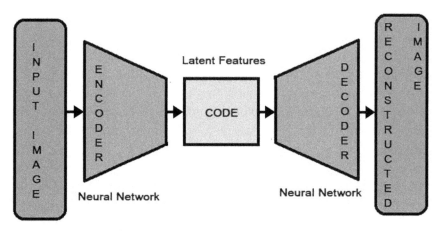

FIGURE 8.3   Latent features are extracted from input image.

Before going further, we need to understand what a code is in autoencoder architecture. Code or bottleneck, or as otherwise called, latent features, are very important in the context of autoencoders. For this, we would take you through a story from almost 1,500 years ago, from "The Allegory of the Cave" by Plato (Figure 8.4).

FIGURE 8.4   The Allegory (Myth) of the Cave.

"The Allegory of the Cave" tells about prisoners in a cave and unable even to move their heads as they are chained. All they can see is the wall before them. Behind them, there is a fire, which burns all through. Behind the prisoners are puppeteers with puppets. They cast shadows on the wall in front of prisoners. Prisoners are unaware of either the puppeteers or the fire behind. All they can see are the images cast on the walls. In the story, Plato's story is very relevant for understanding latent features in the context of autoencoders. To make it clear, the prisoners' reality is only the shadow of the puppets, for they are ignorant about the puppeteers and the fire behind. These are just the "observed variables," and the "real variables" are behind, casting shadows making the observed variables. Here, the real variables are hidden, not visible to the eyes of prisoners. The real variables are not directly observable, but they are the true explanatory factors that are creating the observed variables. These real variables are the true latent variables in autoencoders.

So, what is the challenge now? We need to learn the true explanatory factors; that is latent variables, only when observed variables are given. In order to understand how latent features looks like in a real time example, one could refer to the Figure 8.5.

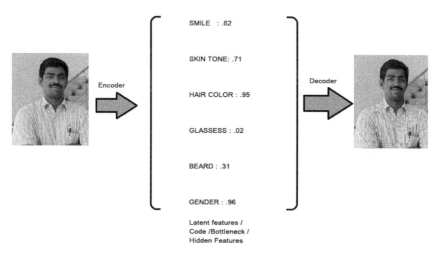

FIGURE 8.5   Real time example for latent features.

In addition, it is important to be aware that each of the latent features has a probability distribution associated with it, which helps autoencoders to clearly understand the whole distribution of data that is fed into the network. The working of autoencoders is very simple now. The image is fed into the encoder neural network, which encodes and maps the various latent features – say Z associated with the input image, say X. The decoder then maps from the latent representation of data and produces the reconstructed image, say Y.

It is as simple as mapping the input, X, to a latent space representation, Y, and training the model in such a way so as to reconstruct the original image, Z, from these features. That is, the decoder model reconstructs the image from the latent space representations. At this point, two more terminologies are to be introduced about the dimensionality of latent space representations and the loss function.

The dimensionality of latent space representation is directly related to the quality of the reconstructed image. Lower dimensionality of the reconstructed image will force a larger training bottleneck because of poor quality of reconstruction. The loss function helps to understand the difference in terms of loss from the original image to the reconstructed image. Normally, in a standard autoencoder, mean squared error is used as the loss function,

$$L(X,Z) = \|X - Z\|^2$$

This loss function, also termed as reconstruction loss, insists the latent space representation to learn as many features as possible from the data. The loss functions indirectly help the reconstructed image to follow the distribution of the original image without much deviation.

8.2.2 Properties of Autoencoders

There are three properties/features one should remember with autoencoders:

- Data Specific Behavior
- Lossy Compression Nature
- Unsupervised in Nature.

Data-specific: This can work only on the data that are similar to what the system is already trained on. (Also, this is not like GZIP or WINRAR, where the compression happens and packaging is done.) For instance, if an autoencoder is trained on compressing cat images, it may not work well with donkey images.

Lossy: Well, the expectation may not always happen. This is the case with Autoencoders. The output may not be exact as the input. Nevertheless, it will be very much closer. It will certainly be a degraded version. This is a lossy version. In addition, if you want lossless compression, well then, find out different methods.

Unsupervised/self-supervised: We can call this unsupervised, as we need not do anything other than feed the raw input. No explicit labelling required. To be precise – they are Self-supervised. They generate their own labels from training.

8.3 APPLICATIONS OF AUTOENCODERS

An autoencoder architecture has mainly three parts: encoder neural network, code, and a decoder neural network. Now, let us see some applications of autoencoders in real time scenarios. The major applications that we are going to see here are

- Data Compression
- Dimensionality Reduction
- Image De-noising
- Feature Extraction
- Image Generation
- Image Colorization

8.3.1 Data Compression and Dimensionality Reduction

Autoencoders are used for data compression before the reconstruction of data (Figure 8.6). This is one of the very first applications of autoencoders. This has already been well discussed in the previous sections of this chapter. Still, one major drawback is the lossy compression and the data-specific nature

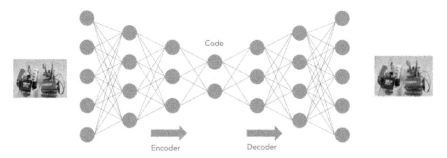

FIGURE 8.6   Neural network representation of Encoder – Code – Decoder.

8.3.2 Image Denoising

Autoencoders are widely used for image de-noising. There can be much noise included in the images and they become corrupted. Image de-noising needs to be done to get the right content from the image. Sometimes, we have salt and pepper noise in the images, so we may need to remove that for further processing. In such scenarios, we need to use image de-noising techniques.

8.3.3   Feature Extraction

In autoencoders, we extract latent features from the original image. The majority of the features are extracted so that it makes the task easier for the decoder to map from the latent representations to a reconstructed image. Underlying explanatory factors have to be very well understood for generating meaningful images as output. If the hidden features are identified properly, then the reconstruction error is reduced automatically. So, by encoding a new set of features are generated from original image and by decoding a new variant of the original image is reconstructed from the features extracted. If new features are generated, they could be used for new sample generation. This greatly helps in generating new volumes of datasets.

8.3.4   Image Generation

Autoencoders, as generative models, is a new research area for generating new samples as close to the original samples. As autoencoders use the probability distribution of data, it is highly useful for generating new samples of data that confine and do not deviate much from the distribution of original data. We will learn more about this while exploring the types of autoencoders, such as Variational Autoencoders and Generative Adversarial Networks.

8.3.5   Image Colorization

Autoencoders are mainly used to convert a black and white image into a colored image or convert a colored image into a grayscale image. This has been well used in the restoration of black and white images. Another major application of autoencoders include automatic colorization of specific areas of images where the color has been faded or not represented properly.

8.4   TYPES OF AUTOENCODERS

There are different types of autoencoders available, namely,

- Denoising Autoencoder
- Vanilla Autoencoder
- Deep Autoencoder

- Sparse Autoencoder
- Undercomplete Autoencoder
- Stacked Autoencoder
- Variational Autoencoder
- Convolutional Autoencoder

8.4.1 Denoising Autoencoder

Denoising Autoencoders produce a corrupted (noised) copy of the input through the introduction of noise. That is, noise added to corrupt the input! Why do we need to do this? Autoencoders with more hidden layers than inputs run the risk of learning the identity function – where the output simply equals the input – thereby becoming useless. That is, no learning of features will happen. Therefore, this random noise inclusion is meant to avoid that. Here, we force the autoencoder to learn the original data after the noise has been removed. The autoencoder identifies the noise, removes it, and learns the important features from the input data as shown in Figure 8.7.

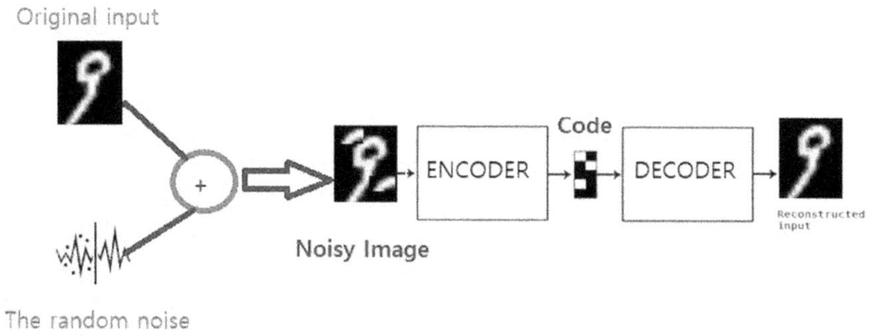

FIGURE 8.7   Denoising autoencoder.

8.4.2 Vanilla Autoencoder

It is the simplest version of autoencoders. It has two layers (ignoring the input layer). Input, hidden and output layers are there. Just to note:

- The hidden layer is smaller < input and output layer.
- Input and Output layer are of same size.

One can understand this from the diagram (Figure 8.8). The hidden layer is compressed representation, and with two sets of weights (and biases), we encode our input data into the compressed representation and decode our compressed representation back into input space.

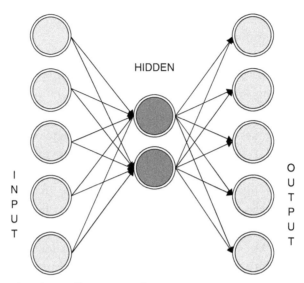

FIGURE 8.8   Simple vanilla autoencoder.

8.4.3   Deep Autoencoder

In deep autoencoder, there are two neural networks, one for encoding and another one for decoding as shown in Figure 8.6. These neural networks usually have 5 to 6 layers of encoding and an almost similar number of decoding layers. They produce a compressed image of the original image by passing through the encoding layer. From that compressed representation, it generates a reconstructed image by passing through the decoder network. As discussed earlier, the decoder network uses a compressed representation for the generation of the new image constructed.

8.4.4   Sparse Autoencoder

Sparse autoencoders have more hidden layers than input layers. The special aspect of sparse autoencoders is that, even with lots of hidden layers in the architecture, they are normally able to identify significant features from the data used. Generally, a constraint is introduced in the hidden layers so that the output layer may not copy from the input layer as such. This constraint is named as sparsity constraint and is mainly identified from various factors, including loss function during the training process. Some of the major AI applications rely on stacked sparse autoencoder architecture.

8.4.5 Undercomplete Autoencoder

Undercomplete autoencoders have a smaller dimension for hidden layers than input layers. For this reason, these autoencoders are famous for bagging the predominant features in the data, in turn minimizing the loss function. Nevertheless, overfitting is normally a disadvantage for this type of autoencoders.

8.4.6 Stacked Autoencoder

This autoencoder consists of several layers of sparse autoencoders, where the output of each hidden layer is associated to the input layer of consecutive hidden layer. This mainly aids in pretraining of layers in the architecture in an unsupervised fashion. In a stacked autoencoder, training of layers happens in a particular way. Initially, the individual hidden layers are trained, followed by final layer and then all the layers join to form a stacked architecture. The final step is to train all the layers together once in a supervised manner, which depends on the application. Stacked autoencoders are used for image classification applications and more.

8.4.7 Variational Autoencoder (VAEs)

This is one of the most commonly used autoencoders in most of the applications. Traditional autoencoders are more deterministic in nature. However, VAEs are more probabilistic in nature, which is their major advantage as well. Let us see how VAEs differ from traditional autoencoders (Figure 8.9).

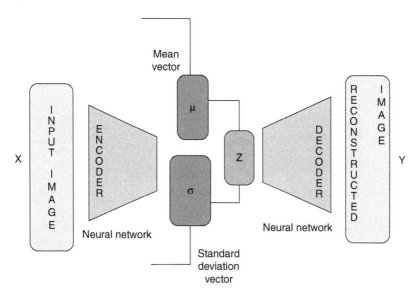

FIGURE 8.9   Variational autoencoders.

In Variational Autoencoders, the deterministic bottleneck layer Z, is replaced by, a stochastic sampling approach. That is, parameterizing the Latent Vector Z with Mean Vector and Standard Deviation vector, which describes the probability distribution, associated with each of these latent variables Z. Encoder computes latent variable Z given the input X, whereas decoder computes Y given the latent variable Z. So, this can be represented as a simple conditional probability. Decoder uses reverse inference from latent space Z to compute Y. Encoder function computes $P_\phi(Z|X)$ and the decoder function computes $Q_\theta(Y|Z)$.

As it is probabilistic in nature, loss functions are also different from the traditional autoencoder mean squared error.

Loss function = Reconstruction loss + Regularization term

Reconstruction loss computes the pixel-wise difference of the input and reconstructed output; mean squared error; it is a matrix, which shows how well the network is generating outputs similar to inputs. Regularization term puts constraints on how the probability distribution is computed; done by placing a prior $P(Z)$ an initial guess or hypothesis about how the probability distribution will look. Regularization is added to prevent overfitting. A common choice of prior is Gaussian prior. $D(P_\phi(Z|X)||P(Z))$, where $P_\phi(Z|X)$ is the inferred latent distribution and $P(Z)$ is the fixed prior on latent distribution.

8.4.8 Convolutional Autoencoder

A convolutional autoencoder is unsupervised learning version of convolutional neural networks using convolution filters (Figure 8.10). Major applications where convolutional autoencoders are used are in the area of image reconstruction in order to reduce errors.

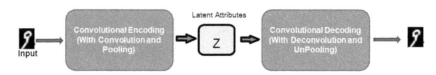

FIGURE 8.10   Convolutional autoencoder.

Here in the convolutional autoencoder architecture there is an encoding part, which does the convolutions accompanied by pooling techniques, and there exists a decoding part that consists of deconvolution followed by an un-pooling part. Let us implement and see how a convolutional autoencoder works using Keras. In this dataset, we are using the MNIST dataset, which contains the alphabet images with labels. A convolutional autoencoder is used to reconstruct the image from the original images inputted. The autoencoder also uses an encoding architecture and a decoding architecture for the whole process.

```
▶ #All imports
  '''
  A function that opens the gzip file, reads the file using bytestream.read()

  '''
  import keras
  from matplotlib import pyplot as plt
  import numpy as np
  import gzip
  %matplotlib inline
  from keras.layers import Input,Conv2D,MaxPooling2D,UpSampling2D
  #upsampling for reshaping and to repeat rows and columns of the data
  from keras.models import Model
  from keras.optimizers import RMSprop

  Using TensorFlow backend.
```

CODE 8.1   Imports.

In Code 8.1, we can see that all the required packages and headers have been imported for the smooth functioning of the program. In the Code 8.2, we are defining a function extract data, which accepts filename and no of images as input, and return a numpy array of data as output. Here, in this function, we use a function named gzip.open to open the file with filename passed as argument and read the data as byte stream. Each of the data read is converted into a 3D tensor as dimensions of image and no of images as arguments. Reshaping of the data is done here.

```
▶ ...
Pass the image dimension and the total number of images to this function

using np.frombuffer(), you convert the string stored in variable buf
into a NumPy array of type float32

Reshape the array into a three-dimensional array or tensor
where the first dimension is number of images,
and the second and third dimension being the dimension of the image.

Finally, return the NumPy array data
...
```

```
def extract_data(filename, num_images):
    with gzip.open(filename) as bytestream:
        bytestream.read(16)
        buf = bytestream.read(28 * 28 * num_images)
        data = np.frombuffer(buf, dtype=np.uint8).astype(np.float32)
        data = data.reshape(num_images, 28,28)
        return data
```

CODE 8.2   Reshape.

```
▶ ...
call the function extract_data() by passing

the training and testing files along with their corresponding number of images

...
train_data = extract_data('D:/ML_DL_NLP/MLCourse/notMNIST-to-MNIST-master/train-images-idx3-ubyte.gz', 60000)
test_data = extract_data('D:/ML_DL_NLP/MLCourse/notMNIST-to-MNIST-master/t10k-images-idx3-ubyte.gz', 10000)
```

CODE 8.3   Extract.

In the Code 8.3, 60,000 training data and 10,000 test data are extracted by using the function extract data (). In the Code 8.4, we can see the same but defining a new function named extract_labels() and applying the training and testing data to the function. The shape function gives the dimensions of training and testing data.

```
▶ def extract_labels(filename, num_images):
      with gzip.open(filename) as bytestream:
          bytestream.read(8)
          buf = bytestream.read(1 * num_images)
          labels = np.frombuffer(buf, dtype=np.uint8).astype(np.int64)
          return labels
```

```
▶ train_labels = extract_labels('D:/ML_DL_NLP/MLCourse/notMNIST-to-MNIST-master/train-labels-idx1-ubyte.gz',60000)
  test_labels = extract_labels('D:/ML_DL_NLP/MLCourse/notMNIST-to-MNIST-master/t10k-labels-idx1-ubyte.gz',10000)
```

```
▶ '''
  analyze how images in the dataset look like and also see the dimension of the images
  '''
  # Shapes of training set
  print("Training set (images) shape: {shape}".format(shape=train_data.shape))

  Training set (images) shape: (60000, 28, 28)
```

```
▶ # Shapes of test set
  print("Test set (images) shape: {shape}".format(shape=test_data.shape))

  Test set (images) shape: (10000, 28, 28)
```

CODE 8.4   Analyze.

In the Code 8.5, we can see the labels and images in dataset displayed.

```
  #create a dictionary that will have class names with their corresponding categorical class labels
  label_dict = {
      0: 'A',
      1: 'B',
      2: 'C',
      3: 'D',
      4: 'E',
      5: 'F',
      6: 'G',
      7: 'H',
      8: 'I',
      9: 'J',
  }
```

```
▶ plt.figure(figsize=[5,5])
```

```
4]:  <Figure size 360x360 with 0 Axes>

     <Figure size 360x360 with 0 Axes>
```

```
▶ # Display the first image in training data
  plt.subplot(121)
  curr_img = np.reshape(train_data[0], (28,28))
  curr_lbl = train_labels[0]
  plt.imshow(curr_img, cmap='gray')
  plt.title("(Label: " + str(label_dict[curr_lbl]) + ")")
```

```
5]:  Text(0.5, 1.0, '(Label: F)')
```

CODE 8.5   Display.

```
#Data Preprocessing
'''
first convert each 28 x 28 image of train and test set

into a matrix of size 28 x 28 x 1,

which you can feed into the network

'''

train_data = train_data.reshape(-1, 28,28, 1)
test_data = test_data.reshape(-1, 28,28, 1)
train_data.shape, test_data.shape
```
```
((60000, 28, 28, 1), (10000, 28, 28, 1))
```
```
'''

make sure to check the data type of the training and testing NumPy arrays,

it should be in float32 format, if not you will need to convert it into this format
'''
train_data.dtype, test_data.dtype
```
```
(dtype('float32'), dtype('float32'))
```
```
'''
rescale the training and testing data with the

maximum pixel value of the training and testing data

Maximum pixel value was 255

'''
np.max(train_data), np.max(test_data)
```
```
(255.0, 255.0)
```
```
train_data = train_data / np.max(train_data)
test_data = test_data / np.max(test_data)
```
```
'''
verify the maximum value of training and testing data

which should be 1.0 after rescaling it

'''

np.max(train_data), np.max(test_data)
```
```
(1.0, 1.0)
```

CODE 8.6   Pre-processing.

In the Code 8.6, the pre-processing of data is done; initially the 3D
tensor is converted into a 4D tensor dataset, both training and testing. The
datatype is float32 itself. As they are images, their max size of pixels are
displayed as 255. Then the data is normalized and rescaled to a max size of
the pixel as 1.

```
▶ ...
  train the model on 80% of the data and validate it on 20% of the remaining training data
  ...
  from sklearn.model_selection import train_test_split
  train_X,valid_X,train_ground,valid_ground = train_test_split(train_data,
                                                               train_data,
                                                               test_size=0.2,
                                                               random_state=13)
```

```
▶ #The Convolutional Autoencoder
  ...
  The images are of size 28 x 28 x 1 or a 784-dimensional vector
  Convert the image matrix to an array, rescale it between 0 and 1,
  reshape it so that it's of size 28 x 28 x 1, and
  feed this as an input to the network
```

```
▶ ...
  will use a batch size of 128
  using a higher batch size of 256 or 512 is also preferable
  it all depends on the system you train your model
  It contributes heavily in determining the learning parameters and affects the prediction accuracy.
  train your network for 50 epochs.
  ...
  batch_size = 128
  epochs = 50
  inChannel = 1
  x, y = 28, 28
  input_img = Input(shape = (x, y, inChannel))
```

```
▶ ...
  Autoencoder is divided into two parts: there's an encoder and a decoder
  Encoder
  The first layer will have 32 filters of size 3 x 3, followed by a downsampling (max-pooling) layer,
  The second layer will have 64 filters of size 3 x 3, followed by another downsampling layer,
  The final layer of encoder will have 128 filters of size 3 x 3.
  Decoder
  The first layer will have 128 filters of size 3 x 3 followed by a upsampling layer,/li>
  The second layer will have 64 filters of size 3 x 3 followed by another upsampling layer,
  The final layer of encoder will have 1 filter of size 3 x 3.
```

CODE 8.7   Initial setting.

In the Code 8.7, it is clearly stated about the training and testing split of dataset with 80 percent of training data and 20 percent of testing data. Followed by the initial settings required for the autoencoder like the batch size, number of epochs, and so forth.

```
M  # Defining the autoencoder module

   def autoencoder(input_img):
       #encoder
       #input = 28 x 28 x 1 (wide and thin)
       conv1 = Conv2D(32, (3, 3), activation='relu', padding='same')(input_img) #28 x 28 x 32
       pool1 = MaxPooling2D(pool_size=(2, 2))(conv1) #14 x 14 x 32
       conv2 = Conv2D(64, (3, 3), activation='relu', padding='same')(pool1) #14 x 14 x 64
       pool2 = MaxPooling2D(pool_size=(2, 2))(conv2) #7 x 7 x 64
       conv3 = Conv2D(128, (3, 3), activation='relu', padding='same')(pool2) #7 x 7 x 128 (sma

       #decoder
       conv4 = Conv2D(128, (3, 3), activation='relu', padding='same')(conv3) #7 x 7 x 128
       up1 = UpSampling2D((2,2))(conv4) # 14 x 14 x 128
       conv5 = Conv2D(64, (3, 3), activation='relu', padding='same')(up1) # 14 x 14 x 64
       up2 = UpSampling2D((2,2))(conv5) # 28 x 28 x 64
       decoded = Conv2D(1, (3, 3), activation='sigmoid', padding='same')(up2) # 28 x 28 x 1
       return decoded

M  ...
   After the model is created,

   compile it using the optimizer to be RMSProp.
   ...
   autoencoder = Model(input_img, autoencoder(input_img))
   autoencoder.compile(loss='mean_squared_error', optimizer = RMSprop())
```

CODE 8.8   Convolutional autoencoder.

In the Code 8.8, this is the main function of the convolutional autoencoder, where there is an encoding part and a decoding part as you can see. The convolution layer, max-pooling layers and activation functions are used in various layers in the encoding part, whereas in the decoding part, the convolution and up-sampling part and various activation functions are used. Then the model is compiled using the loss function, an optimization function passed as arguments to the compile function. The summary of the model is given below in the Code 8.9.

```
ℍ #visualize the layers created
  autoencoder.summary()

  Model: "model_1"
```

Layer (type)	Output Shape	Param #
input_1 (InputLayer)	(None, 28, 28, 1)	0
conv2d_1 (Conv2D)	(None, 28, 28, 32)	320
max_pooling2d_1 (MaxPooling2	(None, 14, 14, 32)	0
conv2d_2 (Conv2D)	(None, 14, 14, 64)	18496
max_pooling2d_2 (MaxPooling2	(None, 7, 7, 64)	0
conv2d_3 (Conv2D)	(None, 7, 7, 128)	73856
conv2d_4 (Conv2D)	(None, 7, 7, 128)	147584
up_sampling2d_1 (UpSampling2	(None, 14, 14, 128)	0
conv2d_5 (Conv2D)	(None, 14, 14, 64)	73792
up_sampling2d_2 (UpSampling2	(None, 28, 28, 64)	0
conv2d_6 (Conv2D)	(None, 28, 28, 1)	577

```
Total params: 314,625
Trainable params: 314,625
Non-trainable params: 0
```

CODE 8.9   Summary.

The autoencoder fits the model with the training and testing data by using this code:

$$utoencoder\_train = autoencoder.fit(train_X, train_{ground}, batch_{size} =$$
$$batch\_size, epochsepochs, verbose = 1, validation\_data =$$
$$(valid\_X, valid\_ground))$$

```
ℍ autoencoder_train = autoencoder.fit(train_X, train_ground, batch_size=batch_size,epochs=epochs,verbose=1,validation_data=(val

Train on 48000 samples, validate on 12000 samples
Epoch 1/50
48000/48000 [==============================] - 363s 8ms/step - loss: 0.0348 - val_loss: 0.0127
Epoch 2/50
48000/48000 [==============================] - 358s 7ms/step - loss: 0.0101 - val_loss: 0.0092
Epoch 3/50
48000/48000 [==============================] - 363s 8ms/step - loss: 0.0072 - val_loss: 0.0066
Epoch 4/50
48000/48000 [==============================] - 339s 7ms/step - loss: 0.0059 - val_loss: 0.0052
Epoch 5/50
48000/48000 [==============================] - 352s 7ms/step - loss: 0.0050 - val_loss: 0.0044
```

CODE 8.10   Epochs.

This code snippet shows the epochs; it goes up to 50 epochs as training, and we can see the loss and validation accuracy calculated at each epoch. In the Code 8.11, we can see the visualization of loss.

```
loss = autoencoder_train.history['loss']
val_loss = autoencoder_train.history['val_loss']
epochs = range(epochs)
plt.figure()
plt.plot(epochs, loss, 'bo', label='Training loss')
plt.plot(epochs, val_loss, 'b', label='Validation loss')
plt.title('Training and validation loss')
plt.legend()
plt.show()
```

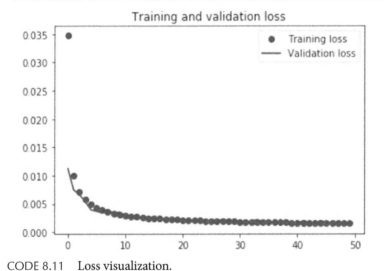

CODE 8.11   Loss visualization.

The next step is to predict the test images by applying the model. Let us see how well the reconstruction of images happen. The test images and reconstructed images can be seen in the Code 8.12.

```
M   pred = autoencoder.predict(test_data)

M   pred.shape

]:  (10000, 28, 28, 1)

M   plt.figure(figsize=(20, 4))
    print("Test Images")
    for i in range(10):
        plt.subplot(2, 10, i+1)
        plt.imshow(test_data[i, ..., 0], cmap='gray')
        curr_lbl = test_labels[i]
        plt.title("(Label: " + str(label_dict[curr_lbl]) + ")")
    plt.show()
```

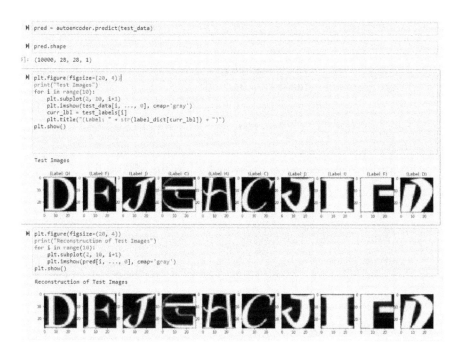

```
M   plt.figure(figsize=(20, 4))
    print("Reconstruction of Test Images")
    for i in range(10):
        plt.subplot(2, 10, i+1)
        plt.imshow(pred[i, ..., 0], cmap='gray')
    plt.show()
```

CODE 8.12   Test and reconstructed images.

By this example, it would be clear how the convolutional autoencoder has to be implemented using Keras–Tensor flow backend.

YouTube links for complete

- Autoencoder Introduction Implementation: *https://youtu.be/ IzxkDgPlXiA*
- Autoencoder Types: *https://youtu.be/r4oP657zQtY*
- Autoencoder Implementation: *https://youtu.be/uc5IcURNqf4*

KEY POINTS TO REMEMBER

- An autoencoder takes an input image and reconstructs the original image in a lower dimension.
- The autoencoder has mainly 3 parts: encoder, code / bottleneck / hidden features /latent features and the last part is the decoder.
- The encoder computes over original image to generate latent features.
- Latent features are the hidden features, which are the compressed representation.

- Lower latent space gives poor quality representation of image and vice versa.
- Decoders take on the challenging task of reconstructing the original image from latent features generated.
- The loss function determines how well the reconstructed image has been revived from latent features. Loss function differs from one technique to another.
- Traditional autoencoders follow deterministic approach.
- The major applications of autoencoders include
  - Data Compression
  - Dimensionality Reduction
  - Image De-noising
  - Feature Extraction
  - Image Generation
  - Image Colorization
- There are various types of autoencoders available:
  - Denoising Autoencoder
  - Vanilla Autoencoder
  - Deep Autoencoder
  - Sparse Autoencoder
  - Undercomplete Autoencoder
  - Stacked Autoencoder
  - Variational Autoencoder
  - Convolutional Autoencoder
- Variational Autoencoders are a probabilistic twist to the traditional autoencoders with mean vector and standard deviation vector.
- Complete implementation of convolutional neural network using Tensor flow – Keras are given.

QUIZ

1. What is an autoencoder?
2. How does an autoencoder work?
3. What is the significance of latent features in autoencoders?

4. What is the difference between latent features and observed features?

5. What are the major applications of autoencoders?

6. What are the various types of autoencoders?

7. How variational autoencoders (VAEs) differ from traditional autoencoders?

8. Can you describe the architecture of a convolutional autoencoder?

FURTHER READING

✓ Baldi, Pierre. "Autoencoders, unsupervised learning, and deep architectures." *Proceedings of ICML Workshop on Unsupervised and Transfer Learning.* JMLR Workshop and Conference Proceedings, 2012.

✓ Pu, Yunchen, et al. "Variational autoencoder for deep learning of images, labels and captions." *arXiv preprint arXiv:1609.08976* (2016).

✓ Pinaya, Walter Hugo Lopez, et al. "Autoencoders." *Machine learning.* Academic Press, 2020. 193–208.

✓ Sewak, Mohit, Sanjay K. Sahay, and Hemant Rathore. "An overview of deep learning architecture of deep neural networks and autoencoders." *Journal of Computational and Theoretical Nanoscience* 17.1 (2020): 182–188.

✓ Guo, Xifeng, et al. "Deep clustering with convolutional autoencoders." International Conference on Neural Information Processing. Springer, Cham, 2017.

✓ Bao, Wei, Jun Yue, and Yulei Rao. "A deep learning framework for financial time series using stacked autoencoders and long-short term memory." *PloS one* 12.7 (2017): e0180944.

## CHAPTER 9

Generative Models

LEARNING OBJECTIVES

After this chapter, the reader will be able to understand:

- What is a Generative model?
- Generative Adversarial Networks
- Types of GAN
- Applications of GAN
- Implementation of GAN

9.1 INTRODUCTION

In the previous chapter, "Autoencoders," we have learned about the working, types, applications, and implementation of the standard convolutional autoencoder. It is already seen that, in autoencoders, we use latent variables for feature extraction. These features are used by decoder networks for the reconstruction of images. Therefore, we could say we already know about latent models. Latent models like autoencoders are mainly used for density estimation of data, as they capture the probability distribution of data being used. Another major application of latent models like autoencoders is to generate new samples of data. However, in order to perform this task, there is another variant of autoencoders, called generative models. Generative models are a part of the statistical approach and have been in use for a long time. This is what we are going to cover in this chapter.

9.2 WHAT IS A GENERATIVE MODEL?

Generative models are part of a statistical classification approach. This model has been widely used in prediction of the next sentence or word in a sequence, where the probability of adjacent word/s matter a lot. Generative models help to find the foundational level of explanatory factors of underlying data by keeping track of the distribution of the data. This concept is extended and used for the generation of new samples, which follow the data distribution of an original dataset.

Generative models are judged to be powerful tools for exploring data distribution or the density estimation of datasets. Generative models follow unsupervised learning that automatically discovers the patterns or irregularities of the data being analyzed. This helps to generate new data that resemble mainly the original dataset. To be precise, Generative models aim at learning the true data distribution of the training set to generate new data points, with some variations.

Generative models are mainly used for density estimation and sample generation, where it takes a few input training samples following some distribution and generating new samples, which follow the same distribution as input training samples. Another major application of generative models is outlier detection. Here the major question is: How can we learn a generative model as similar as the true distribution of original data? This is achieved by identifying the overrepresented and underrepresented features. What are overrepresented and underrepresented features? Let us understand that with help of an example, as shown in Figure 9.1.

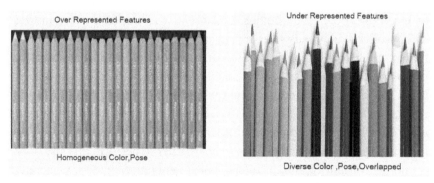

FIGURE 9.1 Overrepresented and underrepresented features.

The overrepresented features are all same in color, and the positions of all the pencils are the same, whereas in the underrepresented features, the colors and poses are diverse and there are lot of overlapping, too. Therefore, the challenge of generative models is to consider both these homogenous and diverse features to generate fair and representative datasets. Another major advantage of generative models is that they detect the outliers when encountering something new or rare in the dataset. This could be done by observing the distribution of data and the insight from outliers could be used to improve the quality of generated data while training. To summarize, the major applications of generative models include density estimation, sample generation, and outlier detection.

9.3 WHAT ARE GENERATIVE ADVERSARIAL NETWORKS (GAN)?

Generative Adversarial Networks are a type of generative models, which sample from a simple noise and learns transformation to the training distribution as shown in Figure 9.2.

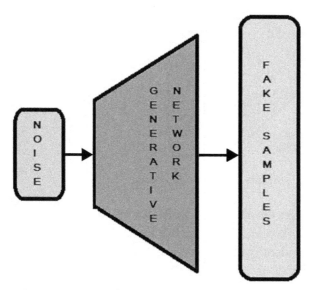

FIGURE 9.2   Generative network takes noise to generate fake samples.

GAN uses two neural networks, which compete with each other, thereby generating new samples. GAN architecture is shown in Figure 9.3.

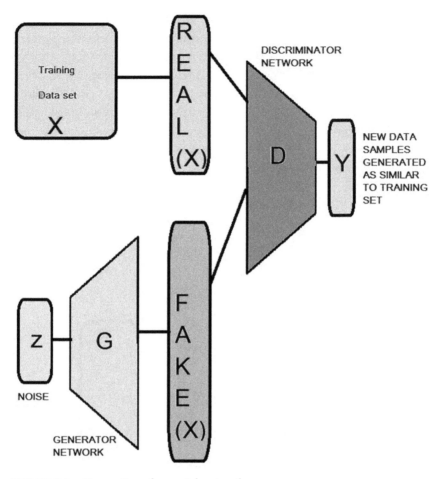

FIGURE 9.3   Generative adversarial networks.

In generative adversarial networks, a noise is induced to the generative neural network, which creates fake samples. The job of the discriminator network is to identify the fake samples generated by the generator network. This is identified by checking with training samples to see how different is the sample generated from the real samples. The networks act like two adversaries trying to compete with each other. In the initial stages, the discriminator network would be easily able to identify the fake samples generated by the network. Then the competing generator network works hard to reduce the difference in the fake samples generated from the real data. They try to generate samples as close to training samples, making the task for discriminator network bit challenging. Still the discriminator network tries to find that the generated data is fake. Both networks compete each other until the discriminator network finds it entirely too difficult to distinguish which of the samples generated by the generator network is fake and whichreal.

In short, GAN tries to improve the closeness to the original data. Discriminator works well and trains in such a way that it can identify the fake ones clearly. Now, generator tries to move the fake points as close to the real points that discriminator would be unable to identify. Discriminator attempts to classify real data from fakes made by the generator. Generator attempts to produce the copy of data to make the discriminator predictions false. After complete training, the generator network would be able to produce new samples that are not at all available. This is how the adversarial networks work, generating brand new data.

9.4   TYPES OF GAN

There are different types of Generative Adversarial Networks available and suitable for variable applications. Before moving into applications, let us have a look over to the various types of GAN.

- Deep Convolutional GANs (DCGANs)
- Stack GAN
- Cycle GAN
- Conditional GAN
- Info GAN

There are many more types of GAN, but they are out of the scope of this book.

9.4.1   Deep Convolutional GANs (DCGANs)

Deep Convolutional GANs (DCGANs) are the most widely used GAN architecture. They use convolution layers. Max pooling and fully connected layers are not used in this architecture. Instead, some advanced techniques like convolutional stride and transposed convolutions are used for up-sampling and down-sampling. To make it simple, this is a variant of standard GAN, which uses convolutional neural networks for generator and discriminator networks. Activation functions like RELU and Leaky RELU are used in the generator and discriminator networks according to the applications for better feature extraction.

9.4.2 Stack GAN

Stacked Generative Networks (StackGAN) is mainly used for generating images from text. They are stacked architecture, which uses a stack of conditional GAN models. They have mainly two levels, one layer conditioned on text, which is normally called Stage-1 GAN, and the second level conditioned on both text and image. The output of the first level, as mentioned, is of low resolution. The output of the second level is high-resolution image, produced from the text, and the generated low-resolution image.

9.4.3 Cycle GAN

Cycle GAN uses two generator and two discriminator networks. They work like reversible networks as each could be used to convert one image to another and vice versa. The G1 generator maps from X to Y, whereas the G2 generator network maps from Y to X. Dx and Dy are the two adversarial discriminator networks, which fake images generated by generators from real images. The architecture for the cycle GAN is shown in Figure 9 .4.

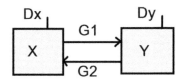

FIGURE 9.4   Cycle GAN.

9.4.4 Conditional GAN (cGAN)

cGAN is a type of generative adversarial network where the generator and discriminator are trained on some extra-useful information. This extra information is conditioned to both networks like extra layers in the network. It could be the information of labels or something which can act on the network, so that they are fed as inputs.

9.4.5 Info GAN

Info GAN are used when the dataset is complex. This is mainly used when the data are not labelled in an unsupervised manner. This uses lot of information, which helps the architecture to learn the most complex representations more easily.

9.5 APPLICATIONS OF GAN

There are many applications for GAN, but we are going to restrict ourselves to discussing a few applications here.

- Fake Image Generation
- Image Modification
- Text to Image/Image to Image Generation
- Speech Modification
- Assisting Artists

9.5.1 Fake Image Generation

www.thispersondoesnotexist.com/ is an imaginary website that generates the faces of people (who do not exist) by a GAN StyleGAN2 (Dec 2019) – Karras and associates and NVidia. This is one of the major applications of Fake Image Generation by GAN.

9.5.2 Image Modification

Image Modification is a beautiful field where a lot of techniques like photograph editing, face aging, photo blending, super resolution, photo in painting and so forth can be done by using GANs and its variants.

9.5.3 Text to Image/Image to Image Generation

Text to image generation has become a very well-known application of GAN, where the texts are given, and images need to be drawn from the texts. Applications also do Image to Image Generation using GANs.

9.5.4 Speech Modification

Speech Modification is a research area where the sound waves of one person are mapped to the sound waves of another person to produce a new speech generated with the voice of another person.

9.5.5 Assisting Artists

Assisting Artists becomes part of Fake Image Generation, to create new cartoon characters, deep dream projects such as inducing hallucination-like features to normal images to have a dreamy look. All these are various applications of GAN (Figure 9.5).

FIGURE 9.5   Applications of GAN.

9.6   IMPLEMENTATION OF GAN

In this section we are going to see how to implement a basic Generative Adversarial Network using Tensor Flow – Keras.

```
from numpy import vstack
from numpy.random import randn
from numpy.random import randint
from keras.datasets.mnist import load_data
from keras.optimizers import Adam
from keras.models import Sequential
from keras.layers import Dense
from keras.layers import Reshape
from keras.layers import Flatten
from keras.layers import Conv2D
from keras.layers import Conv2DTranspose
from keras.layers import LeakyReLU
from keras.layers import Dropout
from matplotlib import pyplot
```

CODE 9.1   Import the libraries.

In Code 9.1, we import all the required libraries for the implementation of GAN. In this we have used, vstack from Numpy to stack arrays in sequence row-wise vertically. We are already familiar with the other libraries. In Code 9.2, we are building the discriminator neural network.

```
def define_discriminator(in_shape=(28,28,1)):
  model = Sequential()
  model.add(Conv2D(64, (3,3), strides=(2, 2), padding='same', input_shape=in_shape))
  model.add(LeakyReLU(alpha=0.2))
  model.add(Dropout(0.4))
  model.add(Conv2D(64, (3,3), strides=(2, 2), padding='same'))
  model.add(LeakyReLU(alpha=0.2))
  model.add(Dropout(0.4))
  model.add(Flatten())
  model.add(Dense(1, activation='sigmoid'))
  # compile model
  opt = Adam(lr=0.0002, beta_1=0.5)
  model.compile(loss='binary_crossentropy', optimizer=opt, metrics=['accuracy'])
  return model
```

CODE 9.2   Discriminator neural network.

Here the network is a simple convolutional neural network, with activation functions as Leaky RELU(). In Code 9.3, we can see the generator neural network which takes the latent dimensions as input and outputs the generator model.

```
def define_generator(latent_dim):
  model = Sequential()
  # foundation for 7x7 image
  n_nodes = 128 * 7 * 7
  model.add(Dense(n_nodes, input_dim=latent_dim))
  model.add(LeakyReLU(alpha=0.2))
  model.add(Reshape((7, 7, 128)))
  # upsample to 14x14
  model.add(Conv2DTranspose(128, (4,4), strides=(2,2), padding='same'))
  model.add(LeakyReLU(alpha=0.2))
  # upsample to 28x28
  model.add(Conv2DTranspose(128, (4,4), strides=(2,2), padding='same'))
  model.add(LeakyReLU(alpha=0.2))
  model.add(Conv2D(1, (7,7), activation='sigmoid', padding='same'))
  return model
```

CODE 9.3   Generator neural network.

In Code 9.4, we can see the combined generator and discriminator model that is the complete GAN module.

```python
def define_gan(g_model, d_model):
    # make weights in the discriminator not trainable
    d_model.trainable = False
    # connect them
    model = Sequential()
    # add generator
    model.add(g_model)
    # add the discriminator
    model.add(d_model)
    # compile model
    opt = Adam(lr=0.0002, beta_1=0.5)
    model.compile(loss='binary_crossentropy', optimizer=opt)
    return model
```

CODE 9.4   GAN module.

In Code 9.5, preprocessing of the MNIST dataset is performed.

```
# load and pre-process mnist training images
def load_real_samples():
  # load mnist dataset
  (trainX, _), (_, _) = load_data()
  # expand to 3d, e.g. add channels dimension
  X = expand_dims(trainX, axis=-1)
  # convert from unsigned ints to floats
  X = X.astype('float32')
  # scale from [0,255] to [0,1]
  X = X / 255.0
  return X

# select real samples randomly
def generate_real_samples(dataset, n_samples):
  # choose random instances
  ix = randint(0, dataset.shape[0], n_samples)
  # retrieve selected images
  X = dataset[ix]
  # generate 'real' class labels (1)
  y = ones((n_samples, 1))
  return X, y
```

CODE 9.5   Pre-processing.

In Code 9.6, generate points in latent space as input for the generator.

```
def generate_latent_points(latent_dim, n_samples):
  # generate points in the latent space
  x_input = randn(latent_dim * n_samples)
  # reshape into a batch of inputs for the network
  x_input = x_input.reshape(n_samples, latent_dim)
  return x_input
```

CODE 9.6   Generate points in latent space.

In Code 9.7, use the generator to generate *n* fake examples, with class labels.

```python
def generate_fake_samples(g_model, latent_dim, n_samples):
  # generate points in latent space
  x_input = generate_latent_points(latent_dim, n_samples)
  # predict outputs
  X = g_model.predict(x_input)
  # create 'fake' class labels (0)
  y = zeros((n_samples, 1))
  return X, y
```

CODE 9.7   Generate fake samples.

In Code 9.8, create and save a plot of generated images.

```python
def save_plot(examples, epoch, n=10):
  # plot images
  for i in range(n * n):
    # define subplot
    pyplot.subplot(n, n, 1 + i)
    # turn off axis
    pyplot.axis('off')
    # plot raw pixel data
    pyplot.imshow(examples[i, :, :, 0], cmap='gray_r')
  # save plot to file
  filename = 'generated_plot_e%03d.png' % (epoch+1)
  pyplot.savefig(filename)
  pyplot.close()
```

CODE 9.8   Plot images.

In Code 9.9, evaluate the discriminator and generated images and save the generator model.

```python
def summarize_performance(epoch, g_model, d_model, dataset, latent_dim, n_samples=100):
    # prepare real samples
    X_real, y_real = generate_real_samples(dataset, n_samples)
    # evaluate discriminator on real examples
    _, acc_real = d_model.evaluate(X_real, y_real, verbose=0)
    # prepare fake examples
    x_fake, y_fake = generate_fake_samples(g_model, latent_dim, n_samples)
    # evaluate discriminator on fake examples
    _, acc_fake = d_model.evaluate(x_fake, y_fake, verbose=0)
    # summarize discriminator performance
    print('>Accuracy real: %.0f%%, fake: %.0f%%' % (acc_real*100, acc_fake*100))
    # save plot
    save_plot(x_fake, epoch)
    # save the generator model tile file
    filename = 'generator_model_%03d.h5' % (epoch + 1)
    g_model.save(filename)
```

CODE 9.9   Evaluate and save.

In Code 9.10, we are training both generator network and discriminator network.

```python
def train(g_model, d_model, gan_model, dataset, latent_dim, n_epochs=100, n_batch=256):
    bat_per_epo = int(dataset.shape[0] / n_batch)
    half_batch = int(n_batch / 2)
    # manually enumerate epochs
    for i in range(n_epochs):
        # enumerate batches over the training set
        for j in range(bat_per_epo):
            # get randomly selected 'real' samples
            X_real, y_real = generate_real_samples(dataset, half_batch)
            # generate 'fake' examples
            X_fake, y_fake = generate_fake_samples(g_model, latent_dim, half_batch)
            # create training set for the discriminator
            X, y = vstack((X_real, X_fake)), vstack((y_real, y_fake))
            # update discriminator model weights
            d_loss, _ = d_model.train_on_batch(X, y)
            # prepare points in latent space as input for the generator
            X_gan = generate_latent_points(latent_dim, n_batch)
            # create inverted labels for the fake samples
            y_gan = ones((n_batch, 1))
            # update the generator via the discriminator's error
            g_loss = gan_model.train_on_batch(X_gan, y_gan)
            # summarize loss on this batch
            print('>%d, %d/%d, d=%.3f, g=%.3f' % (i+1, j+1, bat_per_epo, d_loss, g_loss))
        # evaluate the model performance, sometimes
        if (i+1) % 10 == 0:
            summarize_performance(i, g_model, d_model, dataset, latent_dim)
```

CODE 9.10   Training.

In Code 9.11, we can see the major function calls.

```
# size of the latent space
latent_dim = 100
# create the discriminator
d_model = define_discriminator()
# create the generator
g_model = define_generator(latent_dim)
# create the gan
gan_model = define_gan(g_model, d_model)
# load image data
dataset = load_real_samples()
# train model
train(g_model, d_model, gan_model, dataset, latent_dim)
```

CODE 9.11   Function calls.

In Code 9.12, this is how it initially looks. The generator produces images, and the discriminator is able to identify it is fake with 70 percentage accuracy.

```
...   Downloading data from https://st
      11493376/11490434 [==============
      >1, 1/234, d=0.694, g=0.709
      >1, 2/234, d=0.689, g=0.720
      >1, 3/234, d=0.685, g=0.737
      >1, 4/234, d=0.679, g=0.750
      >1, 5/234, d=0.670, g=0.759
      >1, 6/234, d=0.662, g=0.774
      >1, 7/234, d=0.661, g=0.786
      >1, 8/234, d=0.653, g=0.789
      >1, 9/234, d=0.650, g=0.800
      >1, 10/234, d=0.650, g=0.797
```

CODE 9.12   Results.

As it goes, we could notice the generator getting better accuracy than the discriminator network. That means, at one particular stage, the discriminator is no longer able to distinguish fake images from real ones.

KEY POINTS TO REMEMBER

- Generative models are part of a statistical classification approach.
- GAN uses two neural networks, which compete with each other, generator networks, and discriminator networks.
- Overrepresented and underrepresented features in a dataset.
- There are different types of GAN
  - Deep Convolutional GANs (DCGANs)
  - Stack GAN
  - Cycle GAN
  - Conditional GAN
  - Info GAN
- Applications of GAN include
  - Fake Image Generation
  - Image Modification
  - Text to Image/Image to Image Generation
  - Speech Modification
  - Assisting Artists

QUIZ

1. Definite Generative Models.
2. What is GAN?
3. Can we generate a fair dataset from overrepresented and underrepresented features? If so how?
4. Can you list a few variants of GAN?
5. What are the major applications of GAN?

FURTHER READING

- ✓ Zhong, Shi, and Joydeep Ghosh. "Generative model-based document clustering: a comparative study." *Knowledge and Information Systems* 8.3 (2005): 374–384.
- ✓ Goodfellow, Ian J., et al. "Generative networks." *arXiv preprint arXiv:1406.2661* (2014).

✓ Radford, Alec, Luke Metz, and Soumith Chintala. "Unsupervised representation learning with deep convolutional generative networks." *arXiv preprint arXiv:1511.06434* (2015).

✓ Xi, et al. "Infogan: Interpretable representation learning by information maximizing generative nets." *arXiv preprint arXiv:1606.03657* (2016).

✓ Zhang, Han, et al. "Stackgan: Text to photo-realistic image synthesis with stacked generative networks." *Proceedings of the IEEE International Conference on Computer Vision.* 2017.

✓ Palsson, Sveinn, et al. "Generative style transfer networks for face aging." *Proceedings of the IEEE Conference on Computer Vision and Pattern Recognition Workshops.* 2018.

✓ Li, Yitong, et al. "Storygan: A sequential conditional GAN for story visualization." *Proceedings of the IEEE/CVF Conference on Computer Vision and Pattern Recognition.* 2019.

✓ Wu, Jianyuan, and Wei Sun. "Towards multi-operation image anti-forensics with generative networks." *Computers & Security* 100 (2021): 102083.

## CHAPTER 10

Transfer Learning

LEARNING OBJECTIVES

After this chapter, the reader will be able to answer the following questions.

- What is Transfer Learning?
- The need for Transfer Learning.
- Application areas of Transfer Learning.
- How to leverage Transfer Learning for identifying friends and family?

10.1   WHAT IS TRANSFER LEARNING?

Transfer Learning is the process of transferring the knowledge acquired in implementing or learning one task to implement another related task. For example, if we know to ride a bicycle (task A), we can use the knowledge we gained to learn bike (task B) (Figure 10.1). Here task B is related to task A. In both the cases, the number of wheels will be 2. The way we balance both are also the same. Similarly, if we know to do simple mathematics, we can apply those basics to study Deep Learning \ Machine Learning (ML) algorithms.

DOI: 10.1201/9781003185635-10

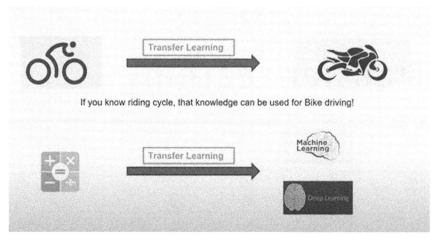

FIGURE 10.1   Transfer Learning.

Where Deep Learning is concerned, if we have a state-of-the-art algorithm that resolves a problem with the utmost accuracy, we can make use of that algorithm to resolve other related problems (e.g., many state-of-the-art algorithms like VGG16, GoogLeNet, and InceptionNetare meant for solving computer vision problems). These pre-trained models are used as the base layer for implementing similar computer vision and natural language processing problems. On top of the pre-trained models, we can make modifications according to the problem in hand to save computing resources, time, and money as the authors of these state-of-the-art models have spent days together before arriving at the details of each of those architectures. Transfer Learning makes it easier for us to leverage those architectures for solving similar problems.

In short, traditional ML algorithms were targeted to solve a specific problem, and they kept the knowledge they acquired within themselves. They also were trained, tested on specific datasets. If tested with a different dataset, they would not perform as well as expected. Due to this, Transfer Learning was introduced. We can make use of the pre-trained models' features and weights, and do some customization and make them work for different dataset/ problem domains.

10.2   WHEN CAN WE USE TRANSFER LEARNING?

In general, we can consider the below points to decide whether to apply Transfer Learning techniques or not:

- We are short of the vast set of labelled data needed to train our network from the beginning.
- We already have a pre-trained network that solves a problem similar to the one in hand.
- When the inputs of task 1 and 2 are same.

10.3 EXAMPLE – 1: CAT OR DOG USING TRANSFER LEARNING WITH VGG 16

The first and foremost step is to import the required libraries. In the below code snippet, we can see that we have to import Keras, Numpy, and VGG16from keras.applications (Keras is the library that provides us the ability to use pre-trained models and Numpy for numerical operations).

Once we are done with the libraries import, we can go ahead with the initialization of the VGG16 model with the weights of Imagenet dataset, using the below lines:

#Load the VGG16 model

vgg_model = vgg16.VGG16(weights='imagenet')

```
import keras
import numpy as np
from keras.applications import vgg16
#Load the VGG16 model
vgg_model = vgg16.VGG16(weights='imagenet')
```

CODE 10.1   Import libraries required.

Code 10.1 shows the first step to importing the libraries and initializing the VGG16 model.

> *Tip: If we want to use the other models like ResNet, Inception, we should be using the below lines of code.*
>
> **#Load the Inception_V3 model**
> *inception_model = inception_v3.InceptionV3(weights='imagenet')*
>
> **#Load the ResNet50 model**
> *resnet_model = resnet50.ResNet50(weights='imagenet')*
>
> **#Load the MobileNet model**
> *mobilenet_model = mobilenet.MobileNet(weights='imagenet')*

When the initialization step is completed, it is time for us to load the test image and do some pre-processing. Code 10.2 does just that. Here, we are loading the test image cat_or_dog_1.jpg from C: drive and initialized filename variable.

```
'''
Load and pre-process an image
'''
#Load the image using load_img() function specifying the target size.
from keras.preprocessing.image import load_img
from keras.preprocessing.image import img_to_array
from keras.applications.imagenet_utils import decode_predictions
import matplotlib.pyplot as plt
import numpy as np
%matplotlib inline
filename = 'C:/ML/cat-and-dog/cat_or_dog_1.jpg'
```

CODE 10.2   Pre-process test image.

Then we fix the dimension of the test image to 224*224 as is the recommended dimension in VGG16 architecture, and convert the original_ image to Python Imaging Library (PIL) format before it is converted to a numpy array named numpy_image. Code 10.3 shows the steps mentioned.

```
'''
Keras loads the image in PIL format (width, height) which shall be converted into
NumPy format (height, width, channels) using image_to_array() function.
'''
# load an image in PIL format
original_image = load_img(filename, target_size=(224, 224))
# convert the PIL image (width, height) to a NumPy array (height, width, channel)
numpy_image = img_to_array(original_image)
```

CODE 10.3   Pre-process test image.

Next, we expand the dimensions of the NumPy image by adding an axis layer. And then we print the sizes of input image, PIL image and NumPy image, just for the understanding purpose. Code 10.4 shows the steps mentioned.

```
# Convert the image into 4D Tensor
#(samples, height, width, channels) by adding an extra dimension to the axis 0.
input_image = np.expand_dims(numpy_image, axis=0)
# To get the image suitable for all the models
#print the size of the image after each processing
print('PIL image size = ', original_image.size) # Python Imaging Lib, Helps in resizing
print('NumPy image size = ', numpy_image.shape)
print('Input image size = ', input_image.shape)
plt.imshow(np.uint8(input_image[0]))
```

CODE 10.4   Expand dimensions.

The print statements presented in the code snippet would be producing the text below.

PIL image size = (224, 224)

NumPy image size = (224, 224, 3)

Input image size = (1, 224, 224, 3)

Along with the above text, we also show the image from the input file for our reference using the imshow() method as shown in the Figure 10.2.

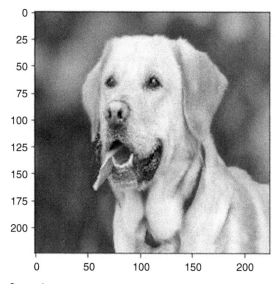

FIGURE 10.2   Input image.

Next, we need to normalize the image as we are trying to use multiple pre-trained models to identify the input image, and each of those pre-trained models uses different ranges of pixels. Some use from 0 to 1 and some use from -1 to 1 while some other use "caffe" style. In the VGG16 class, we have a method called preprocess_input() that does the normalization process as shown below.

processed_image_vgg16 = vgg16.preprocess_input(input_image. copy())

The next step is to let the model predict what the input image is. Model. predict() function helps us classify the input image, and the same is decoded into labels using the decode_predictions() method. Code 10.5 shows the steps from normalization.

```
#preprocess for vgg16
processed_image_vgg16 = vgg16.preprocess_input(input_image.copy())

# vgg16
predictions_vgg16 = vgg_model.predict(processed_image_vgg16)
label_vgg16 = decode_predictions(predictions_vgg16)
print ('label_vgg16 = ', label_vgg16)
```

CODE 10.5   Normalize the input and predict.

Tip: For other models, we would use appropriate classes as below.

#preprocess for inception_v3
processed_image_inception_v3 = inception_v3.preprocess_input(input_image.copy())
predictions_inception_v3 = inception_model.predict(processed_image_inception_v3)
label_inception_v3 = decode_predictions(predictions_inception_v3)
print ('label_inception_v3 = ', label_inception_v3)

#preprocess for resnet50

processed_image_resnet50 = resnet50.preprocess_input(input_image.copy())
predictions_resnet50 = resnet_model.predict(processed_image_resnet50)
label_resnet50 = decode_predictions(predictions_resnet50)
print ('label_resnet50 = ', label_resnet50)

#preprocess for mobilenet
processed_image_mobilenet = mobilenet.preprocess_input(input_image.copy())

```
predictions_mobilenet=mobilenet_model.predict(processed_image_
mobilenet)
label_mobilenet = decode_predictions(predictions_mobilenet)
print ('label_mobilenet = ', label_mobilenet)
```

Output of the predict function using the models would be the breed of the input image (dog) and the probability. It will be similar to the below lines for VGG16:

Label_vgg16 = [[('n02099712', 'Labrador_retriever', 0.5967783), ('n02088601', 'golden_retriever', 0.24647361), ...

So, we are done with the input image classification using the VGG16 model. In the same way, we can predict the input image using Inception_v3, ResNet, and so forth, and do a comparison of the models.

Readers are requested to run the above lines of code and compare and contrast the performance of each model.

10.4   EXAMPLE – 2: IDENTIFY YOUR RELATIVES' FACES USING TRANSFER LEARNING

The objective of this example is to identify the faces of our near and dears using Transfer Learning techniques. We are going to leverage the VGG16 process again for this example. Before we can see the code snippets, we need to recap the VGG16 architecture a bit.

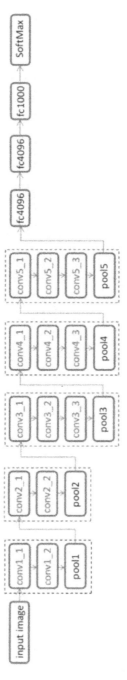

FIGURE 10.3   VGG16 layer details.

VGG16 architecture won the Imagenet contest held in 2014. It had 13 convolution layers, 3 fully connected layers (fc4096, fc4096, fc1000) (Figure 10.3). The number of output classes identified is 1000. This means that the model is able to correctly classify 1000 categories of inputs. Hence, we see the fc1000 in the last layer.

In this example of Transfer Learning, we want to just identify our friends/ relatives. For instance, if we want to find out 6 persons, the number of output classes will be 6. If we have 10 friends who need to be identified, the number of output classes will be 10. So, we need to decide on the number of output classes as per our requirement.

In order for us to use VGG16 architecture for customized problems like this, we need to remove the 1000 fully connected layer and replace it with a fully connected layer of number of persons we want to detect.

Prerequisite:

In our example, if we are going to identify 5 persons named Smaran, Hari, Peter, Mary, Vishnu, we need to create folders, as mentioned below.

Root folder: C:\ML_DL\Datasets

Sub Folders:

1. *<rootfolder>\Test*
2. *<rootfolder>\Train*

Under each subfolder, we will have 5 folders as mentioned,

1. *Smaran*
2. *Hari*
3. *Peter*
4. *Mary*
5. *Vishnu*

Under each folder we will have the pictures of the persons. In short, we are labeling the dataset. Once we are done with the dataset labeling, we can start coding.

```
from keras.layers import  Dense, Flatten
from keras.models import Model
from keras.applications.vgg16 import VGG16
from keras.preprocessing import image
from keras.preprocessing.image import ImageDataGenerator
import numpy as np
from glob import glob
```

CODE 10.6   Import required libraries.

The above Code 10.6 shows the required modules for this exercise. Table 10.1 points out the usage of each of the modules used.

TABLE 10.1   Usage of Module

Library Name	Purpose
Keras	Has classes for using pre-trained models like VGG, add or remove layers from the pre-trained model, etc.
Numpy	For numerical operations
Glob	For dealing with files\folders.

The Glob module is used to identify the number of output classes. In our case, it is going to be determined by the number of folders under Test and Training folders, and Glob is the module that finds the total number of folders.

```
# re-size all the images to this
IMAGE_SIZE = [224, 224]

train_path = 'Datasets/Train'
valid_path = 'Datasets/Test'
```

CODE 10.7   Dataset paths.

Code 10.7 declares the image size to be used for all the images. As VGG16 architecture was originally handling images of size 224*224, we are also abiding by that dimension. Also, we see the path of Test and Train folders above.

```
# Remove last layer
vgg = VGG16(input_shape=IMAGE_SIZE + [3], weights='imagenet', include_top=False)

# don't train existing weights
for layer in vgg.layers:
  layer.trainable = False
```

CODE 10.8   Removing top layer.

Code 10.8 shows how we remove the last fully connected layer as mentioned at the beginning of this section. *include_top=False* will tell the model to ignore the last layer of the pre-trained model.

```
foldercount = glob('Datasets/Train/*')

# Flatten and add fully connected layer
x = Flatten()(vgg.output)
prediction = Dense(len(foldercount), activation='softmax')(x)

# create a model object
model = Model(inputs=vgg.input, outputs=prediction)

# view the structure of the model
model.summary()
```

CODE 10.9   Add fully connected layer in the top layer.

Since we have mentioned *include_top=False*, we need to add the topmost layer by ourselves. For that we need to know how many output classes there are for the current dataset. *Foldercount* variable holds the number of output classes using glob(). In our case, it is going to be 5.

We can then flatten the whole array and add a fully connected layer using Dense() function. We then initialize the model with the chosen pre-trained model and the number of output classes.

Finally we add a *model.summary()* to understand how features are extracted from the input image, how the dimension of the images changes in each layer. Code 10.9 shows the above steps. Once the model object is initialized, we can compile the model by passing the below parameters –

- Loss function
- Optimizer function
- Metrics to be used

In our case, we are using *Categorical_crossentropy*loss function, the *adam* optimizer and the metrics we want to focus on is *accuracy*. Code 10.10 shows the syntax of compiling the model.

```
# tell the model what cost and optimization method to use
model.compile(
    loss='categorical_crossentropy',
    optimizer='adam',
    metrics=['accuracy']
)
```

CODE 10.10   Compile the model.

Data augmentation is the process of increasing the dataset by applying some changes to the existing images. This is done to have various flavors of the same image for training the model with a vast number of images. Code 10.11 shows the way we use data augmentation with the *Image Data Generator()* method on the training and test datasets.

```
#Data augmentation

train_datagen = ImageDataGenerator(rescale = 1./255,
                                   shear_range = 0.2,
                                   zoom_range = 0.2,
                                   horizontal_flip = True)

test_datagen = ImageDataGenerator(rescale = 1./255)

training_set = train_datagen.flow_from_directory('Datasets/Train',
                                   target_size = (224, 224),
                                   batch_size = 10,
                                   class_mode = 'categorical')

test_set = test_datagen.flow_from_directory('Datasets/Test',
                                   target_size = (224, 224),
                                   batch_size = 10,
                                   class_mode = 'categorical')
```

CODE 10.11   Data augmentation.

Next comes the fitting part of the model. It is done to understand how well our model is able to generalize to datasets similar to the ones on which it was trained.

```
# fit the model
r = model.fit_generator(
    training_set,
    validation data=test set,
    epochs=5

    steps_per_epoch=len(training_set),
    validation_steps=len(test_set)
)
```

CODE 10.12   Fitting the model.

Code 10.12 shows the fitting step. The parameters required for fitting a model would be the test data set, training data set, number of epochs, steps per epoch, and validation.

```
labels = ['Smaran','Hari','Peter','Mary','Vishnu']
test_imgs = 'C:/████████████████████████//Datasets//Test//test.jpg'
img = image.load_img(test_imgs, target_size=(224, 224))
x = image.img_to_array(img)
x = np.expand_dims(x, axis=0)
x /= 255.
classes = model.predict(x)
result = np.squeeze(classes)
result_indices = np.argmax(result)

plt.title("{}, {:.2f}%".format(labels[result_indices], result[result_indices]*100))
plt.imshow(img)
```

CODE 10.13   Predict the person.

The last set of code snippet is given in Code 10.13. In this, we see that we are declaring the labels of the datasets, followed by the image to be tested (test.jpg). After the dimensionality changes, we ask the model to predict. And, finally, we print the name of the person in test.jpg.

In this example, we are using the VGG16 model for predicting friends and family. The readers are requested to try the above exercise with other pre-trained models, such as resNet, Inception, and so forth.

10.5   THE DIFFERENCE BETWEEN TRANSFER LEARNING AND FINE TUNING

The whole process of any neural network model is classified into two parts (Figure 10.4).

1. Feature extraction

2. Classification/Prediction.

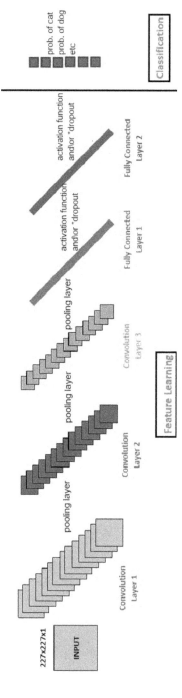

FIGURE 10.4   Outline of CNN architecture.

As we have seen in Section 10.4 (Example 2), in Transfer Learning, we do not touch the feature extraction part of the original model anywhere in the code we write. To be precise, we do not change the number of Convolution layers/Pooling layers that the original model had.

We still go with 13+3 for the VGG16 model. Just that, we make some changes to the final fully connected layer and modify the number of output classes according to the problem in hand.

But with respect to fine tuning, in addition to modifying the last layer of CNN architecture (fully connected layer), we have the flexibility to change the feature extraction part as well.

So, whenever we are given a situation to choose between Transfer Learning and fine tuning, the first choice would be to go with Transfer Learning, and if the results are not as impressive as the original model, we can fine tune the early layers of the network.

10.6   TRANSFER LEARNING STRATEGIES

Based on source domain, target domain, source task and target task, we can classify the Transfer Learning techniques to different types.
What is a domain?

Domain is about a random variable X and the values X may take. Mathematically, Domain (D) is represented as follows:

$$D = \{X, P(X)\}$$

Where,
- X = Feature Space (X1, X2, X3, X4, … .,Xn)
- P(X) = Probability distribution of X.

To make it simpler, if our domain is Animals (X), the domain space will contain animals such as Cat, Dog, Giraffe, Elephant, and so forth. In this case, X1, X2, X3 denotes an animal.

All right, what is a task then?
A task is the objective, or what our model is supposed to identify. For instance, a cat or dog from the given picture. So, for a given target Domain Dt and the task Tt, if we use the knowledge gained from source Domain Ds and the task Ts, then coming back to the first statement of the section, we can classify the Transfer Learning techniques to different types. We are going to see these techniques in detail.

10.6.1 Same Domain, Task

When the source and target domains are the same (animals), and the task is also the same (identifying cat or dog), then it falls under conventional Deep Learning. There is no point in applying Transfer Learning technique.

10.6.2 Same Domain, Different Task

When the domain is the same, but the task is different, this is termed multi-task learning. For example, from an image, if the first task is to identify just animals, and from the same set of images, if we are asked to identify the tree, vehicles around, in the second task, then we could transfer the knowledge gained in the first task to implement the second.

10.6.3 Different Domain, Same Task

When the task is same, but it is on different but related domains, we classify it to be domain adaptation. There are certain subcategories for domain adaptation based on whether or not the source dataset and target dataset are labeled. When we have labeled data in both source and target, it is called Supervised Learning. When source has labeled data, but target does not, it is called Semi-supervised. When there are no labeled data at all, it is called Unsupervised Learning.

Based on the problem in hand and the domain it belongs to, if there has been a model in the same domain and/or for solving same task, we can leverage Transfer Learning technique.

KEY POINTS TO REMEMBER

- Transfer Learning is the process of utilizing pre-trained models to solve a problem similar to the ones previously solved by those pre-trained models.

- Before we try to use a state-of-the-art model, we need to think about the domain and task of the requirement in hand versus state-of-the-art models,

- Keras library has modules for all the famous models that can be used for Transfer Learning.

QUIZ

1. When the domain of the problem in hand is same as a pre-trained model, but the task is different, what is it termed to be?

2. What are the differences between fine tuning and Transfer Learning.

3. What are the benefits of Transfer Learning?

4. How can we measure the accuracy of a model that uses Transfer Learning?

5. If we do not have enough dataset available to train the model; we cannot use Transfer Learning. True or false.

FURTHER READING

✓ www.cse.ust.hk/~qyang/Docs/2009/tkde_transfer_learning.pdf

✓ W. Dai, Q. Yang, G. Xue, and Y. Yu, "Boosting for Transfer Learning," in Proceedings of the 24th International Conference on Machine Learning, Corvalis, Oregon, June 2007, pp. 193–200.

✓ K. Nigam, A. K. McCallum, S. Thrun, and T. Mitchell, "Text classification from labeled and unlabeled documents using EM," *Machine Learning*, vol. 39, no. 2–3, pp. 103–134, 2000. Blum and T. Mitchell, "Combining labeled and unlabeled data with co-training," in *Proceedings of the Eleventh Annual Conference on Computational Learning Theory*,1998, pp. 92–100.

✓ T. Joachims, "Transductive inference for text classification using support vector machines," in *Proceedings of Sixteenth International Conference on Machine Learning*, Bled, Slovenia, 1999, pp. 825–830.

✓ S. J. Pan, V. W. Zheng, Q. Yang, and D. H. Hu, "Transfer learning for wifi-based indoor localization," in *Proceedings of the Workshop on Transfer Learning for Complex Task of the 23rd AAAI Conference on Artificial Intelligence*, Chicago, July 2008.

## CHAPTER 11

Intel OpenVino: A Must-Know Deep Learning Toolkit

LEARNING OBJECTIVES

After this chapter, the reader will be able to understand the following:

- What is OpenVino?
- How to install and set up Intel OpenVino?
- Sample applications with Intel OpenVino.

11.1   INTRODUCTION

OpenVino is from Intel: Expanded as Open Visual Inference and Neural Network Optimization toolkit. This is regarded as now the fastest on the market. It was earlier called Intel Computer Vision SDK. OpenVino provides improved neural network performance. To be precise, the performance is ensured on variety of intel platforms and processors.

One can say, for sure that OpenVino is cost-effective and most suitable for real-time computer vision applications. Also, OpenVino enables Deep Learning Inference and Heterogeneous execution a reality. OpenVino also can really enable the developers to innovate with the Deep Learning and AI solutions. One good thing, this is easier to try, install, and practice. Also,

DOI: 10.1201/9781003185635-11

this is compatible with Neural Compute Sticks, both versions. This chapter is focused toward getting readers a clear idea and guideline about how to use OpenVino.

11.2 OPENVINO INSTALLATION GUIDELINES

This is a bit tricky, and you need a good machine with nice configuration. Otherwise, this might not be a good show for you. OpenVino is compatible with Linux/Windows 10/MAC. Guidelines are pretty easy, and installation can be completed in an hour provided you do not get to many errors.

The hardware requirements for installation are to be met and the users are supposed to have one of the following hardware components available.

- 6th–8th Generation Intel Core
- Intel Xeon v5 family
- Intel Xeon v6 family
- IntelMovidius Neural Compute Stick
- Intel Neural Compute Stick 2
- Intel Vision Accelerator Design with IntelMovidius VPUs

The entire installation process for Windows 10 is explained in this section. For Linux, the procedure is slightly different. All materials are available online on installation and support. The links and details will be presented at the end of the chapter. Let us start the installation process.

https://software.intel.com/en-us/openvino-toolkit/documentation/get-started– This is where you get all the contents that can be installed. and documentation is also available there. One can get to see the landing page as shown below in Figure 11.1

FIGURE 11.1   OpenVinoLanding page.

Complete Windows Installation Guide is present @ *https://docs. openvinotoolkit.org/latest/_docs_install_guides_installing_openvino_ windows.html*

The installation is to be followed after installing the dependency software clearly one after another. The list of prerequisites:

- Microsoft Visual Studio* with C++ 2019, 2017, or 2015 with MSBuildo9i
- CMake* 3.4 or higher
- Python* 3.6.5 with the Python libraries, 64-bit

We shall see Microsoft Visual Studio* with C++ 2019, 2017, or 2015 with MSBuild download and installation.

One should visit – *https://visualstudio.microsoft.com/downloads/*. The landing page would be similar to the one presented below in Figure 11.2. One should select the free download option as presented below.

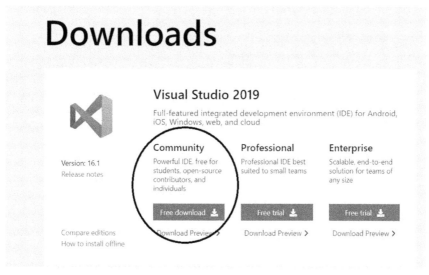

FIGURE 11.2   Visual studio landing page.

From the workloads section during the visual studio installation, select the highlighted options as presented below in Figure 11.3. These are essential and must be done.

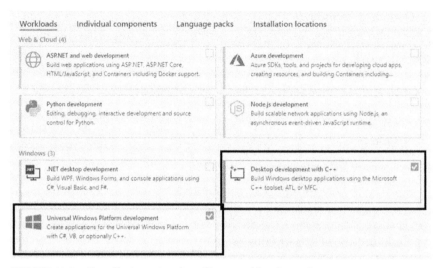

FIGURE 11.3   Installation: visual studio – workloads section.

Now, under the individual components section, select the ticked options as presented in the Figure 11.4.

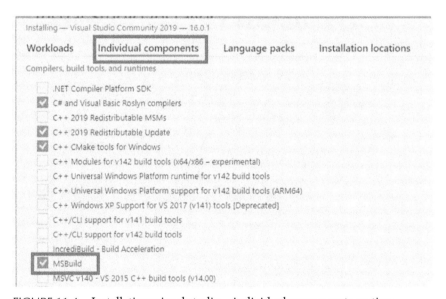

FIGURE 11.4   Installation: visual studio – individual components section.

Next in the sequence is the installation of C-Make. For the installable to be downloaded, one should visit the Installation Site: *https://cmake.org/download/*. As presented in the Figure 11.5, select the highlighted option.

FIGURE 11.5   Installation: CMake installation.

Add path for all the users as it is preferred. The same is presented as Figure 11.6.

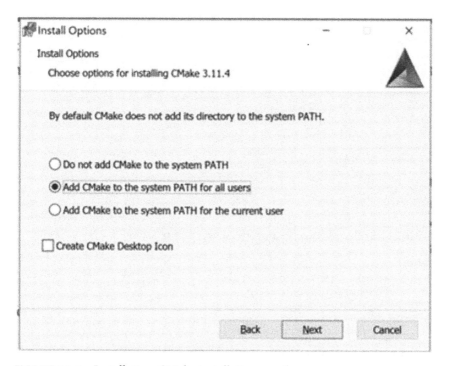

FIGURE 11.6   Installation: CMake installation – path.

It is time for the installation of Python. If you have installed it already, you may ignore this section. One should visit the official python site: *www.python.org/downloads/release/python-365* (Figure 11.7).

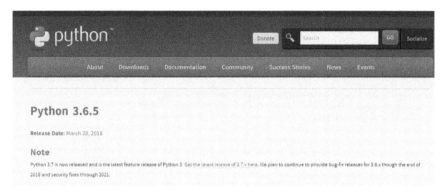

FIGURE 11.7   Installation: Python installation.

Select the appropriate version files for the installation. One can refer to Figure 11.8 for a quicker understanding.

FIGURE 11.8   Installation: Python executable files selection.

After adding the path, installation can be completed (Figure 11.9).

FIGURE 11.9   Installation: Python installation completion.

The real installation starts now. The core OpenVino components are to be installed and the same can be found from the link: *http://software.intel. com/en-us/openvino-toolkit/choose-download/free-download-windows?_ ga=2.118944013.509865441.1560578777-1273749604.1560486217&elq_ cid=3591353&erpm_id=6399395*

w_openvino_toolkit_p_<version>.exe will be the name of the file. You should register and download. Keep the key safe (Figure 11.10).

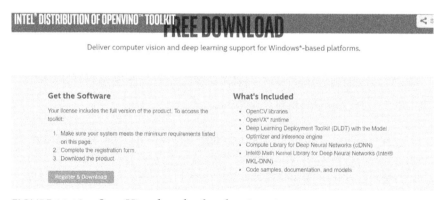

FIGURE 11.10   OpenVino download and registration.

Let the installation go on as presented below in Figures 11.11 and 11.12.

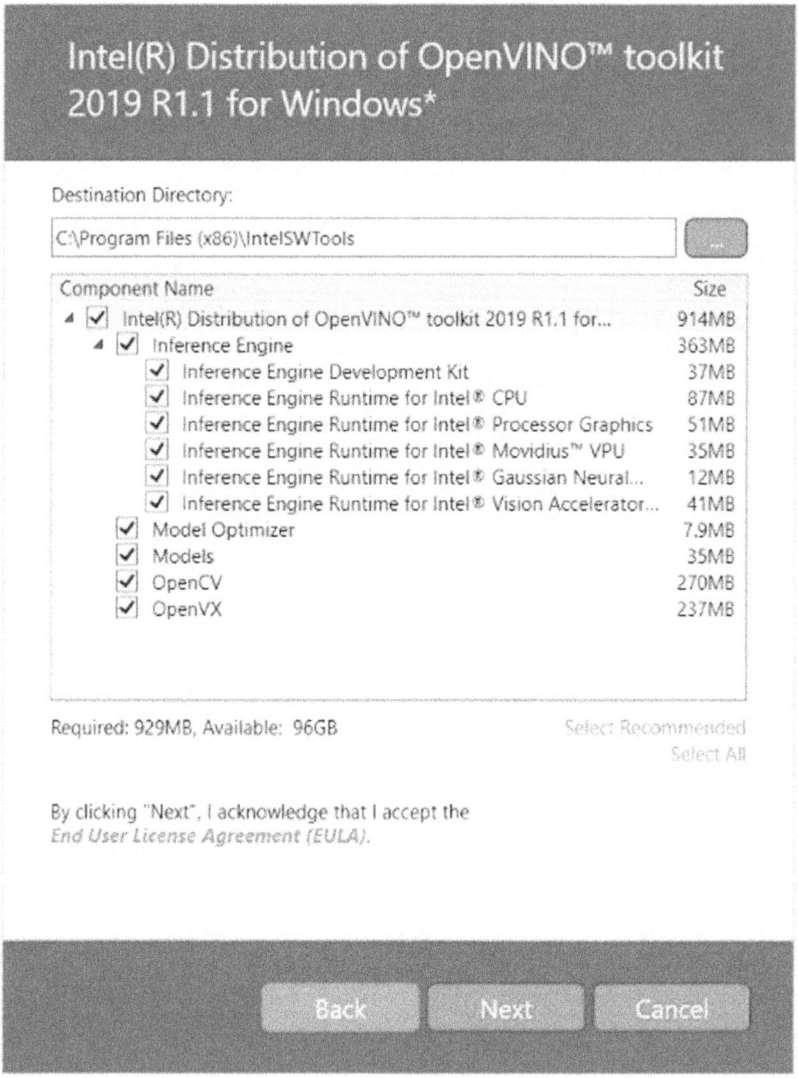

FIGURE 11.11   Installation of OpenVino.

The following warning should not appear, as the installation of prerequisites is already complete. If you see this warning, there is something wrong with the process. Have a re-look.

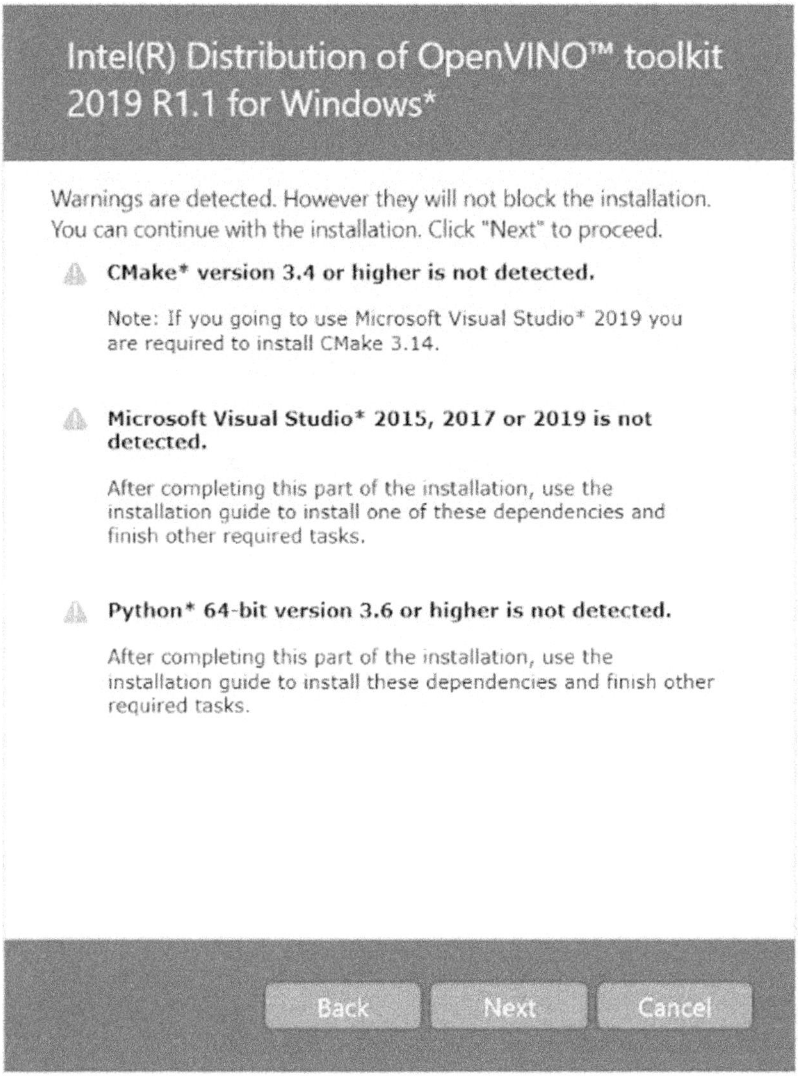

Intel(R) Distribution of OpenVINO™ toolkit
2019 R1.1 for Windows*

Warnings are detected. However they will not block the installation. You can continue with the installation. Click "Next" to proceed.

⚠ **CMake* version 3.4 or higher is not detected.**

Note: If you going to use Microsoft Visual Studio* 2019 you are required to install CMake 3.14.

⚠ **Microsoft Visual Studio* 2015, 2017 or 2019 is not detected.**

After completing this part of the installation, use the installation guide to install one of these dependencies and finish other required tasks.

⚠ **Python* 64-bit version 3.6 or higher is not detected.**

After completing this part of the installation, use the installation guide to install these dependencies and finish other required tasks.

[Back]   [Next]   [Cancel]

FIGURE 11.12   Warnings.

You must update several environment variables before you can compile and run OpenVino applications. Open the Command Prompt, and run the setupvars.bat batch file to temporarily set your environment variables:

>cd C:\Program Files (x86)\IntelSWTools\openvino\bin\ (this is must, else it wont work)

>setupvars.bat

The same has been presented as a screenshot for the quicker reference below as Figure11.13.

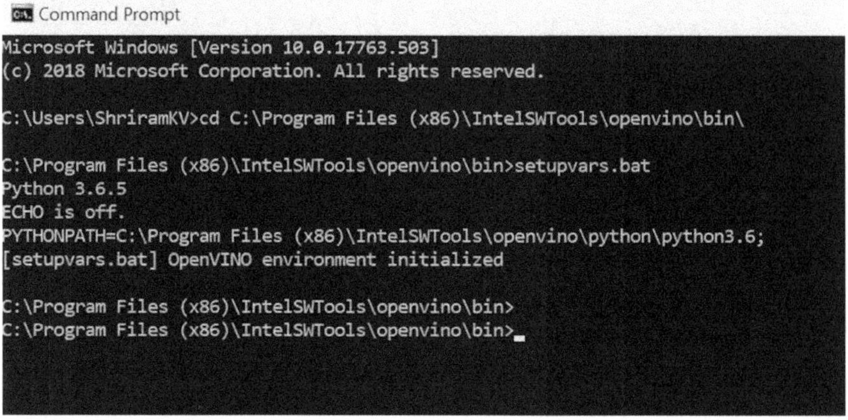

```
Command Prompt
Microsoft Windows [Version 10.0.17763.503]
(c) 2018 Microsoft Corporation. All rights reserved.

C:\Users\ShriramKV>cd C:\Program Files (x86)\IntelSWTools\openvino\bin\

C:\Program Files (x86)\IntelSWTools\openvino\bin>setupvars.bat
Python 3.6.5
ECHO is off.
PYTHONPATH=C:\Program Files (x86)\IntelSWTools\openvino\python\python3.6;
[setupvars.bat] OpenVINO environment initialized

C:\Program Files (x86)\IntelSWTools\openvino\bin>
C:\Program Files (x86)\IntelSWTools\openvino\bin>_
```

FIGURE 11.13   Environment variables setup.

The next step is to configure the Model Optimizer. It has to be configured for "One Framework" at least or else, it may not work the way we want. The Model Optimizer is a key player that helps in the inferencing. Inferencing happens on the trained model, when the model is run through the Model Optimizer.

Readers have to understand this: With the pre-trained model we run through the model optimizer, and Intermediate Representation of the network is arrived at. IR is nothing more than the pair of files that represent the whole model.

- .xml: Describes the network topology
- .bin: Contains the weights and biases binary data

The Model Optimizer is a Python based command line tool (mo.py), which is located in *C:\Program Files (x86)\IntelSWTools\openvino\deployment_tools\model_optimizer*. Use this tool on models trained with popular Deep Learning frameworks such as Caffe*, TensorFlow*, MXNet*, and ONNX* to convert them to an optimized IR format that the Inference Engine can use.

Configuration of the Model Optimizer can be done with the following commands:

*cd   C:\Program   Files[CE:(x86)\IntelSWTools\openvino\deploy-
ment_tools\model_optimizer\install_prerequisites]*

install_prerequisites.bat

Again, make sure the below-mentioned path is reached.

*cd C:\Program Files (x86)\IntelSWTools\openvino\deployment_
tools\model_optimizer\install_prerequisites*

For each framework: We need to now go ahead with the configuration.

install_prerequisites_caffe.bat – For caffe

install_prerequisites_tf.bat – For Tensorflow

install_prerequisites_mxnet.bat – For Mx Net

install_prerequisites_onnx.bat – For Onnx.

install_prerequisites_kaldi.bat – For Kaldi

One would get the message as shown below in the prompt (Figure 11.14).

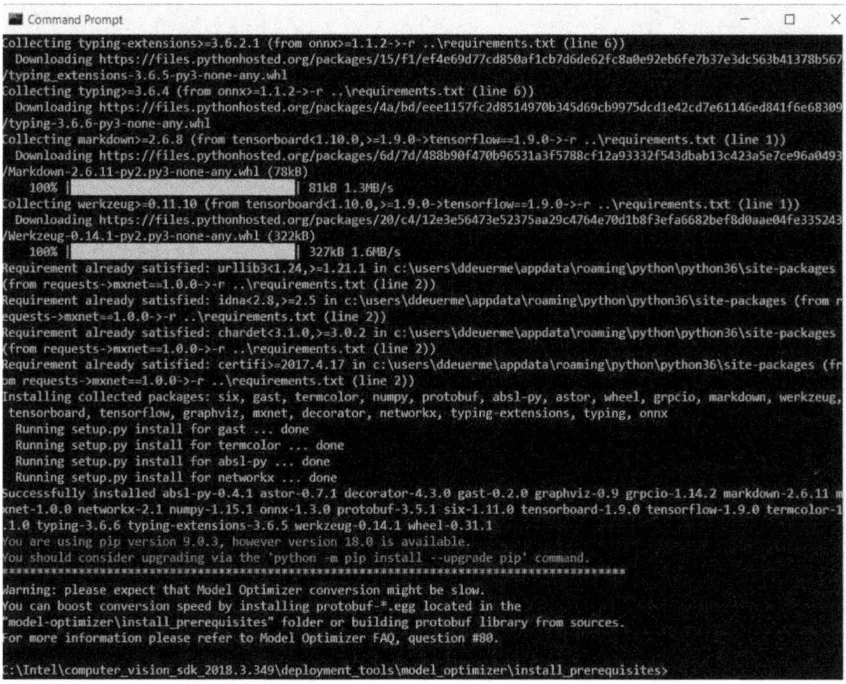

FIGURE 11.14   Framework installation.

Two samples are there, by default, and the same can be tested. One has to navigate to:

cd C:\Program Files (x86)\IntelSWTools\openvino\deployment_ tools\demo

Issue the following commandfor running the first demo.

demo_squeezenet_download_convert_run.bat

When the verification script completes, you will have the label and confi- dence for the top-10 categories as shown in Figure 11.15.

```
Top 10 results:

Image C:\Program Files (x86)\IntelSWTools\openvino\deployment_tools\demo\\car.png

classid probability label
------- ----------- -----
817     0.8363345   sports car, sport car
511     0.0946488   convertible
479     0.0419131   car wheel
751     0.0091071   racer, race car, racing car
436     0.0068161   beach wagon, station wagon, wagon, estate car, beach waggon, station waggon, waggon
656     0.0037564   minivan
586     0.0025741   half track
717     0.0016069   pickup, pickup truck
864     0.0012027   tow truck, tow car, wrecker
581     0.0005882   grille, radiator grille


total inference time: 8.6094001
Average running time of one iteration: 8.6094001 ms

Throughput: 116.1521110 FPS

[ INFO ] Execution successful

##############||  Classification demo completed successfully ||##############

Waiting for  5 seconds, press a key to continue ...
```

FIGURE 11.15   Demo – 1: classification demo.

The next demo is interesting as well, and to run that one should issue *demo_security_barrier_camera.bat*command. Immediately the result appears on screen and the same is presented as Figure 11.16.

FIGURE 11.16   Demo – 2: identification.

If you have seen these results on screen, that is it. You have installed the software and is ready to be used. There are many scenarios one could use OpenVino with. Two such examples are presented below as a simple reference. One can recognize and predict the posture of a person with OpenVino, and it is presented as a screenshot in Figure 11.17, followed by real-time emotion analysis as presented in Figure 11.18. Opportunities are endless when it comes to OpenVino. Start exploring.

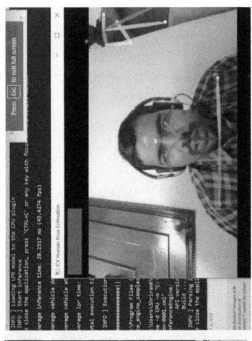

FIGURE 11.17 Posture recognition.

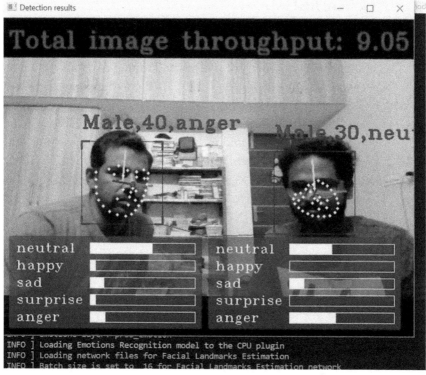

FIGURE 11.18   Emotion recognition with OpenVino.

KEY POINTS TO REMEMBER

- OpenVino is from Intel – Expanded as Open Visual Inference and Neural Network Optimization toolkit.
- OpenVino provides improved neural network performance.
- Model Optimizer is a key player, which helps in the inferencing. Inferencing happens on the trained model when the model is run through the Model Optimizer.
- .xml: Describes the network topology
- .bin: Contains the weights and biases binary data

QUIZ

1. How do you install the Intel OpenVino on Linux boxes?
2. What is a model optimizer, and what is the purpose of the same?
3. What are the frameworks supported by OpenVino?

FURTHER READING

- ✓ Gorbachev, Yury, Mikhail Fedorov, Iliya Slavutin, Artyom Tugarev, Marat Fatekhov, and Yaroslav Tarkan. "Openvino deep learning workbench: Comprehensive analysis and tuning of neural networks inference." In *Proceedings of the IEEE/CVF International Conference on Computer Vision Workshops*, pp. 783–787, Korea. 2019.
- ✓ Castro-Zunti, R.D., Yépez, J. and Ko, S.B., 2020. "License plate segmentation and recognition system using deep learning and OpenVINO." *IET Intelligent Transport Systems, 14*(2), pp.119–126.
- ✓ Kustikova, V., Vasiliev, E., Khvatov, A., Kumbrasiev, P., Vikhrev, I., Utkin, K., Dudchenko, A. and Gladilov, G., 2019, July. "Intel Distribution of OpenVINO Toolkit: A Case Study of Semantic Segmentation." In *International Conference on Analysis of Images, Social Networks and Texts* (pp. 11–23). Springer, Cham.
- ✓ Yew Shun, O.O.I., 2018. High Density Deep Learning – Lite, with Intel OpenVino.
- ✓ https://docs.openvinotoolkit.org/latest/index.html
- ✓ https://software.intel.com/content/www/us/en/develop/tools/openvino-toolkit.html

## CHAPTER 12

Interview Questions and Answers

LEARNING OBJECTIVES

After this chapter, the reader will be

- familiar with the most commonly asked industry interview questions;
- ready to attend interviews confidently.

Q1. Define Deep Learning.

A: In Deep Learning, the human brain is imitated in processing the data and understanding the same. Solutions also be in a way the brain thinks. This is fully based on Neural Networks (Brain is full of neurons!). People also call this Deep Neural Learning or Deep Neural Networks.

Q2. What is the relationship you could draw between Deep Learning, AI, and Machine Learning?

A:

The Relationship for a quicker understanding

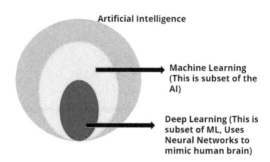

FIGURE 12.1   Relationship between AI, ML and DL.

Q3. Define underfitting, overfitting, correct fitting.

A: *Underfitting–* The line does not cover all the points shown in the graph. Underfitting is also referred to as "High Bias."

Overfitting– The graph shows the predicted line covers all the points in the graph. Is this not perfect and okay to go? No. It is ideally not possible. It covers all the points. This means it could as well miss the noise and outliers. Therefore, this is not a good approach. This model certainly will give poor results. Avoiding this is mandatory! This is a "high variance" approach. One can understand the concepts by referring Figure 12.2.

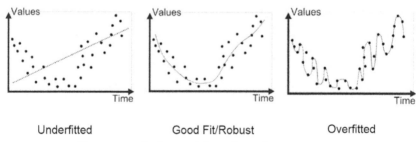

FIGURE 12.2   Fitting – underfit, good fit and overfit.

What is correct fit? – The name says it all! It is the perfect fit. This will not have High Bias/Variance.

Q4. What is bias?

A: Bias is how far the predicted values are from the actual values. If the average predicted values are far from the actual values, then the bias is high. This is what is seen with the underfitting. This is to be avoided!

What is the side effect of High Bias? – The model is said to be too simple and will not capture all the complexity of the data. This will lead to underfitting.

Q5. What is variance?

A: Variance occurs when the model performs very well with the trained dataset but, on the other hand, does not do well on a dataset that the model has not trained on, such as a test dataset or validation dataset. Variance tells us how scattered is the predicted value from the actual value.

What is the side effect? Simple noise/outliers would be included and will be regarded as overfitting.

Q6. Explain the structure of the human neuron.

A: The neuron has dendrites, a nucleus, axon, and terminal axon (Figure 12.3). To make it simple, a neuron has a cell body and as you can see a nucleus inside.

Cell body – round polygon: This is where the signal processing happens.

It is all about signals! When there is a message or communication from one neuron to another, it produces electrical signals. These signals are to be transmitted from the source neuron to the destination neuron. This happens through the long structure shown in the figure called the axon.

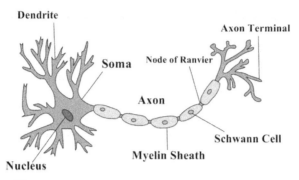

Dendrite

Axon Terminal

Soma   Node of Ranvier

Axon

Schwann Cell

Myelin Sheath

Nucleus

FIGURE 12.3   The neuron structure.

Many signals can be received at an instance from other neurons. For this the dendrites are attached to the cell body.

Q7. Draw a simple structure of ANN.

A: The first layer is the input layer. The last column is the output layer. Anything in between is hidden and called *hidden layers*. Having very limited, or just one, hidden layer makes your ANN shallow. If you have many hidden layers, we call it Deep Neural Network (Figure 12.4).

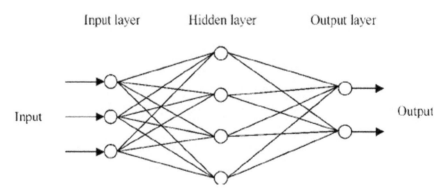

Input layer   Hidden layer   Output layer

Input   Output

FIGURE 12.4   Structure of ANN.

Q8. Define convolution.

A: In mathematics (in particular, functional analysis) convolution is a mathematical operation on two functions (f and g), which produce a third function expressing how the shape of one is modified by the other.

Q9. How convolution works?

A: The first hidden layer is the convolution layer, and we have to specify the filter. A filter is a matrix. We can have a 3 * 3 filter like the one shown below (Figure 12.5):

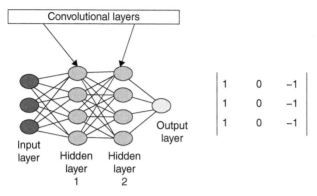

FIGURE 12.5   Convolution layers and filter.

The filter shown above will slide over the input block (matrix). Sliding is called convolving (Figure 12.6). The filter is going to convolve, and is the crux!

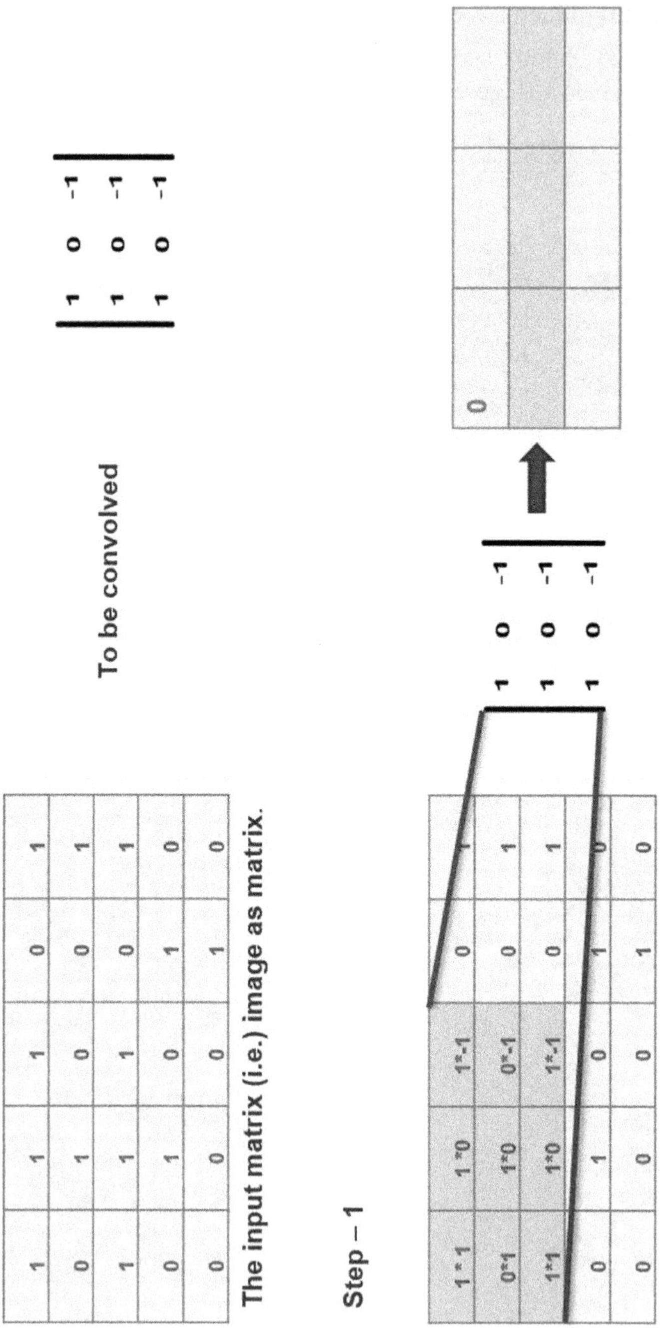

The input matrix (i.e.) image as matrix.

To be convolved

Step – 1

FIGURE 12.6 The convolving operation.

Q10. Define Depth

A: Depth – As conveyed earlier, depth is fundamentally based on the number of filters used. When I use n different filters, the depth of the feature map is also n.

Q11. Define Striding.

A: Stride – We moved the matrix over the input image, right? That sliding is important here. Moving one pixel at a time corresponds to Stride 1. An example will be handy (Figure 12.7).

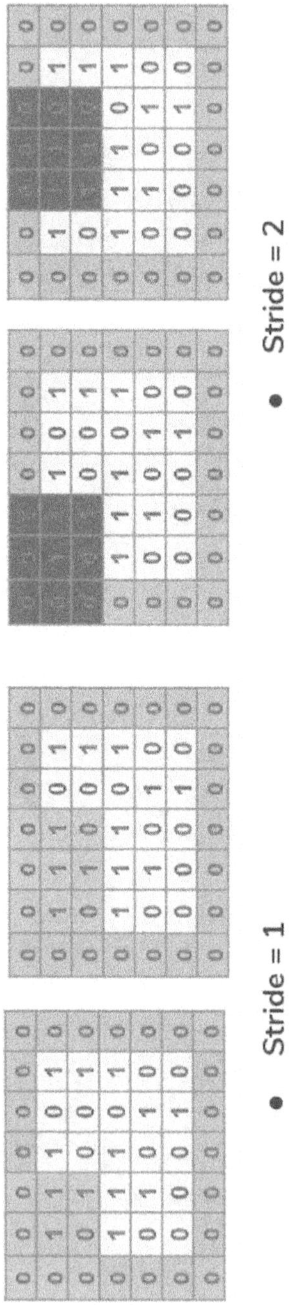

- Stride = 2

- Stride = 1

FIGURE 12.7   Striding operation.

Q12. What is max pooling?

A: It is purely math and, after the max pooling process, the dimensions of the image (i.e. the result) will be reduced (Figure 12.8). The number of pixels will be reduced when comparing them with the previous stage.

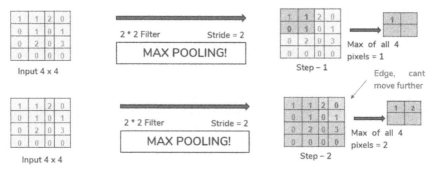

FIGURE 12.8   Pooling operation.

Q13. What is average pooling?

A: Average pooling – This is like the max pooling, but with a slight deviation in the approach: Instead of taking the maximum values from the identified region, it is now the average of all the values in the region. Therefore, the name, *average pooling*. This is not preferred over max pooling as it fails with the detection of sharp edges and other complex features.

Q14. What is sum pooling?

A: This is again a variation of the max pooling. Here, instead of average or max value, the sum of all the pixels in the chosen region is calculated. Sum pooling also is preferred next to the max pooling in applications.

Q15. What are the steps in the CNN?

A:

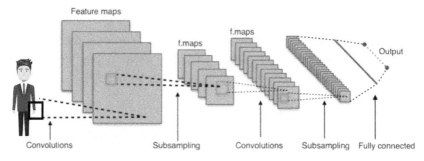

Feature maps

f.maps

f.maps

Output

Convolutions | Subsampling | Convolutions | Subsampling | Fully connected

FIGURE 12.9   CNN step by step.

Q16. What is flattening? Why is it important?

A: Output from previous layers are flattened to a single vector so they can be input to the next level.

Q17. What is the role of the activation function in the ANN?

A: In ANN the activation function of a neuron defines the output of the neuron given a set of inputs. The activation function operates on the value, which can be then transformed to anything between the lower limit and the upper limit (Say 0 and 1). (It fires or none)

Q18. What is the Sigmoid activation function?

A: For Sigmoid, zero is the lower limit. One is the upper limit (Figure 12.10).
  • If the input is negative – Transforms this number close to 0.
  • If input is positive – Transforms this number close to 1.
  • If the input is close to 0– Transforms this number close to 0 and 1.

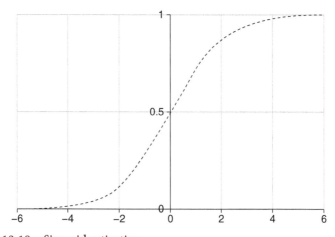

FIGURE 12.10   Sigmoid activation.

Q19. What is ReLU? How does it work?

A: It is expanded as a Rectified Linear Unit. It actually transforms the input to 0 or input value itself. When the input value is negative (i.e., less than 0 or equal to 0), it will make it the output as 0 and 0. If the input is greater than 0, then the output will be the given input.

```
If(x<=0)
{
    return 0;
}else
{
    return x;
}
```

Q20. What percentage should be test dataset and how much should go for training?

A: There is no hard and fast rule. Normally it is preferred as 70 percent/30 percent – 70 percent for the training and 30 for the testing. Therefore, the best combination can be arrived at by trial and error.

Q21. What names of 5 CNN architectures are you aware of?

A:
- LeNet
- AlexNet
- ZFNet
- GoogleLeNet
- VGGNet

Q22. Explain the structure of VGG – 16.

A:

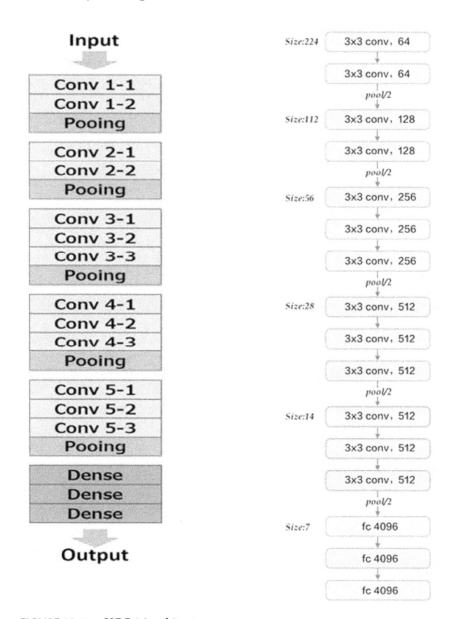

FIGURE 12.11   VGG 16 architecture.

Q23. Explain the architecture of AlexNet

A:

CVL = Convolution Layer
MP = Max Pooling
FC = Fully Connected
SM = Softmax Layer

FIGURE 12.12   AlexNet architecture.

Q24. How can you enable padding in the Python code? Can you present the code for the same?

A:

One can understand the process by referring Figure 12.13

```
import keras
from keras.models import Sequential
from keras.layers import Activation
from keras.layers.core import Dense, Flatten
from keras.layers.convolutional import *
# ALL the above shall be explained with the code for CNN, Shortly.

model = Sequential([
    Dense(16, input_shape=(30,30,3), activation='relu'),
    Conv2D(32, kernel_size=(4,4), activation='relu', padding='same'),
    Conv2D(64, kernel_size=(5,5), activation='relu', padding='same'),
    Conv2D(128, kernel_size=(6,6), activation='relu', padding='same'),
    Flatten(),
    Dense(2, activation='softmax')
])

# Remember this, 'valid' as the option for padding, the size will shrink.
# with 'same' for padding, zero padding happens and dimension gets retained.
model.summary()
```

Layer (type)	Output Shape	Param #
dense_22 (Dense)	(None, 30, 30, 16)	64
conv2d_28 (Conv2D)	(None, 30, 30, 32)	8224
conv2d_29 (Conv2D)	(None, 30, 30, 64)	51264
conv2d_30 (Conv2D)	(None, 30, 30, 128)	295040
flatten_10 (Flatten)	(None, 115200)	0
dense_23 (Dense)	(None, 2)	230402

```
import keras
from keras.models import Sequential
from keras.layers import Activation
from keras.layers.core import Dense, Flatten
from keras.layers.convolutional import *
# ALL the above shall be explained with the code for CNN, Shortly.

model = Sequential([
    Dense(16, input_shape=(30,30,3), activation='relu'),
    Conv2D(32, kernel_size=(4,4), activation='relu', padding='valid'),
    Conv2D(64, kernel_size=(5,5), activation='relu', padding='valid'),
    Conv2D(128, kernel_size=(6,6), activation='relu', padding='valid'),
    Flatten(),
    Dense(2, activation='softmax')
])

# Remember this, Valid as the option for padding, the size will shrink. No padding happens with valid.
# with same for padding, zero padding happens and dimension gets retained.
model.summary()
```

Layer (type)	Output Shape	Param #
dense_1 (Dense)	(None, 30, 30, 16)	64
conv2d_1 (Conv2D)	(None, 27, 27, 32)	8224
conv2d_2 (Conv2D)	(None, 23, 23, 64)	51264
conv2d_3 (Conv2D)	(None, 18, 18, 128)	295040
flatten_1 (Flatten)	(None, 41472)	0
dense_2 (Dense)	(None, 2)	82946

FIGURE 12.13 Padding with the Python code.

Q25. Differentiate traditional neural networks and recurrent neural networks

A: RNN is one of the types of ANN. Here, the output of the previous step is fed as the input (i.e., feedback) to the current step. It is definitely different from the traditional approach, or even CNN, which we dealt with. Traditionally, the input and output are independent of each other. Remember CNN, we never fully remembered the previous state to advance further. But RNN is not that. It remembers. This means it has memory like you and I! (Figure 12.14)

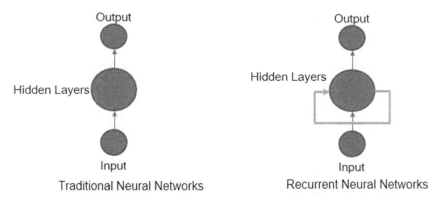

FIGURE 12.14   Traditional neural networks and recurrent neural networks.

Q26. Differentiate RNN and FNN.

A: When it comes to Feedforward Neural Networks, the data navigates from the input layer to the output layer (i.e., from left to right). The data moves through the hidden layers, which are structured in between.

The information (i.e. the flow of the data) will be only from left to right, that is, no looking back. Also, remember, never, ever does information reach a particular node twice in the entire cycle.

When it comes to RNN, we should remember there is a loop! The information goes through the loop! Memory comes in.

The decision on the data is arrived at through the current state input and the previous outputs. That is, the prediction of markets will be done through the consideration of current and historical data. Only then, it is prediction! (Figure 12.15)

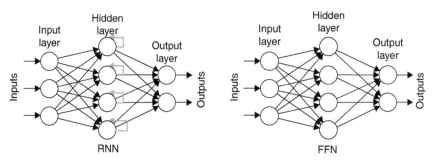

FIGURE 12.15   RNN vs. FFN.

Q27. Give one common application of RNN with an appropriate example.

A: Many say, when they talk about RNN, "I had a good time in France. I also learned to speak some _____." If someone asks you to predict what would be the answer for the blank space, how would you answer? Simple: You will remember the previous phrase. The previous phrase says it was France. Therefore, the prediction would be *French*. We needed memory to calculate the next word. This is the case with RNN. It has memory and it helps prediction! The previous stage output plays a role in deriving the current output!

Q28. What is linear activation function?

A: It is a straight-line function, and one can see that is linear.

Values can become very large and cannot be confined within some specific range.

The linear function alone does not capture complex patterns – or one can say is not used as frequently as the nonlinear activation functions being used (Figure 12.16).

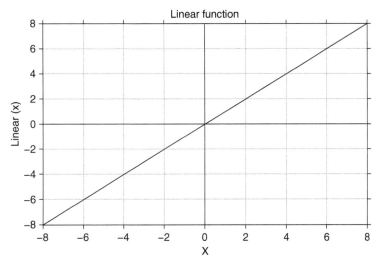

FIGURE 12.16   Linear activation function.

Q29. What is the nonlinear activation function?

A: The main aspect of the nonlinear activation function is that it is nonlinear (Figure 12.17).

One can refer to the below graph to understand what the nonlinear activation function will look like.

The model can be adapted with variety of data and, hence, is useful for analyzing complex patterns. Some of the commonly used nonlinear activation functions are Sigmoid, ReLU, and Tanh.

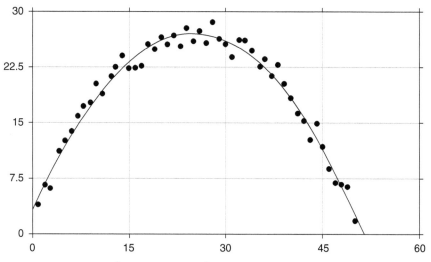

FIGURE 12.17 Non-linear activation function.

Q30. What is a vanishing gradient?

A:

FIGURE 12.18   Vanishing gradient.

A vanishing gradient is an inclined part of a road or railway, a slope (Figure 12.18). So, the gradient is small or none when the aforesaid situation occurs. When this situation occurs, the network definitely refuses to learn and becomes slow. This is referred to as a vanishing gradient problem, and Sigmoid is a victim to it.

Q31. Differentiate LSTM and GRU

A: Number of Gates – 3 in LSTM and 2 in GRU. Gates – Forget, Input and Output in LSTM, and Reset and Update in GRU.

Use of Hidden States is the prominent difference, which was not followed in LSTM. Also, there is no Output gate concept.

Q32. What is an autoencoder significantly used for?

A: An autoencoder is a relatively simple ML algorithm that acquires an input image and will reconstruct the same (i.e., the image is compressed). This is also called *dimensionality reduction*. The dimensionality reduction is used in data preprocessing (reduce/

compress). The process of dimensionality reduction reduces the dimensionality of the considered dataset (Figure 12.19).

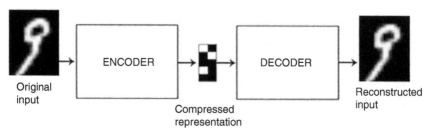

FIGURE 12.19   The autoencoder.

Q33. List the three major layers in an autoencoder.

A:

1. Input Layer
2. Hidden Layer (bottleneck/code)
3. Output Layer

Q34. What are the three properties/features one should remember with autoencoders?

A:

1. Data-specific behavior
2. Lossy Compression nature
3. Unsupervised in nature

Q35. What is a latent feature?

A: These are the true explanatory factors extracted from the input image (Figure 12.20).

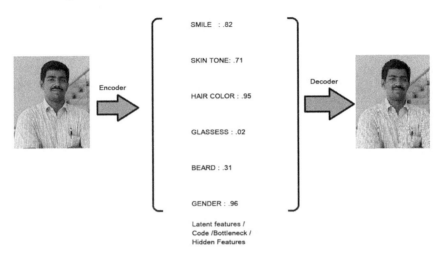

SMILE : .82

SKIN TONE: .71

HAIR COLOR : .95

GLASSESS : .02

BEARD : .31

GENDER : .96

Encoder

Decoder

Latent features /
Code /Bottleneck /
Hidden Features

FIGURE 12.20   The latent features.

Q36. Distinguish between observed variables and latent variables.

A: "Real variables" are hidden, or they are not visible (Figure 12.21). These are not directly observable but are the true explanatory factors that make the observed variables. These real variables are the true latent variables in autoencoders. Observed variables are cast by the real variables, which are hidden.

FIGURE 12.21   Observed features vs. latent features.

Q37. Can you explain the relationship between the dimensionality of latent space and the reconstructed image in an autoencoder?

A: Dimensionality of latent space representation is directly related to the quality of the reconstructed image. Lower dimensionality of the reconstructed image will force a larger training bottleneck because of poor quality of reconstruction.

Q38. What determines the difference from the original image to the reconstructed image in an autoencoder?

A: Loss function helps to understand the difference in terms of loss from the original image to the reconstructed image. Mean squared error is used as the loss function,

$$L(X,Z) = \|X - Z\|^2$$

Q39. List different types of autoencoders

A:
- Denoising Autoencoder
- Vanilla Autoencoder
- Deep Autoencoder
- Sparse Autoencoder
- Undercomplete Autoencoder
- Stacked Autoencoder
- Variational Autoencoder
- Convolutional Autoencoder

Q40. How does a Denoising Autoencoder work?

A: Denoising Autoencoders produce a corrupted (noised) copy of the input through the introduction of some noise (i.e., noise added to corrupt the input) (Figure 12.22).

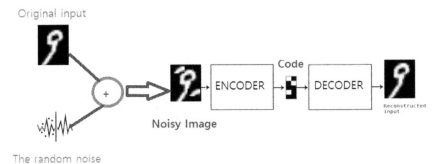

FIGURE 12.22 Denoising Autoencoders.

Q41. How does a Variational Autoencoder (VAE) work?

A: VAE works by parameterizing the Latent vector Z with Mean vector and standard deviation vector, which describes the probability distribution associated with each of these latent variables, Z. The encoder computes latent variable Z given the input X, whereas the decoder computes Y given the latent variable Z. So, this can be represented as a simple conditional probability. Decoder uses reverse inference from latent space Z to compute Y. One can refer to the Figure 12.23 to understand the concept.

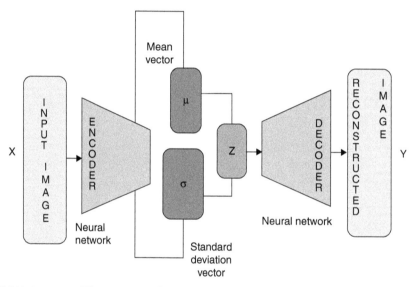

FIGURE 12.23   The Variational Autoencoder.

Q42. Differentiate between a Standard Autoencoder and VAE.

A: Standard Autoencoders are deterministic in nature. VAE have a probabilistic twist to the Standard Autoencoders by parameterizing the Latent vector Z with Mean vector and standard deviation vector, which describes the probability distribution associated with each of these latent variables, Z.

Q43. How does a Convolutional Autoencoder work?

A: A Convolutional Autoencoder is an unsupervised learning version of convolutional neural networks using convolution filters (Figure 12.24).

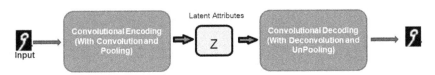

FIGURE 12.24 The Convolutional Autoencoder.

Q44. What is Generative Adversarial Networks (GAN)?

A: Generative Adversarial Networks are a type of generative model, which uses two neural networks that compete with each other, thereby generating new samples (Figure 12.25).

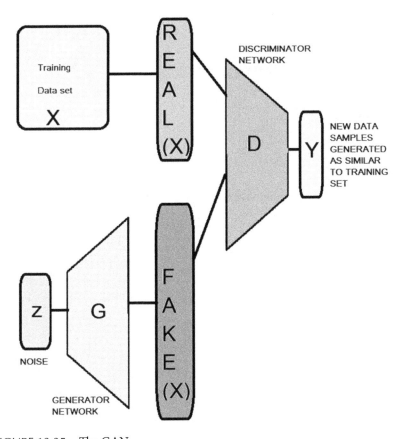

FIGURE 12.25 The GAN.

Q45. List the different types of GAN.

A:

- Deep Convolutional GANs (DCGANs)
- Stack GAN
- Cycle GAN
- Conditional GAN
- Info GAN

Q46. What is Transfer Learning?

A: In Transfer Learning, all we have learned can be transferred, that is, from one model to another (Figure 12.26). The features or weights and so forth. can be used for other models. Therefore, the advantage is reusability, no need to learning everything from scratch and, even with a limited dataset, it will become easier.

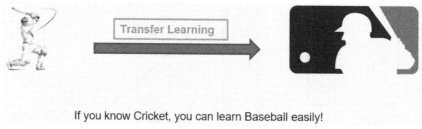

If you know Cricket, you can learn Baseball easily!

FIGURE 12.26   The Transfer Learning.

Q47. Differentiate between Transfer Learning and Fine Tuning?

A: In Transfer Learning, we take advantage of the knowledge of another problem to solve the one we are dealing with by using the feature extraction stage and Fine Tuning the classifier part.

In Fine Tuning, retrain not only the classifier layer but also retrain the feature extraction stage (the convolutional and pooling layers).

Q48. How would you decide whether Transfer Learning or Fine Tuning is best suited for a problem?

A: Start with Transfer Learning and, if needed, move to Fine Tuning other detailed layers.

Q49. What is One-shot Learning?

A: Developing a computer vision system that uses two images it has never seen before and predict whether both look similar or not (Figure 12.27).

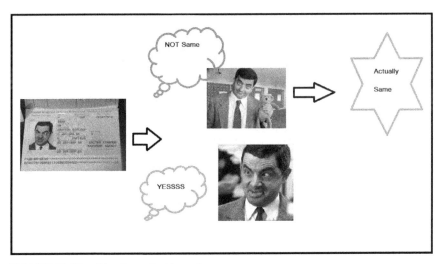

FIGURE 12.27   The One-shot learning.

Q50. Which are common applications of Deep Learning in AI?

A:

- Self-driving Cars
- Emotion Detection
- Natural Language Processing
- Entertainment
- Health Care

YOUTUBE SESSIONS ON DEEP LEARNING APPLICATIONS:

- *https://youtu.be/kFEckWpbXOU*
- *https://youtu.be/DGxmmMaI1oo*
- *https://youtu.be/dKKI_NVr0Ds*
- *https://youtu.be/SzG_i3L9icU*

Index

Lightning Source UK Ltd.
Milton Keynes UK
UKHW050810250722
406270UK00004BA/71